Other books by Anne LaBastille

BEYOND BLACK BEAR LAKE

WOMEN AND WILDERNESS

WOODSWOMAN

MAMA POC

MAMA POC

AN ECOLOGIST'S ACCOUNT OF
THE EXTINCTION OF A SPECIES

Anne LaBastille

W · W · NORTON & COMPANY · *NEW YORK* · *LONDON*

The names of certain persons in this book have been changed to protect their privacy.

THE TEXT OF THIS BOOK *is composed in Electra, with display type set in Neuland and Willow. Composition and manufacturing by the Haddon Craftsmen Inc. Book design by Marjorie J. Flock.*

First published as a Norton paperback 1991

Library of Congress Cataloging in Publication Data
LaBastille, Anne.
  Mama Poc / Anne LaBastille.—1st ed.
     p.   cm.
  1. Podilymbus gigas. 2. LaBastille, Anne.   I. Title.
WL696.P586L33   1990
598 443—dc20   89-22843

ISBN 0-393-30800-6

W. W. Norton & Company, Inc., 500 Fifth Avenue, New York, N. Y. 10110
W. W. Norton & Company Ltd., 10 Coptic Street, London WC1A 1PU

2 3 4 5 6 7 8 9 0

For Daniel Q. Thompson,
Leader, Cooperative Wildlife Research Unit,
AND
for the Adirondack Park Agency

Contents

Contents

Foreword

By THOMAS E. LOVEJOY, *Smithsonian Institution*

PECIES COME INTO EXISTENCE but ultimately vanish from the face of the Earth. So it has been since the dawn of life on our planet. Why then do people concern themselves with endangered species such as the grebe of Lake Atitlán, whose lamentable story is the subject of this book?

A major reason, of course, is that each and every species is intrinsically beautiful, a source of fascination, wonder, and aesthetic enjoyment. It is the same reason that propels some of us to be concerned with historic preservation and the monuments and artworks of people past and present. There is, in the case of plants and animals, the additional pull on our psyche because they are living. Deep in us, at a level barely conscious, if at all, is a sense of community with other forms of life—a profound primordial tug.

That really should be sufficient in itself. But there is much more than that: our lives are very much bound up in the fate of other forms of life, yet we *ourselves* have tilted the balance between speciation and extinction to the point where the latter predominates by orders of magnitude. Largely, but not entirely because of destruction of natural areas in the tropics, extinction rates are soaring exponentially. And hovering on the horizon is a second tsunami of extinction as the building greenhouse effect generates climate change more rapid than has occurred on earth for millions of years.

These great, disastrous global trends are played out at the level of the individual species such as the grebe for which Anne LaBastille labored both assiduously and eloquently for so long. Typically it is a saga of multiple threats that spring up Hydra-headed and not at all predictable to type or timing. The task of conservation is indeed eternal vigilance; battles may be won, truces may be declared, but the war is never won. The tale of the grebe is no exception: a problem not just of introduced species altering the lake ecology but also of pollution, hunting, and altered lake levels entering the picture singly, yet all acting synergistically. One wonders what might have been next?

The vulnerability of species to myriad factors is what confers yet additional importance to them, for they are like litmus paper designed to detect environmental problems. That is why, as we struggle to redefine our relationship to nature and to live on a sustainable basis, diversity of plant and animal life becomes the *ultimate assay* of the sustainability of our lifestyle.

Environment and economics will dominate the agenda for at least decades to come. Much of the tale will, directly or indirectly, play itself out at the species level. Many of the battles will be as hard and lonely as that of the grebe on a faraway volcanic lake in Guatemala. The struggle will require vision, commitment, endurance, and eloquence of the sort we have become accustomed to expect of Mama Poc. We cannot, however, leave it to those few who pioneer as she did. This must be an effort that involves the larger part of humanity and draws upon synergies yet greater than the destructive ones of our own making, which constitute the very challenge. The measure of our success will be in the number of species that survive. They will also be our reward.

From Author to Reader

THOSE OF YOU who may have read *Woodswoman* and *Beyond Black Bear Lake,* books describing my life in two hand-built log cabins beside an Adirondack wilderness tract, will surely wonder why I ever went to Guatemala and what I did there. Basically, I've spent twenty-five years off and on living in the Adirondack Mountains, the largest park in the continental United States. I've also spent twenty-five years off and on researching an endangered water bird on Lake Atitlán, Guatemala, one of the most beautiful lakes on earth. When I wasn't writing and working out of my Adirondack cabins, I was often at Atitlán studying giant grebes.

Yet this doesn't tell you, the reader, how I initially arrived in Guatemala. Very simply, my first real job out of college (with a B.S. in Conservation of Natural Resources) was with the National Audubon Society, which ran two-day trips in south Florida around Lake Okeechobee and Fish-eating Creek and through the Everglades National Park and Florida Keys. I was eager to be a wildlife tour leader. The Society hired me—first woman ever—for the winter season. I reveled in showing people snowy egrets and smooth-billed anis, stalking wild turkeys through live oak hammocks, and cruising among mangrove islets.

By the end of that tour season, I had fallen in love with one of the other guides, Morgan Brown. He owned and operated a small rustic resort lodge in the Adirondacks, and I went to work there summers. When we eventually married, we decided to spend spring, summer, and fall running the inn and wintertime conducting natural history tours of our own. Rather than tie up again with the Audubon Society, we decided to organize our own personalized, adventure trips *out* of the country for a week or two at a time. We had already gone to the Caribbean on a short birding-and-caving honeymoon and loved it. We could start there and expand to Central America, Mexico, and perhaps northern South America. As far as I know, we were the first naturalists to operate nature tours *outside* the United States. Today, of course, such trips are numerous and go to far-flung corners of the world.

Over the years, we sampled Jamaica, Trinidad, Tobago, the Netherland Antilles, Yucatan, Costa Rica, and Guatemala. Each place offered a wildlife spectacle, like the scarlet ibis of Caroni Swamp, birds of paradise on Little Tobago, flamingos stalking the Bonaire salt pans, and oil birds deep in a cleft of the Arima Valley.

Of all the places we traveled, I liked Guatemala the best. And one event that stands out in my mind happened in early 1960, when we were boating along the rocky shores of Lake Atitlán and I focused my binoculars on a strange-looking waterbird near the reed beds. It was nearly as big as a wood duck and had a large white beak with a black pied mark and a jaunty appearance. Neither Morgan nor I could identify it. None of our field guides showed such a species. That night, back in the Indian village of Panajachel, the natives told us it was a "funny duck" that never flew and could stay under water for half an hour!

Full of curiosity, we visited the Museum of Natural History in Guatemala City. Its Director, a charming, blue-eyed Spanish man named Jorge Ibarra, immediately identified the mysterious bird as the giant pied-billed grebe, or in scientific jargon, *Podilymbus gigas.* He produced his only museum specimen, a grotesquely stuffed creature with a neck as long as a heron's.

"This bird lives *only* at Lake Atitlán," Mr. Ibarra said, "and is very rare. I was there in 1958, observing them. Dr. Ludlow Griscom, your famous American ornithologist, wrote a fine description of them in 1929. He named them and counted about 200 grebes. Dr. Alexander Wetmore of the Smithsonian Institution came here in 1936 and estimated roughly the same number of birds. But neither scientist made a complete census."

Before the afternoon was out, Morgan and I had arranged to take Jorge to the lake and to conduct a new short census of giant grebes. We actually *saw* 99 birds and estimated 200 or more lived at Atitlán. We figured that many may have been diving, sleeping, roosting, or nesting so we missed counting them. This turned out to be only the fourth time anyone had ever counted giant grebes.

Back in the States, I delved into the ornithological literature and found a few paragraphs in old journals. This bird lived only on Lake Atitlán, was apparently flightless, could barely walk, and was almost twice the size of the common pied-billed grebe *(Podilymbus podiceps),* found throughout most of the United States. No photographs or drawings of this curious creature existed. And no one had ever written an article about it.

How extraordinary, I thought, to find an animal today so little studied and documented. The idea of going to Guatemala, not as a tour guide but as a trained wildlife biologist, started to form. The challenge of researching this species, photographing the grebes, and producing a popular article lingered in the back of my mind. And it never left during the seven years of being a wife, innkeeper, and wildlife tour leader.

Glamorous as Morgan's and my lives seemed, running a resort lodge and jetting around the Caribbean, our marriage was not sound. In 1965 we were divorced. Suddenly I was single and free to follow my dreams. Despite deep feelings of despair at losing both a husband and my father, who died that year, there were two things I wanted to do. One was to build a little cabin in the woods, as Henry David Thoreau had at Walden Pond, Massachusetts. The other was to spend four to eight weeks in Guatemala taking pictures and preparing a story about giant grebes.

I set about making my log home on the shores of Black Bear Lake, one and a half miles from the nearest road. I moved into it on July 4th, just as Thoreau had done 145 years before. All that is written in *Woodswoman*. But as autumn arrived and nights chilled down, I thought increasingly of Guatemala. Living isolated in one room and a loft, without electricity or indoor plumbing, was wonderful in warm weather, but would be difficult, if not dangerous, in winter. Therefore, just before Christmastime, I closed up my cabin and flew to Central America. Little did I realize that my four to eight weeks would stretch to four *years* and be the start of a twenty-four-year campaign to save the giant grebes, let alone that I would have the opportunity to document the entire process of an extraordinary extinction of a species. As best as can be determined, I am the first ecologist to have systematically observed an animal go from a balanced, healthy population to zero and its habitat shift from ecologically sound to badly deteriorated within two and a half decades.

MAMA ROC

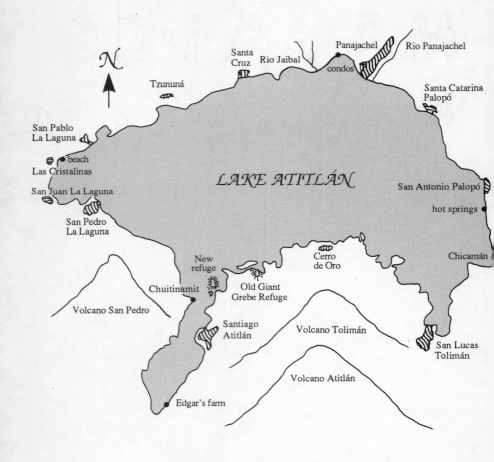

N

Tzununá

Santa
Cruz   Rio Jaibal   Panajachel   Rio Panajachel

condos

San Pablo
La Laguna

Santa Catarina
Palopó

beach

Las Cristalinas

LAKE ATITLÁN

San Antonio Palopó

San Juan La Laguna

hot springs

San Pedro
La Laguna

Cerro
de Oro

Chicamán

New
refuge

Old Giant
Grebe Refuge

Chuitinamit

Volcano San Pedro

Santiago
Atitlán

Volcano Tolimán

San Lucas
Tolimán

Edgar's farm

Volcano Atitlán

Lake Atitlán

GUATEMALA

1
Giant Grebes and Big Water

I CLAMBERED DOWN from the old bus at twilight in the Indian village of Panajachel, Guatemala. For the past forty-eight hours all I had heard were engines. Now my nerves calmed as I walked toward the shore of Lake Atitlán—my final destination. An unexpected afternoon storm had pushed across the lake, in spite of it being early December and the dry season. Immense pewter thunderheads, their tops tinged with peach, towered above the three volcanoes which are the backdrop of the lake. From time to time, flashes of lightning lit up their inky interiors. Distant thunder rumbled over the Pacific coast far behind the volcanoes. The lake was restless; small wavelets lapped incessantly at the edge of the beach.

I dropped my three heavy bags on the sand and stumbled toward the water. Its surface was gunmetal gray with highlights of electric blue. A patch of clear sky opened directly over my head. That dramatic scene and colors were mirrored in a large rain puddle near where I stood.

Not a sound beside the lake's murmur. All the local Indians were home eating supper. The huts closest to shore and the villages far across the lake glimmered softly with candlelight. Electricity was scarce in this remote countryside. And the few foreign tourists in town were probably having drinks at their hotels and listening to marimba bands. Gradually, my weariness dissolved.

Atitlán. Big Water! How aptly named. A mile high and 1,200 feet deep. Volcanoes rising to 11,300 feet and 75 miles of shoreline in an oval shape. Turbulent afternoon winds sweep up from the southern coast and funnel between the volcanoes to collide over the lake and produce the "fury of the demons," or *chocomil.* Or else cold fronts pour down from the north, following our winter blizzards in the States, to shove four- and five-foot waves against the far shore. These dreaded *nortes* may blow for days, making travel by dugout canoes or small boats hazardous. Yet tomorrow I would have to find a boat and start looking for the rare flightless giant grebes on that huge, awesome body of water.

Now the lake was calming. Small night noises could be heard above the wavelets. Crickets, an owl in oaks up the hill, a date palm rustling in the warm tropical breeze. How rich these sounds seemed after the Adirondacks. Four nights ago I'd listened to a somber winter wind in bare branches, then awakened to five inches of fresh snow on Black Bear Lake's newly iced surface. Spruces and firs were draped in fluffy cloaks, and the heavily laden toboggan slid along easily as I snowshoed down the lake. After a month of November gloom, the first sun had strewn snow sequins in my path.

Behind me, the cabin stood darkly curtained, its wood stove cooling down. I glanced back and sighed. How I hated to leave my new log home. Yet I knew that the subzero nights and keening winds of December were imminent. Already the max-min thermometer by my door had registered 11° F. at dawn today. More than that, living alone for the first time in seven years with my

Jorge Ibarra, director of the Museum of Natural History in Guatemala City, with the country's only specimen of a giant grebe prior to my arrival in the 1960s.

nearest neighbor five miles away was bound to lead to psychological depression. I felt emotionally raw that winter of 1964–65.

Resolutely, I turned and headed south down the lake. A friend was waiting with his four-wheel-drive at the landing one and a half miles away to help me load baggage and drive out to the main road. Then it would be south to sun, 70° temperatures, blooming poinsettias, and the sparkling water of Lake Atitlán. South to the three friends I knew who I hoped would help—Jorge Ibarra at the Museum of Natural History, a kindly Catholic priest, and Doña Rosa, an outdoorsy woman who rented rooms in Panajachel.

I turned from the darkening lake and headed toward Doña Rosa's house to greet her and get settled. Reaching for my luggage, I loaded up. Carefully, I slung the khaki dufflebag over my shoulder, for it contained indispensable field equipment: 7×35 binoculars, a life jacket, tape recorder, rubber boots, two 35 mm. cameras and lenses, waterproof pens and notebooks, film, tapes, and batteries. The basic tools of an ecologist. In my suitcase I carried field clothes, a few gifts, shoes, and a dress. Latin women in the mid-1960s never appeared in town wearing pants. So if ever I went into Guatemala City, neither would I. A large cardboard box completed my baggage and was the heaviest. It held my newly published book, *Birds of the Mayas,* a collection of Maya Indian folk tales about tropical birds. I had heard these tales during the wildlife tours that Morgan and I used to run. I hoped to sell the books to help pay for my stay in Guatemala. One hundred dollars a month support was all I had to cover room and board, a rental boat and motor, with gas and oil to run it, plus occasional bus trips to the city, and incidentals.

Panting from the exertion of hauling my bags at the 5,000-foot elevation, I arrived at Doña Rosa's rambling home. I knocked at the heavy wooden door and it flew open immediately. Doña Rosa was waiting and happy to see me. Tall, with dark curly hair and green eyes, she tossed the bags inside, gave me a hug, and beckoned me to the supper table. "You're just in time," she beamed. "How was the trip?"

I caught my breath and smiled. "It was fine, Rosa, but exhausting." It felt good to be in a warm house with spicy smells coming from the kitchen. A fire crackled on the stone hearth. I glanced around the room with its whitewashed walls, dark handhewn timbers, well-used furniture, and gay Guatemalan cushions. Two of Doña Rosa's dogs lay in front of the fireplace, a couple of cats curled on the sofa, a parrot shuffled sleepily on its perch. They were just part of the menagerie that lived here, along with Doña Rosa's children, roomers, and house help.

She clapped her hands sharply. An Indïan man slipped into the living room. "Take Doña Anna's bags to the back bedroom," she told him, "and tell the cook we're ready to eat." Turning to me, she said, "Run and wash up, Anna. I want to hear your plans about the grebes. *And* what happened with Morgan."

During dinner, I filled her in on events. I had not seen Doña Rosa for over a year, or since my last wildlife trip here. More than once she had accompanied our groups onto the lake birdwatching. So my letter to her in November announcing I was coming back to the lake alone to study giant grebes was a bombshell.

"Sad," was her only comment. "But you'll get over it, Anna," she said matter-of-factly. "Now where will you go to find a boat?"

Together we discussed the various possibilities and costs. After deciding on the best place, I excused myself and went to my room. My eyes would barely stay open. A small fire was burning in that hearth and two thick woolen blankets covered the bed. After hanging a few clothes on hooks, I tumbled into bed.

Next morning I was chugging along in a rickety wooden row-boat with an ancient 25 h.p. engine. I had rented both from a small inn. Cautiously, I decided to try out the boat and test the mood of Atitlán. I headed west from the village of Panajachel and slowly scanned the lakeshore. After a scattering of picturesque cottages and weekend homes, habitation ended abruptly at the edge of a mountain. From there on, the shoreline stretched wild, stark, and precipitous. Yet in a small cove not two miles from town I encountered a pair of grebes. They were preening on a floating mat of aquatic plants near an isolated strand of reeds. Through my binoculars, they appeared to be resting on a water-bed.

I stopped the motor and drifted on the calm surface. Fumbling with my knapsack, I took out notebook and pen while keeping the glasses trained on the two birds. They looked dark, chunky, with very large white beaks striped in black pied marks. From time to time, they stropped their wing feathers or scratched around their heads. Each time, the movements disclosed pearly gray underparts, which flashed in the strong sunlight. It reminded me of the way loons (to which grebes are closely related) roll on their sides to preen on Adirondack lakes.

For over an hour I watched, wondering if they'd dive. And, if they did, how long would these grebes stay underwater? Not for a moment did I believe the Indian folk tale of half an hour or more. But I had forgotten my stopwatch and the birds were too lazy that

An adult male giant grebe scans his territory for intruders. Note the heavy, broad bill, adapted for eating small fish and crabs, and the handsome white eye ring. Photo by David G. Allen

morning to move. So I set off in the other direction from town toward the tiny fishing hamlet of Santa Catarina. There I found three pairs of grebes and one lone adult in the bay. All told, I was thrilled with my morning's explorations. Both places were connected to Panajachel by foot trails which twisted over the steep slopes. If all else failed, both groups of grebes were close enough to Doña Rosa's house so I could "walk to work."

I was determined to find all the grebes on Lake Atitlán and choose the best ones for photography and observation. So I placed my faith in the old boat and motor and pushed farther around the jagged shoreline every day. One dawn I set off bravely, planning to make a direct crossing to the end of the Bay of Santiago Atitlán—a distance of eighteen miles. Although Guatemala lies at 14° above the equator, nights are cold and I was bundled in a wool jacket and windbreaker. Doña Rosa had insisted on preparing a large thermos of hot coffee, extra food, and water.

The bay was a bonanza. I discovered more giant grebes here than on all the rest of the lake. Because of the shallow depth, reeds and cattails flourished, providing ideal habitat for aquatic birds. The lake was staying calmer much longer than usual, so I did not hurry home to avoid the midday *chocomil.* The grebes were definitely hard to find and to follow with binoculars. I was reminded of another Indian tale in which grebes, if hunted or wounded, will commit suicide. They dive down to a water weed patch, grab on, and drown themselves. No wonder, given the birds' wary nature, that they escape detection easily.

It was way past lunchtime when I decided to go back to Panajachel. No one had warned me always to check the tops of the volcanoes for tell-tale flat, circular clouds, which cling like caps to the peaks. They always signal a *norte.* At the mouth of the bay, near a jagged shoal called Lions Rocks, I felt the first ruffle of wind. By the time I reached the center of Atitlán, right over its deepest part, I was in the teeth of a strong norther.

The water was an angry blue. Crosswinds collided and waves

leapt every which way. The boat creaked and groaned as it bucked up and sidled down each crest. My hat had long since blown overboard and my jeans were soaking wet. I still had miles to go. There was no other course than to plow straight on toward Pana-jachel. As I knelt in the bottom for greater stability, the first fear I'd known on this beautiful lake washed over me. I now understood why Atitlán is considered a perilous place and why a dozen or more people drown here yearly. Bodies that go down in those depths can never be recovered.

Shortly after I began fieldwork at Lake Atitlán, I found this emaciated juvenile and tried to nurse it back to health.

The hot sun beat on my bare head, making me giddy. Despite my newly acquired tan, my face and arms were burning. I realized how easy it would be to succumb to severe sunburn or sunstroke. Hundreds do, especially fair-skinned Americans, in that clear air at 5,200 feet of altitude. I was a prisoner in the boat, gripping the motor handle for dear life. The trip which had taken thirty minutes at dawn had already stretched to two hours.

Abruptly, the motor faltered, then died. A large wave broke over the transom, leaving the floorboards awash. Slowly my boat veered sideways and began rolling heavily in the troughs. More water spilled over the gunwales. Binoculars, tape recorder, and cameras fell off the seats into the bilge water. Without power, I doubted I could last till the wind blew me to shore. The waves would get worse the closer I came to the northern coast. Either rowing or drifting, I would probably end up smashing against the rocks miles from anywhere.

After pumping the gas tank, checking fuel line and tank, and repeatedly choking the motor, I got it to cough reluctantly. As soon as the boat was underway again, I lunged forward to retrieve my field gear. The next hour was a struggle to keep the engine running, dry my equipment, to bail, and to stave off flooding. I came close to sinking twice.

When I finally reached Panajachel and tied up, I was shaking from fright, sun, and exertion. I stood several moments on the shore, letting the volcanoes and lake stop rocking in my head. The wind began drying my clothes. I reflected that the boat's owner should never have rented out a craft and motor in such condition and should have coached me about conditions on the lake. Crossing to the other side was high-risk travel. There had to be a better and safer way to do my research. Yet this old rowboat was all I could afford. Larger speedboats cost as much per *day*, as I was paying per week. Glumly, I walked down the beach toward Doña Rosa's house, kicking white pieces of pumice that had floated ashore. Rounding a hedge of hibiscus, I looked up and was startled to see a tall, lean, white-bearded man gazing out over the lake. He wore a faded blue cotton shirt, scuffed leather riding boots, and the red sash of a Basque. I murmured, *"Buenas tardes, señor."*

He turned and tipped his wide straw sombrero. *"Buenas tardes, señorita,"* he replied in a deep voice. Then he admitted he had been watching me battle my way across the lake. He sternly chastised me for being out there in a boat alone. I shrugged helplessly.

"What can I do? The motor is very old, but I have to go all around the lake in this rowboat. I can't afford a fancy speedboat from the big hotel."

The old man glared down the beach toward the inn and dock where my boat was tied and muttered something under his breath. "A señorita should not be out by herself on this lake. It is not safe. I've lived here over seventy years, since I came from Spain as a boy. I know how capricious Atitlán can be."

Then he introduced himself. "I'm Don Emilio. At your service. And you are the crazy bird lady. The little *gringita* (Yankee girl) who goes barefoot and wears pigtails like an Indian woman and loves animals."

I grinned at the accurate description, and the speed of small-town gossip. "Yes, Don Emilio," I answered. "I'm Anna and I'm not so crazy. My purpose is to study a certain diving bird, so I can write a story about them. They're not easy to see from shore due to the thick reeds, so I *have* to use a boat."

"I know, I know," he said testily. "I've been watching those *zambullidors* (diving birds) all my life."

"Besides," I continued, "no one else would enjoy sitting in that boat six or seven hours a day without talking, getting sunburned, and having to cross the lake in the *chocomil.*"

I will speak to my son about you," Don Emilio said. "Perhaps Armando can fix you a good boat and motor." Then he turned abruptly and strode toward a simple adobe and tile house which commanded a striking view of Atitlán. I heard a child crying inside. Later I learned that the Basque had several children; the youngest had recently been born—on his eighty-second birthday!

Next morning I was lugging a full five-gallon gas tank and my knapsack down to the dock when a Land Rover pulled up beside me. Its driver was a short, muscular man with a deep tan and twinkling blue eyes. *"Óla,"* he greeted me, pearly white teeth flashing. "Do you want a ride, señorita?" He leaped out and of-

Don Emilio with his youngest child. He lived most of his eighty-five years on the shores of Lake Atitlán.

fered me his hand. "I'm Armando," he said courteously. "My father told me you are having troubles with your rental boat. Perhaps I can help?"

He took the heavy gas tank from me and placed it in the back of the jeep, then opened the door for me.

"Oh, yes, thank you so much," I answered, flustered by the unexpected chivalry and kindness.

As we drove to the dock, I explained the erratic behavior of the motor and the various leaks in the rowboat. Armando shook his head disapprovingly.

"The owner is wrong to rent such a boat. He's only thinking of the money. The spark plugs are probably old, the carburetor dirty, and the tank full of water. You must not take chances on the lake. You must not go alone."

I was rapidly learning that most Latins are accustomed to traveling in groups and are very protective toward women. They could not understand why I worked alone, especially at a time when women were always chaperoned. I found this concern touching, and also a little stifling. Living among the rugged and independent people of the Adirondacks, I was quite used to fending for myself.

I explained to Armando how a field ecologist carries out observations on birds and obtains data on ecosystems. "Besides working from a boat," I told him, "I'll have to crawl into the reeds, looking for grebe nests, animals, and plants, shooting pictures, and taking specimens for a collection."

He looked at me with new respect but shook his head worriedly. He offered to dig out an old engine he had in storage and repair it for free. He also volunteered to refinish his boat and rent it to me. Armando had been planning to put it back in service but had been too busy with his local trucking service. I was delighted until he mentioned the fee. Rent would be $45 a month. That was more than the dollar a day I'd been paying for the inn's boat. However, it would be much safer. With room and board at Doña

Rosa's at $10 a week, that only left me $15 for gas and oil out of Morgan's $100 a month. Somewhere I had to find more funds. For now, I accepted eagerly because Armando agreed to stand behind his work and take care of any new repairs gratis.

"Give me a week or so to get things ready," he said as he politely opened my door and set the gas tank on the dock.

The week passed slowly. I continued to cross the lake and pinpoint new grebes, counting as I went. But I was careful to watch for wind and always came home early. Under Armando's tutelage, I strained my gas, cleaned out the fuel tank and carburetor bowl, and changed the plugs. No more breakdowns occurred, but I always felt on edge.

An additional problem lurked in the background. If I *did* break down far from Panajachel, there'd be no commercial motorboat, no Coast Guard, no search-and-rescue service to help me. Only one mail-plus-tourist boat plied daily between Panajachel and Santiago Atitlán. There were no marinas, no safe anchorages, only twelve Indian villages. None of the Indians could afford outboards. They used dugouts and paddles. A few well-to-do Guatemalans from the city owned lakeside houses and speedboats, but they only visited here on weekends or holidays. One day I counted all the fancy vacation homes out of curiosity, making a mental note where help might be found: There were thirty-two "chalets" in 1965 (twenty-eight in 1960) around the seventy-five-mile shoreline.

Moreover, my Spanish was so poor that certainly none of the Indians would understand me if I sought assistance. They spoke the Mayan dialects of Cakchiquel and Tzutujil. Few *ladinos* (Guatemalans of mixed blood who speak Spanish) lived at the lake. With this communications barrier, I might as well have been working in the wilderness. My entire support system consisted of Doña Rosa, Don Emilio, his son, Armando, and the Texaco gas station!

By the time I finished surveying the entire lake, Armando was putting final touches of paint on his boat. The new motor parts had arrived from Guatemala City, seventy-five miles away, and the engine was running smoothly. "Anita," he said proudly, "tomorrow you can start using it. See! I named the boat, *Xelaju*, 'the beautiful one.' Just for you."

I was charmed. But I was also troubled. In covering the lake, I had counted only *80* grebes instead of the 200–300 reported in the 1930s, and the 200-plus Morgan and I estimated in 1960. I had stopped by every stretch of reeds and scanned the surface carefully. I'd kept track of each grebe, American coot, Florida gallinule, and the various ducks on the lake. Something was wrong. I asked Armando what he thought.

"You may have missed some birds with the wind and waves, Anita," he counseled. "They are so shy. You should count them again—at night. With a full moon, no wind, quiet. It'll be better that way. You'll find more."

"But how will I *see* them?" I asked. "It's hard enough to spot them in sunlight."

"You won't. You'll *hear* them," he answered cryptically. "The grebes always call with the full moon. You can call back. Then make sure how many answer and where each one is roosting."

I stared at Armando in admiration. It was a brilliant idea. In fact, if I had a real taped grebe call, I'd be sure of getting better responses. Perhaps I could use the recorder, on which I noted my observations, to capture a male's vocalization.

Armando read my mind. "You have the recorder. Why not spend the next few days trying to get a good call on tape? The moon will be full soon," he added, excitement in his voice. "I will go with you and help count the zambullidors."

Four nights later, Armando and I were steering toward a pitch-black bed of reeds in a remote corner of Lake Atitlán. A cold moon silhouetted the volcanic cones of Atitlán, Tolimán, and San Pedro. Their huge shadows seemed lacquered upon the quicksilver surface. Cutting the motor, I switched on the recorder and played the male grebe's call used to delineate and defend territory.

At once, a challenging "caow, caow, caow-uh, caow-uh" responded near shore. Armando placed a dot on the map. I checked off one adult male. Seconds later, a soft warbling duet floated on the air. The male had met its mate, and they were greeting each other. I checked off one adult female. Then I played the recorder again. No more replies. Methodically, I waited another minute and repeated the process. Silence.

"That's all there are here," whispered Armando. "Let's go on." He started the engine. We cruised past miles of steep, rocky shoreline, keeping well offshore, until we reached another reed patch. This was our third night of conducting the night census, and so far we'd not hit a rock or shoal. Again we went through the precise routine just outside the tall emergent reeds. This is the only habitat where grebes, ducks, and other waterbirds can roost, nest, and hide around the craggy, often violent lake. I gave three plays, three waits, totaling five minutes per stop, to give grebes time to answer. Then we'd move a hundred yards, or roughly the width of a pair's territory, and repeat the process until we ran out of vegetation. I was to use this method of censusing systematically over all my years at Lake Atitlán. By 3 A.M. I was shivering from cold, and Armando was yawning. "Shall we go back and finish up tomorrow?" he asked.

"Not yet," I pleaded. "It's such a perfect night. The weather might change by tomorrow. We're almost done. We still have two or three hours of moon and darkness. I just wish I could get warm."

"Let's go to the hot springs," Armando suggested. "That will warm you up fast."

"Hot springs? In the lake?"

"Yes, sulfur springs bubble up from the bottom. We can soak in a little pool for a while. You'll feel terrific afterward."

He pointed the boat toward a jagged escarpment and eased close to shore. The rank odor of sulfur fumes invaded my nose.

Armando threw an anchor overboard and pulled off his jacket. "I wore a bathing suit, just in case," he said. "Let me swim in and find the spot. You wait here."

With an almost splashless dive, he plunged into the black lake and disappeared. I shuddered. How could he stand the cold? How could I? In a couple of minutes his voice echoed back from the cliffside and I heard him splashing along the edge. A few minutes later, he called to me.

"Here they are, Anita. There's an underwater rock wall that keeps the hot springs from mixing with the lake water. It's like a bathtub. Hot as a sauna. Come on in."

I paused. On the one hand, I didn't want to disappoint this new companion who was being such a help in my work. On the other hand, I'd never done a crazier thing in my life—swim through a cold lake 1,200 feet deep at 3 A.M. Stripping to my underwear and cotton work shirt, I slid over the side, gasping with shock. Although Atitlán stays about 70–72° F. year round due to the tremendous mixing by wind, I was already too chilled to feel anything but colder. A few swift strokes and I was next to Armando. He gave me a hand and helped me slide over the low wall.

"Sit here," he said. Instantly I felt the upwelling of hot water. I could sit right on the pebbly bottom of the lake and be bathed in warm water right up to my neck. The situation and view were magnificent. I stopped shivering and relaxed, sculling the hot and cold water together with my hands. Armando and I watched a corn-colored moon slowly set toward the wild western skyline. It was a magical night.

After an hour of steeping ourselves, we were limp with muscle relaxation from the sulfur. We swam back to the boat, reviving at once in the cold water. Scrambling over the transom with aid of the motor, Armando and I dried ourselves briskly and dressed. Then we cruised on to finish our census before first light, chatting and chuckling like kids.

As we pulled the boat back onto the beach at dawn, I reflected this was the first fun I'd had in months, maybe years. How nice it was to find an adventurous friend like Armando. Moreover, we had double-checked the entire grebe population of Lake Atitlán. Our results? Only eighty-two birds! Our nighttime number matched too well with my daylight census to be a mistake. Something was definitely amiss on this beautiful, bizarre lake. How could the world's only population of these flightless birds have been cut by more than half in less than five years?

2
Binoculars and
Black Magic

I'D ALREADY BEEN AT Lake Atitlán almost four of my allotted eight weeks and had little to show for it—no photographs, limited observations on grebe behavior, movements, and food habits. I knew nothing about the birds' courtship, nesting, or their young. I'd never even *seen* a nest! Most important, I had no clues as to why the population was so low. The realization hit me that I could not begin to write a meaningful article at this point and had been terribly naive to think it was possible in a one-to-two-month span. Too much time had been taken tinkering with motors and boats, locating and counting birds, learning the natural rhythms and perils of the lake, and improving my Spanish.

But then I reflected on what I *did* know. First and foremost, I'd not seen any grebes fly. They did try to patter across the water, beating their wings valiantly, but never became airborne. In order to obtain specimens to study their flightlessness and to send to Cornell University's Lab of Ornithology and Yale University's Peabody Museum, I had a local hunter shoot four adult birds.

Giant grebe specimens collected for Cornell University. Because of the extremely short wings and large bodies, the birds were virtually flightless.

From them I discovered that giant grebes have bodies roughly twice as heavy as those of common pied-billed grebes, yet their wings are almost the same size. Also, their wing bones are small and the pectoral muscles poorly developed. So it is aerodynamically impossible for them actually to fly!

Few birds are truly flightless. Yet, in this respect, grebes are peculiar. Of the twenty-one different species in the world, three *are* flightless. The giants of Guatemala, the short-winged grebes of Lake Titicaca, and the puna grebe of Lake Junín, Peru. All three are endemic and confined to high-altitude lakes. All show fascinating changes through evolution toward becoming excellent divers and swimmers rather than flyers and migrators. Before I pickled the specimens for shipment, I also checked their stomach contents and body organs to note condition. The two pairs seemed well nourished and healthy. I could tentatively rule out starvation and disease as limiting factors.

It also seemed important to measure carefully all parts of the birds—beaks, feet, body length, and so forth—and to write detailed descriptions of their colors. With the population so low, these four birds were the only "benchmark" for giant grebes that any scientific institution would ever own. I would never dare shoot more and would do everything possible to deter other scientists from collecting. My instincts then were to prove valuable years later.

I also debunked the myth that grebes can stay submerged for half an hour and can swim underwater half a mile. By timing dozens of birds over the past month with my stopwatch, I proved that 90 *seconds* was the maximum time and 300 feet the farthest distance. Their top speed above water appeared to be 5 m.p.h.

Giant grebe about to fold up like an accordion before diving.
Photo by David G. Allen

Grebes are superb divers. When a bird folds up in the middle like an accordion and sinks underwater without a ripple or sound, there's no telling where it'll reappear. Often it practices submarine surveillance. It quietly pokes the top of its head and nostrils above the surface like a periscope, peeks around for danger, and resubmerges. If waves cover the lake, an observer usually misses this action. Thus, the bird seems to disappear.

I had discovered that giant grebes are small fish and crab eaters. They dove out in the lake far beyond the reeds for food. Of course, they may have been taking snails, aquatic insects, tadpoles, or young frogs within the reed beds, but I had yet to explore inside this dense vegetation.

I was totally intrigued by my initial contact with the grebes— their sleek dark bodies, smooth powerful dives, startling black and white beaks, and perky, alert stance. Moreover, I wanted time to find out what was causing their decline. For most species, a population of fifty or less means probable early extinction. The Atitlán grebes were treading close to this mark. Therefore, I changed my air ticket, renewed my tourist card, paid Doña Rosa another month's rent, and gave Armando more money for his boat and motor.

There was no authority to turn to for help and no one to ask for advice. I was in a country slightly smaller than New York State (42,042 vs. 49,576 square miles) whose total department of conservation and natural resources in 1965 consisted of four people. None was trained specifically in natural resource management, nor did anyone have a degree higher than a B.S. in agronomy and fishery biology. They had perhaps three cars, three small boats, a few fish hatcheries, and one tiny lab at their disposal. Salaries were pitifully low. There were no official, uniformed game wardens or conservation officers anywhere in Guatemala.

New York State, in comparison, had a department of about 2,000 people, several with doctorates. There were hundreds of state vehicles, uniforms, firearms, even a couple of light planes and helicopters for field investigations. Salaries were respectable. Roughly 250 game wardens covered the state, working out of several regional offices.

This comparison is in no way meant to imply that Guatemala

was slack or backward, but rather to illustrate that the art of
conservation and science of wildlife management were very new,
unsophisticated, and of extremely low priority in Third World
government programs. However, after making this comparison in
my mind, I was spurred to devote my energies and modest training to helping this developing nation, be it to save the grebes or
any other natural resource.

However, none of my graduate classes in wildlife management
had prepared me for the situation I was now in. We had only
learned theoretical techniques of studying and censusing populations, not hands-on fieldwork with endangered species. None of
the Guatemalan universities and colleges had departments in environmental sciences or natural resources. No help there. And no
one, except perhaps Don Emilio, seemed to care about the lake
and the grebes. The Maya Indians living around the lake were
totally engrossed with corn farming, fishing and crabbing, weaving, cutting firewood, and family care. The handful of ladinos
mostly ran small shops and pensions. The smattering of retired
Americans and Europeans who wintered in Panajachel were
chiefly concerned with their tans and cocktail hours. And the few
wealthy chalet owners from Guatemala City came to relax from
business worries. Jorge Ibarra was the only colleague I could seek
out, and he was seventy-five miles away running his museum.

I took to visiting Don Emilio in the afternoons. He was now
probably the oldest resident of Lake Atitlán. Living close to the
water, he knew more about local natural history than anyone else.
I considered him my chief informant. We would sit on his shady
porch, slapping at fleas that hopped from his German shepherds
onto our pants.

"What's wrong with the grebes?" I asked him.

"I'm not sure," he answered. "But when I was young, zambullidors were all around the lake. I could barely sleep on full moon
nights for their serenading. There must have been hundreds. But

as you say, there are not so many birds now, and not so many reeds. Too many people!" He scowled. "What about hunters, or poachers? Have you checked into that? Seems to me I heard about a law to protect the grebes a few years back."

"A law?" I gasped. "That's wonderful. I'll bet Mr. Ibarra helped with it. How can I find out about it?"

"Go to the Secretary in one of the Indian villages, or the Governor of this region, and ask him to show it to you".

This lead sent me off around the lake on a new investigation. With my boat, *Xelaju,* I confidently crossed the lake in all directions looking for hunters. Only once on a Sunday afternoon did I hear shots, but they came from shore. Another time I saw three sportsmen in a smart fiberglass boat shooting at ducks. I figured they were wealthy hunters from the city because no Indian owned a firearm, and guns were generally outlawed among Guatemalan citizens. At any rate, the lake was not exactly crawling with hunters as Don Emilio thought.

Satisfied about this, I cruised over to Santiago Atitlán, the largest Indian town on the lake, to find its Secretary. I tied up to its spindly dock. Leaving my field gear under the boat deck, I walked up the long cobblestoned street toward the central square. Inquisitive eyes watched me from tiny windows in thatched huts. A hundred scrawny dogs barked at me. Several children—exact replicas of their parents in purple-and-white-striped pants or blouses intricately embroidered with bright birds—trailed behind me. Young Indian men lounged in doorways; their black slanted eyes discreetly examining my jeans, long-sleeved shirt, straw sombrero, and pigtails. A woman in pants was unheard of in their culture.

As I walked into the plaza, groups of young barefoot girls padded softly past me with clay jugs on their heads. Their jet-black hair hung lustrous and thick below their waists. From their giggles and glances at the boys, it was easy to see that going to the lake for water was a special event, not a chore. Apparently, it was the best way to do some surreptitious courting. No wonder the youths were standing around and not working.

I headed for the town office, hoping to find the Secretary. A spare, dry-skinned man was writing in a huge record book within an adobe room. I introduced myself. He seemed only too glad to

Stone house in Santiago Atitlán. Plastic jugs are replacing the traditional clay water jugs.

stop writing in an exquisite, feathery script and talk. I asked if he knew anything about the grebes.

"The *what?*"

"The small duck that dives so well and lives in the reeds," I explained. "I think it's called a zambullidor."

"Ah, the *poc,*" he responded rather ostentatiously. "Of *course* I do."

Now it was my turn to be bewildered. "Poc?"

"That is the Tzutujil name for those birds," he said. "Many pocs live in the Bay of Santiago Atitlán. Sometimes the people try to hunt them with slingshots and sell them in the market for food."

"They *eat* grebes?" Fish-eating birds are usually rank and sinewy.

"Certainly," he said importantly. "They eat ducks, coots, gallinules, herons, eggs, any meat they can get. You see, señorita, having nothing but black beans and tortillas three times a day becomes monotonous." With an air of disdain he added, "If waterbirds are smoked, they're not too bad. One only costs a quetzal (one dollar)."

I noticed that he was a ladino and apparently considered himself above eating smoked birds.

"Of course," he said. "It's against the law."

"What law?"

He unbent his cadaverous frame from the desk and pulled an enormous cardboard file off a shelf. Sucking in his breath between yellowed teeth, he rifled through sheaves of official papers. Dust gently floated into the shafts of sunshine streaming through the open door. I got the feeling no one had looked at these files for ages.

"Here it is," the Secretary declared after some time. With a flourish he read, "President Miguel Ydigoras Fuentes, on 14 January 1959, decreed that hunting or molesting pocs and other water birds at Lake Atitlán was prohibited. He imposed a fine of five to twenty-five quetzals, plus confiscation of firearms or slingshots, on anyone breaking this law."

I was overjoyed to find a legal basis for protecting the giant grebes. "Are there any game wardens working here?" I asked.

"Game wardens?"

"You know, conservation officers, uhhh, wildlife patrolmen, uhhhh, vigilantes, sort of. . . ." I ended lamely, not knowing the Spanish word.

"Ah, *vigilantes,*" exclaimed the Secretary, sucking in his breath again and blinking his green eyes. "There are no vigilantes for *birds* in Guatemala, señorita," he said decisively. "Maybe for the rare *pinabete* (balsam fir) which people steal at Christmas time. And certainly for *people.* Our *aguaciles* (Indian policemen) are sitting right outside this room."

I glanced out the door and saw six handsome, robust Indian men holding long sticks and sitting along a wooden bench.

"Well, can't your men also watch out for the grebes," I asked naively, "if the law protects them?"

He shrugged. "No one cares, señorita."

"But there are only eighty pocs left alive. They are *disappearing,* but I don't know why. This is the only place in the world where they live."

The Secretary looked at me curiously, then said flatly, though courteously, "And what difference does that make?"

His question so shocked me that I fumbled in my inadequate Spanish for an answer. Terms like "conservation conscience," "genetic pool," "scientific enigma," "aesthetics," "moral responsibility," and "ecological support system" raced through my mind. But I sensed that this self-important minor official would never understand why humans have an obligation to cherish wildlife and wildlands.

For a long moment we stared at each other. "It's our duty," I suggested.

"I'm sorry, señorita," he said impatiently. "There's nothing that can be done about the pocs."

We shook hands and I left, crossing self-consciously in front of the row of idle policemen. Each *aguacile* wore his hair cut in a trim line and sported a new sombrero and rubber-soled sandals. I mumbled good morning and headed for the market.

Under a high tin roof I found dozens of women kneeling on the ground next to large wicker baskets filled with vegetables. Everything looked brighter and fresher than in a U.S. supermarket. Scarlet tomatoes, glistening onions, strings of garlic cloves, pale green cabbages, stubby bananas, silvery minnows, blaze-orange carrots, buff eggs, purple eggplants, red crabs, cerise watermelons—it was a kaleidoscope of colors and smells, although lacking in protein foods. Children squatted among the women, as did laying hens. Sloe-eyed babies wrapped in shawls were slung over their mothers' backs, or were suckling at their breasts. A soft murmur filled the air. Nowhere did I hear strident hawkers, discordant shoppers, or Muzak. It was a gentle market.

I hopscotched my way down narrow aisles, shopping casually as I went, yet keeping a sharp eye out for smoked grebes. For less than $2, I soon had enough vegetables and fruits to help Doña Rosa feed me and her family for a week. I did not see wild birds of any type for sale. I asked a few women in Spanish if they had smoked pocs. Each one shook her head in confusion and looked away shyly. Finally, a fat toothless ladino lady pointed to a stall filled with spices and corn. Looking up, I spied a lone leathery bird dangling from a piece of twine. If this was the extent of water birds for sale, then market hunting didn't seem to be a large drain on the poc population.

It was almost lunchtime, so I walked back to my boat and ran it out toward a large reed patch across the bay. I decided to tie up to some stalks, eat my sandwiches, and then observe grebes until the winds started. I was sprawled on the bottom with only my head above the gunwale when an Indian canoe approached and rammed into the reeds. The Indian paddler started slashing the reeds and laying them carefully in his dugout canoe. I continued eating, trying to figure out what he was doing. The man worked methodically and quickly. Within half an hour he had cleared a patch about eight feet square. Could he be cutting a pathway to shore? Or making a mooring spot for his boat? Then it dawned on me that he was harvesting reeds.

Suddenly, a Florida gallinule dashed out panic-stricken. That triggered my imagination. If the Indian was cutting reeds during the pocs' nesting season, would he chop right through their nests, eggs, and young? And what about right *now?* He was destroying the only available habitat on Lake Atitlán not just for grebes but for other water birds, small fishes, crabs, frogs, insects, snails, and turtles. These reeds were wildlife homes and nurseries.

Then I remembered the law prohibited killing *or* molesting water birds. The man should be stopped. I leaped up and shouted at him in Spanish. Startled, he almost dropped his machete overboard. I yelled out an explanation, but he acted as if he didn't understand and kept slashing. "No, no," I called severely. I didn't feel like getting any closer with that gleaming blade between us. Maybe these people didn't like foreigners. Maybe *I* should carry a machete or gun, or at least take a dog along, for protection. Perhaps Don Emilio would give me one of his German shepherds. For the second time on that idyllic lake, I felt apprehensive. Living here was a lot different from visiting on a wildlife tour. With these sobering thoughts, I shut up and decided to go for help.

Rushing back to Santiago Atitlán, I went looking for the Secretary. He was taking a siesta in the large swivel chair, his yellow teeth bared to the ceiling.

Timidly, I tapped on his desk and cleared my throat. He opened one green eye and closed his mouth. Then he struggled to rise and say hello. I explained what I had seen across the bay. "Can't you send your *aguaciles* to stop the man?" I pleaded.

"To stop a man cutting reeds?" He blinked, then regarded me severely. "Unfortunately, señorita, I cannot. In the first place, there's no law against that. Secondly, the police have no boat. Third, it's a six- or seven-mile walk around the entire bay. And—"

"But slashing reeds destroys the grebes' homes and nests," I interrupted. "It's the same thing as 'molesting' them, and the law forbids that."

The Secretary continued coolly, "These people have been using reeds for *petates* (sleeping mats) and little seats for centuries. Many families earn part of their living cutting and weaving reeds."

"You mean those reed beds aren't wild?" I asked incredulously.

"Oh, no," he said. "Every stalk either belongs to, or is rented to, an Indian reed cutter. I have it all here in my files. Lake Atitlán has the best reeds in Guatemala."

A picture of hundreds of men cutting down reeds, of pocs and coots homeless, of fish and crabs looking for spawning grounds flashed through my mind. *This* must be the reason for the grebe decline!

"Well," I fumed. "If you won't arrest that man, then I will!"

The Secretary suddenly realized how serious I was about these odd birds. He sat bolt upright and said firmly, "You do *not* have the authority to do so. I would not advise it. Besides the man has no money for a fine."

At once I saw that he was right. Only an official game warden should do the job. I was getting carried away, and this wasn't even my country. For all I knew, Guatemala did not allow citizen arrests as we do in the States when hunters trespass on private lands.

A bit shamefaced, I apologized to the Secretary and left. But the seed had been planted in my mind that somehow enforcement had to be brought to Lake Atitlán to protect its natural resources, especially the pocs.

Back in my boat, I found the *chocomil* in full force, but it

didn't seem so bad now. I was becoming adept at handling the
boat through the jumbled waves. Thinking of all I'd learned, I
didn't notice the two figures standing on the beach at Panajachel.
I glanced at my watch—3:30 P.M. I'd never come back so late
before alone. Both Armando and his father, looking worried, were
waiting for me. They helped me pull the boat onto the beach. I
blurted out the day's events. Then I noticed Armando feeling
around under the deck.

"Anita," he said in a peculiar way, "Where's your tape recorder and binoculars?"

"In my knapsack under the bow," I answered.

"They're not there," he said. "Did you leave the boat alone at
the dock in Santiago?"

I nodded.

"Well, that's it. Someone stole your things. You must always
pay a boy to watch your boat."

"What will I do?" I began moaning. "Without my gear I'll
have to fly to Miami and buy more—or even go back home." The
severity of the situation hit me. I could not even afford to buy
more field equipment. Without it there could be no more observations, no article. I'd have to spend Christmas all alone in my
cabin . . . in the snow . . . without Armando or Doña Rosa or . . .

While I was imagining the worst, Armando was already tugging the boat back into the water. Don Emilio let out a string of
swear words and waded in up to his thighs to help. "Get in quick!"
Armando ordered, as waves crashed against him. "We're going
right over to Santiago to report this. If we offer a reward through
the town crier, there's a chance you'll get your things back."

With his usual direct logic, he explained, "Either the thief
will leave by bus at dawn to pawn your stuff in the city, or some
poor Indian has no idea what's in the knapsack or what to do with
it. He's probably consulting a shaman right now."

Don Emilio gave the boat a mighty shove and we were pounding our way into the *chocomil.* I was too upset to talk. Here I was

going for the third time that day to the village, making a nuisance of myself. Word was surely going to spread about the "crazy bird lady." However, Armando handled everything smoothly. He went into a huddle immediately with the Secretary and Mayor, persuading them to call out the *aguaciles* and make a *pregon*. Since so few Indians read or write and they do not possess phones, radios, or TV, this was the swiftest way to inform villagers about urgent events. Armando advised them to say that the lady scientist from the States had lost valuable things from her boat. These things were only good for watching the pocs; no use to anyone. She would pay a $5 reward to get them back.

I whispered to Armando that I would gladly pay $25, but he hushed me with a frown. "These people only earn $100–300 a year," he said. "Five dollars is a whole week's wage. Just keep quiet and let me manage this, Anita. Please!"

Twilight was coming on and the wind had dropped. A haze of pine smoke hung over the village, as aromatic as incense. It came from hundreds of small cooking fires where Mayan women were preparing the evening meal of tortillas and beans. Men and small boys were walking tiredly home from their cornfields, hoes and *morrales* (string work bags) over their shoulders. An incandescent glow flared up behind Volcano San Pedro, clear as claret. To the east, the first stars were winking in a darkening sky. The town of 15,000 quieted as suppertime began.

Then I heard the low, muffled boom of a drum. It reverberated eerily against the stone huts and cobblestone streets. Armando and I stepped out of the Secretary's office and saw three Indian policemen parading across the empty plaza. One beat a large wooden drum and another carried a flaming *ocote* (pine heartwood torch). The third was the crier. At every street intersection they stopped and he shouted out the message. Here and there the torchlight caught a glint of eyes peering from shuttered windows.

"If anyone finds a bag with black and silver metal objects in it, bring it to the Secretary's office. These things are of no value. The *gringa* who watches the poc will pay five quetzals reward to have them back," Armando translated for me.

The staccato Indian dialect sounded strange. The night seemed very dark. My chances of ever seeing that equipment were slim indeed. I asked myself what was I really doing in a dilemma like this. Why was I getting so wrapped up in the survival of one silly bird? How many other ecologists were off in foreign lands trying to save a species? Then I sensed Armando's blue eyes smiling at me.

"Do not worry, Anita," he said gently. "You'll get your equipment back. We must wait now. Be patient. Are you hungry?"

"Oh, yes." I suddenly realized how long the day had been. I'd started out on the lake at 5 A.M. and now it was 7:30 P.M. My lunchtime had been halved by the reed cutter.

"Come. We'll find a place that's still open."

We walked along a dirt path till we saw candles flickering in an open window. *"Buenas noches, Doña Susi,"* called Armando. He pushed open the door and led me to some straight chairs inside the shop. Offering me a seat, he laid his jacket over my shoulders. "You look cold, Anita. Let's drink a beer and relax."

A chubby ladino shopkeeper with plastic curlers in her hair came out and greeted Armando. Soon she was back with two lukewarm bottles of beer, some salt, dried river shrimp, and then stacks of hot tortillas, scrambled eggs, rich black beans, and fiery little peppers. Armando had ordered well.

I was so hungry that I ate and drank everything, despite the fact that in those days I never took anything alcoholic and knew the shrimp might harbor hepatitis or amoebas. Who knew what river they came from and how polluted the water was from night soil (human urine and feces) or raw sewage since most Indians defecate directly on the ground. We ate ravenously by candlelight, listening to the *pregon* fade into the distance. The crier must have alerted the whole town by now.

As soon as we finished eating, we hurried back to the Secretary's office. No knapsack, no news. My heart sank. It was almost ten o'clock. The *pregon* was over. The village was asleep. The Secretary yawned unceremoniously. Nothing to do but to return to Panajachel for there were no overnight accommodations in Santiago. Armando left the five quetzal reward and an extra quetzal to telegraph him in case the bag turned up next day. Then we stumbled back toward the dock. There hadn't been time to bring flashlights. Once I bumped into a dog, then almost walked off the end of the dock. I was tipsy from the beer. Armando chuckled. He supported me to the boat and sat me firmly on the seat with a warning not to fall out. Then he started the motor and headed toward the twinkling lights of Panajachel, the only town with electricity.

As we cruised across that immense sheet of water, tiny torches flickered like fireflies all along the dark shoreline. Crabmen were searching the shallows with pinewood flares and long bamboo gigs. The light lured these crustaceans toward the dugouts, where they were speared. Huge stars glowed in a velvet black sky. I saw Orion, the winter hunter, striding out of the east. A cool breeze crinkled the lake with star-shimmer like beaten silver. All three volcanoes had halos of clouds. I felt a nip in the air and was grateful for Armando's jacket. All he wore was a short-sleeved shirt and wet pants. Where he got his stamina and energy I could not imagine.

"A *norte* is coming," said Armando, cocking his head at the volcano tops. "Tomorrow we'll have a strong wind and cold."

Depressed, I didn't care what happened tomorrow because I couldn't continue without my field equipment. At the beach, I helped Armando pull out the boat. As we tugged and hauled, a dark object rolled out from under the bow. Armando grabbed it and examined it under the star glow. Then he shouted, "Here are your things, Anita."

I couldn't believe my ears. But, yes, he was holding my prized knapsack, and everything was inside. Even my precious notebook was in its place. "But, but how . . ." I began.

"A shaman," Armando said. "He must have advised the thief to put things back, or risk an evil eye." He handed me the bag. "Most shamans are very wise men and healers. It's the *brujas* (evil witch doctors) who are malicious with their advice."

"Shamans, brujas. That's nonsense, Armando. Someone just wanted the reward."

"No," said Armando with great conviction. "No one will take your money. It would make the whole village suspicious of that person stealing your things in the first place. More important, the thief knows it is better to be rid of such mysterious objects. You must realize that these Indians have never seen a camera except in the hands of tourists. They refuse to let their pictures be taken unless paid, or the camera might steal their soul. They've never looked through binoculars. How can they comprehend that things look much bigger, or smaller, depending on which end you look into? A tape recorder would be sheer magic to them. It might be stealing their voice." Giving me an exuberant bear hug, he said, "Oh, yes, it was a smart shaman."

Yet, despite Armando's careful explanation, how could I, a university product, with a bachelor's and master's degree in science, believe that? Things worked by cause and effect, not by superstition and black magic. Life was rational and logical: steps a, b, c. So I said to Armando, "Poppycock. It was just luck."

Little did I know how much I had to learn from this experience, and that much of the world does, in fact, act in unscientific and irrational ways. Soon, I, too, would be needing the help of a shaman.

3
Discovery

WHEN I WALKED DOWN TO the shore next morning, the *norte* was blowing so hard that I had doubts about going out in my boat. While I was watching the wind sweep across that royal blue expanse, Don Emilio ran down and sternly ordered me to stay home. I was burning to be out watching grebes, but the old Basque was adamant. He tugged at the clove of garlic around his neck, which he wore to ward off heart attacks, and motioned me toward his house.

"Come in," he said hospitably, "I want to show you something, Anita."

Resigned, I followed him. Maybe I could learn more about the pocs by talking to him. Instead of sitting down, however, Don Emilio began fiddling with the knobs and decorations on a seven-foot-tall wooden chest standing near a plank table on the front porch. Suddenly, a door swung open smoothly. It was an old Spanish safe! Inside I could see a number of tin cans of Nestle's dried milk.

Don Emilio took out four of the cans and pried off their lids. Cascade upon cascade of green jade stones came spilling out onto the rough tabletop! Dozens of carved faces, ear plugs, nose plugs, drilled necklace pieces, and plain polished stones lay in disarray before me—a treasure trove of authentic Mayan artifacts.

"Where did you get them?" I asked in astonishment.

Don Emilio gestured vaguely toward the north. "Oh, up in the mountains when I go to my farm."

More than ever I was impressed by this wiry old character with his long white beard and his flinty blue eyes, for I knew his farm was three days horseback ride away. Don Emilio was in a talkative mood that morning. He picked out various ornaments and told me their uses. Finding him in such a good humor, I settled down on the porch and looked out over the seething lake. "You were right to keep me here," I said amiably, "although I hate to miss a single day on the water." Before long I was telling him my ideas about the grebe decline.

"Hunting and poaching really don't seem to be done much, Don Emilio, from what I've seen. And I doubt the Indians can kill many pocs with their slingshots. But, I think that *reed cutting* may be the problem." And I related the incident of the Indian cutter in the Bay of Santiago Atitlán.

"Well now," the old man said. "Indians have been using the *tul* (reeds) for centuries. They know enough to leave some standing for a new crop. There's bound to be enough shelter for the birds around the lake."

"I'm not so sure. Maybe the human population's growing too fast. Maybe the Indians are overharvesting. How many men cut reeds?"

"On the whole lake I'd guess sixty or seventy men," said Don Emilio. "They cut the stalks, like you saw, then dry them in the sun for at least ten days until tawny brown and canoe them back to the village. The old women and men weave them into *petates* and little seats. Remember, Anita, the Maya don't use beds and have few chairs. They curl up at night on the floor as an entire family, spoon-fashion, to sleep. *Petates are* their beds."

Coming as I did from a developed country, it had never occur-

Reeds enroute to Santiago Atitlán, where they will be woven into sleeping mats and seats. Most Indian houses at Lake Atitlán do not have modern furniture.

red to me that people slept without beds unless they went camping. "How many mats might be made in one year?" I asked.

"A thousand or more. The reeds here grow very tall and thick and make the biggest and nicest *petates* in Guatemala." A dog came rambling by and Don Emilio bent down to pet it.

This gave me a thought. "Don Emilio," I said, "do you think I should have a dog with me in the boat for safety? And would you be able to sell one?"

"Caramba!" Don Emilio began, scooping handfuls of jade back into the tins with his gnarled brown hands. "I won't *sell* you a dog. The next litter my bitch has, you can have a puppy." He set the four Nestlé cans back in the safe and, turning the knobs, added, "You're safe enough, Anita. No one will hurt you."

I began thinking of the reed mat industry again, relieved by his words. "I wonder how many reeds it takes to make a mat and how many miles of reed beds there are around the lake?"

"Why don't you go and measure them," the old man suggested matter-of-factly.

Just then Armando stopped by in his Land Rover to invite Don Emilio to Doña Rosa's for Christmas Eve. It seemed my landlady traditionally gave a party. I'd forgotten that only two days remained till Christmas and made a mental note to buy presents that very day. But I was still thinking about the reeds.

"Armando," I began, "your father says I should measure all the reeds around Atitlán, but I have no idea how to do that unless I walk the whole shoreline. That would take *days.*"

"Simple," he said, with a wink of blue eyes. "Calculate your boat speed along a certain section of shoreline where you know the distance—like the public beach in Panajachel. Then, take your stopwatch and cruise the whole shore at that speed. Turn on the stopwatch whenever you pass some reeds."

"Why that's brilliant," I said, marveling at his mechanical gift. I liked the way he made everything seem simple and practical. He never wasted motions, words, or time.

"Why do you want to know this, Anita?" he asked.

"I have to find out how much habitat there is, and how much is being destroyed by reed cutters. Then maybe I can determine if that is why the grebes are declining."

"That makes sense," he said. "I'll go with you and help whenever you're ready."

With this fresh idea and kind offer warming my mind, I walked on into the village. Highland Guatemala was at its loveliest. Poinsettias bloomed in gardens, brilliant red and creamy white. Calla lilies, which practically grew wild here, stood elegantly in the swales. The sky was the deepest, purest blue I'd ever seen, with fleecy clouds sailing overhead on the north wind. The dry crisp air smelled of pines and oaks. I did my shopping quickly and went back to Doña Rosa's. At sunset, the norther calmed.

Next day, I sped across the flat lake at dawn. The sky was incredibly clear and the tops of the volcanoes looked close enough to touch. They were coated with hoar frost and glistened silver-white in the rising sun. I drove the boat to the end of Santiago Bay, where I'd found a pair of grebes less skittish than most. They seemed used to Indian women washing their clothes in the shallows near the reed beds. Therefore, I could get closer and see more of their behavior than with others. I hunched down in my woolen jacket with hot coffee, binoculars, and notebook and prepared for another interesting day.

As the sun slid over the edge of Volcano Tolimán and warmed the morning air, Indians' canoes were crossing the bay bound for the cornfields on San Pedro's slopes. Each boat held a man paddling near the bow, one or two small boys, and a mongrel dog. (If I used my imagination just a bit, these Indians showed the same intensity as businessmen crossing Grand Central Station in New York from their trains to their offices.) The Maya men would spend all *their* day on the volcano-sides, tending the life-sustaining cornfields and cutting firewood. Back home, the women would be grinding corn kernels into a *masa* (dough), patting out

Early morning at mile-high Lake Atitlán, with Volcanoes Tolimán and Atitlán in the background.

tortillas, and baking dozens upon dozens of these nutritious corn cakes over open fires. Thus, man and woman, corn and wood, made an endless, dependent circle in the Maya culture.

As I waited for displays or calls from the pocs, two dark shapes slowly bobbed toward me at the edge of a bed of submerged water plants. I trained my glasses on them and could see a pipe rising from each round object. The shapes came closer and I heard the sound of air being sucked in. Skin divers! The two snorkelers paid no attention to me and swam up a narrow channel cut through the reeds. Rising, they waded out to shore and stood flailing their arms for warmth. From their belts hung two of the biggest bass I'd ever seen. One must have weighed close to fifteen pounds; the other was nearly as large. The two ladino men began taking off their fins and masks. I rowed in and greeted them.

"Buenos dias, señores."

They looked up in surprise and waved.

"Where did you get such beautiful fish?" I asked.

They walked into the water toward me and held out the larger bass for inspection. It was deep-bellied and fat, with huge jaws that curved downward balefully. Clearly it was a largemouth bass.

"The *lobina negra* (black bass) were put into Lake Atitlán a couple of years ago," said one man. "Now they're all over. We come here to spear them. It's easy to shoot large fish down in the deep waterweed patches."

"What do you do with them?" I asked.

"We take them to Guatemala City to sell in the fish markets."

"Can't you sell them here to the Indians? They seem to eat a lot of fish."

"No. They can't pay enough for these bass. We get 60¢ a pound in the city. Besides, the Indians say they don't like the taste. They're used to minnows and crabs."

Then it hit me. Bass might be the culprits! These carnivorous fish are notorious predators. They eat small fish, crabs, frogs, even young water birds. Records tell of them snatching redwing black-birds, warblers, and swallows on the wing when they fly too close to the water. I had little doubt that bass this size could gobble up young grebes, plus the aquatic food that grebes depended upon. As a scientist, though, I had to confirm my hypothesis.

While I was talking to the divers, a short, swarthy young man in well-polished boots sauntered beneath dense coffee trees toward the lake. He looked quite dapper in pressed pants, green windbreaker, and wide sombrero. The divers greeted him enthusiastically. "Hello, Edgar, how are you?"

I introduced myself and learned that he was the owner of a property at this end of the bay. Behind his farm rose a high escarpment which contained the lake like a natural dam between the two great volcanic masses. Beyond it, the land slanted down steeply 3,000 feet and more to the Pacific lowlands. Lake Atitlán sat like a teacup balanced among the mountains. From Volcano

Atitlán's hoary summit at 11,300 feet, to the Pacific Ocean fifty miles away, the topographic relief was dramatic.

Edgar invited the shivering divers and me up to his farmhouse for coffee. I could see that rich volcanic soil and abundant rainfall made Edgar's land enormously fertile and productive. He grew prize-winning coffee and avocados on his small holding, which was modest compared to some wealthy coastal farms. His widowed mother, with whom he lived, served us demitasses of his finest "essence of coffee."

Finally, both the divers and I were warm. They, however, were anxious to be off with their fresh fish. I decided to stay and see Edgar's farm, at his invitation. Judging from the efficient operation, I could tell that Edgar was an intelligent, well-organized man. His father had been a farmer, too, and taught him a great deal. He also had an agronomy degree.

As we walked about the plantation, I explained what I was doing with the grebes. "You have more birds in front of your farm than anywhere on this lake," I said. "But there are only eighty-two left in all."

"You mean I've had pocs living right here all these years and I never paid any attention?"

"Yes, indeed," I said. "I can show you about them, Edgar, if you're interested. In fact, this would be a great place to search for nests, eggs, and chicks when they start breeding. The reeds are very tall and thick. It's great habitat. No one's described a nest or young of giant grebes."

"Then why not look for them here?" Edgar's brown eyes flashed. "I love animals and being on the lake. I'll help you look. It'll be fun."

"Have you any idea when they mate?" I asked.

He thought a moment. "I've heard them calling a lot in March and April. Maybe then."

This was my first clue as to when to expect reproduction, since breeding habits of tropical birds can vary far more than birds of temperate climates. I was happy to find another person taking an interest in my work and the pocs.

"You must stay for lunch," Edgar said. "Make my farm your home. My mother loves company. She's very isolated here, not driving and having lost my father. Work here as often as you like. I'll be very interested in what you find, Anna."

This generous offer would help tremendously with my field-work because I could zero in on established birds and have a safe place to store my field gear. Also, it was much calmer in the bay than out in the main lake, so I could anchor comfortably for several hours. When I left Edgar's farm that afternoon, we walked slowly down the long cobbled drive lined with immense eucalyptus trees. I felt as if we'd been friends for years. Twirling his mustache tips, Edgar chatted easily. I had the sense that he was bored with his rural lifestyle and that the grebes had captured his imagination. When he pushed my boat back out into the bay and waved goodbye, I felt I'd been blessed.

That night, at 11:45 P.M., I went to the old colonial cathedral with Doña Rosa, her older children home from boarding school, Armando, and Don Emilio to celebrate Christmas Eve Mass. The pungent scent of copal incense filled the air as Indian elders swung censers on the front steps. Others shot off firecrackers, which burst in the starry sky and illuminated the entire church courtyard. Solemn Indian women, with babies on their backs and youngsters in hand, shuffled into the cathedral with their men. All were barefoot but dressed in their finest handwoven clothes. Here and there on the steps were small offerings of flowers, candles, and corn. Armando nudged me pointedly. "Those are for the ancient Maya gods," he whispered.

Inside, a hundred candles bathed the old stone walls in a mellow glow. The altar, which was almost 400 years old, shimmered softly for it was covered with colonial Spanish silver and gold panels. The top was adorned with antique, handembroidered white cloths and the silver chalice. My friend the priest stood reverently beside the alter. He had come to Panajachel to perform this special Mass. Silver-haired, burly, with handsome features, he wore immaculate robes edged in handmade lace and a carmine red surplice.

Throughout the service, babies cried, firecrackers popped, Indians chanted ancient words to pagan deities *outside* on the front steps while the priest droned ancient Latin holy ones *inside*. I had never experienced the mixing of two religions before and found it a confusing, yet dazzling, experience.

After the last chant and prayer, Doña Rosa led the way down the aisle. I was jammed next to Indians, tourists, ladinos, children, and retired folk. I glanced sideways at Armando. His face seemed unusually reflective compared with his normal energetic self. As we reached the front steps, he took my arm to help me down. Giving it a gentle squeeze, he said quietly, "I'm glad you came to Guatemala, and I hope you stay much longer, Anita."

Back at Doña Rosa's home, dozens of friends dropped in, bringing gifts and food and liquor. Everything sparkled with festivity. We ate, drank, and talked till dawn. Even her youngest children stayed up to see the sun rise on Christmas Day. It was the jolliest Christmas I'd ever spent. More importantly, I felt accepted and cared for.

My best presents were discovering the introduction of large-mouth bass to the lake, and finding Edgar and his farm.

4

A Sunstroke and
a Swear Word

MY NEW YEAR'S RESOLUTIONS all had to do with giant
grebes. First of all, I decided to write to conservation
organizations and ask for grants so I could afford to stay
longer at Lake Atitlán. Next, I would tell *National Geographic*
magazine about this rare and endangered bird to see if there was
any interest in an article. I still had no good photos and hoped the
Society might loan me a proper telephoto lens, or possibly a photographer. Third, I planned to prove that largemouth bass *were*
the chief culprit destroying the grebes.

Hesitantly, for I'd never sent such letters, I wrote to World
Wildlife Fund International and the International Council for
Bird Preservation, Pan American Section, explaining the critical
situation I'd found, giving my census figures, and asking for funds
to carry on research. I desperately needed money for film, tapes,
gas and oil, boat rental, and film developing. To my delight, I
received a small grant—enough to carry on for another three or
four months. Surely in that amount of time I could get pictures,

witness the breeding season, and figure out a sound conservation and management scheme for the birds. Then and there, I decided to stay at Lake Atitlán until May 1965.

My letter to *National Geographic* was also lucky. Mary Smith, a wonderful editor who at that time handled free-lance photographers with new story ideas, wrote back, encouraging me to send more data and any photos I had taken so far. All I had to send were some blurry black and white prints and one good color slide of an adult male poc. Explaining that I'd stay a while longer in Guatemala, I offered to update her and send more pictures.

Meanwhile, I had found out that Pan American Airways and the Panajachel Hotel Association had devised a plan to introduce largemouth bass and crappies into the lake in 1958 and 1960. They considered it a means to improve sport fishing and attract more foreign tourists (who, of course, would fly to Guatemala on Pan Am and stay in the local hotels). This was done without any experimentation or research, and against the recommendations of a U.S. Fish and Wildlife Service technician. The first release was several dozen fingerlings; the second, 2,000.

It was important to find out about bass predations and changes in the aquatic ecosystem, if any. Armando and I concocted a plan to survey the local Indian fisherman and crabmen and ladino scuba divers. By asking them five easy, nonbiased questions in simple Spanish, perhaps I could learn what effects they had noticed in the last five years. There seemed no other way to get this information unless a fishery biologist suddenly materialized. I also wanted to check on bass diet by buying or collecting big fish whenever possible and dissecting their intestines. Then, to try and confirm my hunch that bass ate grebe chicks, I made some fake chicks out of ping-pong balls and painted chicken feathers and tethered them outside of reed beds where I knew mated adults lived.

Armando had it all figured out. "Anita," he said "you can ask

fishermen questions as you meet them on your way across the lake.
Then you can stop and check your ping-pong babies. Make your
observations for the day, and watch out for spear fishermen so you
can buy big bass to examine."

This ambitious plan yielded a wealth of information. Though
my Spanish was still poor, the Mayan fishermen understood me.
Day by day I asked them: How are the fish here? Many? Few?
Like always? How are the crabs? How long ago did the fish and
crabs change (if they did)? Why? Where do you find crabs now?
What kinds of fish do you catch now? What's the largest *lobina
negra* you've seen?"

I interviewed fifty-six men, ranging in age from fifteen to sixty
years. The majority told me that they'd been catching fewer fish
and crabs during the last three to six years. (This tied in perfectly
with the bass introductions of 1958 and 1960.) Half the fishermen
blamed the new fish for ruining their fishery—a native observation I found remarkably astute! The fishermen said they used to
catch twenty to fifty pounds of tiny fish per day in small stick
corrals and wicker traps baited with corn. For centuries this had
been the traditional way of fishing at Atitlán. Small fishes *had*
been *the* major source of protein. But these days fishermen only
got two to four pounds of bass and crappies with small hooks and
string lines. No one used nets, as they were very expensive. Now,
said the fishermen, the villagers seldom had fish to eat, thus little
animal protein except for an occasional egg or chicken.

The crabmen also reported a sad tale. In the old days, a night's
catch would bring in five or six dozen crabs, captured by torchlight right along the shoreline with sharp gigs, or by using baited
strings down to 75 feet. But the nightly catch now averaged only
one or two dozen crabs, mainly taken in water as deep as 300 feet.
Again, they told me, the villagers missed their crab *caldo* (soup),
which had been a favorite meal.

The largest bass ever caught had been twenty-five pounds,

with an average of nine pounds. Every indication was that these fish had grown from fingerlings to near record growth-weight adults in only twenty-seven months.

From this survey data, an incredible situation became clear. The huge bass population at Lake Atitlán was virtually untouched and untouchable because the local Indians had neither the means nor the skill to catch them. They could not spear bass because most Indians don't swim. They could not afford scuba and spear fishing gear on incomes of $100–300 a year. Moreover, no one could buy fancy fishing tackle: spinning rods, lures, monofilament line, or nets. Indians had used penny hooks and lines for years, and before that handmade wicker traps baited with corn. That's all.

The more I dug around for facts, the more complicated this ecological puzzle became. I'd uncovered an intricate "web of

Spearfishermen with large-mouth bass captured at about thirty feet down.

My photo with two of the huge fish shows the size of their mouths.

life," where the dependency of one life form upon another was
deeply meshed.

The bass intestines I examined held small fishes, crabs, snails,
frogs, and insects, pure proof that they were competing directly
with giant grebes for food. I never found any ingested water bird
chicks, though I looked carefully. However, with such a huge prey
population and so few grebes alive, my chances were about 1 in 10
million. Similarly, none of my ping-pong poc chicks were devoured.

By the greatest coincidence, two groups of American scientists arrived at Lake Atitlán. One was from Oklahoma State University. They were doing a fishery survey. From them I learned
that of the eighteen species of fish present in Atitlán in the 1950s,
only five species were now common. And these were mainly bass,
crappies, *Tilapia,* and other introduced species.

Since the introduction of the bass, fishing success with hook and line dropped drastically, causing a protein deficiency.

The second group was from Stanford University. For Ph.D. degrees in medical anthropology, they were studying the health of Indians in Santiago Atitlán. Discovering a severe protein deficiency, they traced it to the lack of fish and crabs. Formerly, Indians ate fish two or three times a week, and crab soup perhaps once a week. Some 100–125 families had relied heavily on fishing for income. Now only 30–50 fishermen were engaged in this labor, and fish was eaten just a few times a month. Many men were forced to go down to the lowlands to find seasonal jobs on ranches or coffee farms. Many picked up tropical diseases and parasites there. Thus, one unwise fish introduction had dislocated human health and life.

All in all, the ecological and social ramifications of this exotic introduction were staggering. Within five years, the poc population had fallen from over 200 birds to 80. The number of small minnows, crabs, and other aquatic creatures plummeted as the voracious bass burgeoned. Grebes, especially the young, might starve unless they could adapt to catching and eating bass. I had doubts they could even swallow such finny fish. How could they be expected to thrive? Moreover, there was no question in my mind that big bass could gobble up the tiny chicks of all water birds.

What could a lone, foreign, wildlife ecologist do? I racked my brains, but there seemed no way to rid a lake as large as Atitlán of bass. It would take a thousand trainloads of rotenone (a fish poison derived from an African plant) to kill them all. And then the rest of the fish would die, too, with disastrous results for both Indian and grebes. I finally admitted that largemouth bass could *not* be controlled and were there to stay. One consolation was that nature might, in a few years, force a change. The bass would eat themselves out of house and home, suffer from a population explosion and crash, and eventually readjust to a more balanced ecosystem.

Meanwhile, I reasoned, the giant grebes would probably be

extinct in five to ten years. Whereas it had taken 10,000 years of evolution to turn this once migratory species into a flightless wonder, an Ice Age relic, a scientific curiosity, the bird could be wiped out in a split-second of that time span. It seemed inevitable that the pocs follow the fate of the great auk, passenger pigeon, and dusky seaside sparrow unless I could come up with a solution.

Now it seemed imperative to learn as much as possible about poc reproduction. As a last resort, they might be bred in captivity, or moved to another lake. I increased my hours on the water and picked three groups of grebes to concentrate on. One was my first isolated pair near Panajachel, which I named Luisa and Clark. Another was composed of three mated pairs and a lone male in a sheltered cove on the south shore. The third, and best, were the "tame" couple, called the Organ Grinders because of their hoarse calls, at Edgar's farm. No matter what direction the wind, I could now work safely at one of these locations and stay out as long as possible.

Poor Doña Rosa. Her cook and maid never knew when I'd show up for meals. The houseboy was under strict orders not to touch any of my equipment—unless I asked for assistance. My bedroom looked more like a field bivouac than sleeping quarters. There were pickled grebes, film canisters, cameras, field guides, dried samples of reeds and cattails awaiting identification, jars of aquatic insects, windbreakers, and wet bathing suits. Yet he was supposed to wash the tile floors, lay the fire, and keep the room tidy. Most of all, my friend Doña Rosa lost a willing listener to her stories of animal life in Guatemala. I was so tired at night that I forwent hearing how she tamed monkeys, macaws, and margay cats; or cured sick dogs, horses, even a raccoon and a coati mundi. I just tumbled into bed right after dinner, and at dawn I awoke full of energy to go watch my birds again.

In early March I found that male grebes seemed strongly territorial. They brayed out their weird "gulping cow call" every few minutes. I suspected breeding season was about to begin, although I'd not seen any courting, nest building, or chicks.

One morning the male at Edgar's coffee farm executed a marvelous dive right in front of the reeds. He literally folded in the middle and sank without a ripple. His head and tail were last to disappear. I immediately named this the accordion alarm dive because he seemed nervous about something and was obviously going off on a reconnaissance. A moment later he emerged, cautiously surveying the surroundings with only his eyes and nostrils above the water like a periscope. He dove again.

Soon the male appeared twenty feet from the female, who was fishing offshore. Suddenly, both birds hunched down in the water and puffed up their feathers. They faced each other and dived toward each other. They popped up barely three feet apart, now sleek and trim, and swam rapidly together. A collision seemed so imminent that I almost cried out. At the last second, both birds veered sideways and swam parallel to each other. They gave a sweet warbling call in duet. It was the same song I'd heard in the reeds during our moonlight census—which I'd named the "hen flicker recognition call." Altogether, this was a courtship display of amazing grace.

As I watched, the male abruptly left his mate and performed still a new action. He faced the edge of his reed patch and bent his head forward. The crown was flattened until it almost made a straight line with the top of his beak. The neck crooked into a strong S-curve. The bird's throat swelled like a cobra's, and the black patch showed clearly. The whole effect was that of a coiled snake about to strike. (Not so strange, since birds are descended from reptiles.) This analogy flashed into my mind so I called it the "snakehead aggressive display."

One of the nice things about being the first person to study a species is creating your own names for calls and displays. This gave me a little thrill of scientific discovery.

Another male grebe in the same posture appeared and began advancing upon my poc. He approached like an angry black tor-

pedo, body half-submerged and powerful lobed feet kicking back a
wake. A small ripple preceded the interloper like a miniature tidal
wave. The two males met near the reeds. They pivoted back to
back, side to side, beak to beak. They looked like two bridling
street dogs. Every few minutes the birds repeated this behavior
along a straight line. I could almost imagine their territorial bor-
der as having a barbed wire fence.

Suddenly, both males rose up in the water, beating their small
wings mightily and each slashing at the other's neck and head.
After five minutes of tussling, the invader retreated ignomini-
ously, diving for safety in the reeds. My victorious male swam
slowly "home," kicking water back in spurts. This was the strongest show of aggression and territorial defense that I'd been privi-
leged to see. Surely, the reproductive mood was gripping the
birds.

A day or two later, I noticed that both male and female would
carry bits of rotten reed stalks, old cattail fronds, and fresh-water
plants into the reed beds. They would twitter their duet and make
amorous-sounding calls from deep within these stands. I guessed
they performed sexual functions in this hidden realm on low,
barely floating platforms. I never saw pocs copulating on open
water, nor do other grebe species.

Somehow I had to enter their private world, and one morning
I decided to force my way into those eighteen-foot beds of reeds,
among the tallest and densest on earth. I had quite an audience.
Edgar came down from his farmhouse and put his boat in the
water. He waited well offshore, clad only in his shiny boots and a
bathing suit. One of his Indian laborers paddled me toward the
edge of reeds where the birds called most often. He stood by in
case I needed to be pulled out. Edgar's mother stood on shore
under a red parasol, calling out shrill warnings.

"Be careful of the water scorpions. Watch out for water
snakes." A little later, she yelled, "Do you have your hat on,
Anna? The sun is very strong today."

Meanwhile, several Indian women stopped washing their clothes along the shore to stare at me as I swam through the tallest stalks in ten feet of water. The bottom was firm here, but as I shoved my way through matted patches of reeds, and it got shallower, it turned to oozy mud. The water became murky, fetid gases bubbled up around me. I paused often to look for snakes and scorpions, although common sense told me they probably could not survive on this rough lake. My heart was pounding with apprehension and exertion. The sun beat fiercely on my wet head.

Edgar directed me from his boat, shouting, "More to the right." Then, "Now ten feet forward."

I was practically crawling on my belly over flattened masses of dead reeds, perspiring, itching, in four feet of water. I could see no more than three feet in any direction.

Suddenly, there lay the nest! It measured about eighteen inches across and was anchored to a few reed stalks. Only three inches protruded above the surface, but the rest hung down in a three-foot funnel. Its size and shape gave the nest great stability in the winds and waves of Atitlán. A flimsier one, such as the common pied-billed grebes build, would have soon disintegrated. *This* nest would easily overflow from a bushel basket. I calculated its weight at about one hundred pounds. How did two little birds, less than two pounds each, manage such a feat?

Seeing no eggs inside, I made more measurements and mental notes, then started backing out of the reed bed. It seemed to me that few predators, other than man and his machete, could ever reach this inner sanctum. Certainly the words of Dr. Arthur A. Allen, famed ornithologist and bird photographer, about the common grebes were true for the giants: "Few birds offer greater difficulties to the ornithologist who would become familiar with their lives." How often I would remember these words in the next two years of fieldwork at Atitlán.

After taking a shower at Edgar's farm and eating lunch, I left for Panajachel. A new *norte* was hurling its five-foot waves against

the southern shoreline, and *Xelaju* shuddered from the onslaught.
Again I lost a hat overboard. Again it took me over two hours to
cross the lake. Throughout the trip, a merciless sun beat down.

I beached my boat about 5 P.M. and took a hard scolding from
Don Emilio about being gone so long. I walked back to my room
feeling queasy and lightheaded. No way could I eat the supper
Doña Rosa had prepared for me. All I wanted was cool liquids. At
8 P.M. Armando stopped by. He took one look at me and asked
Doña Rosa for a thermometer: 102° F. By 9 P.M. it was 103°, and I
was shaking with chills. The good woman coaxed me to bed, lit a
fire in the hearth, and wrapped three thick Guatemalan wool
blankets around me. Armando sat on the edge of the bed putting
cold compresses on my head. The cook scurried in with camomile
tea, aspirins, cocoa butter, and ice. Apparently, despite the deep
tan I'd acquired over the weeks, eight hours' exposure to that
high-altitude sun, mostly without a hat, plus the struggle in the
reeds, had caused a sunstroke. In addition, the foul mud had
provoked a skin rash.

Three rough days passed as I wavered near delirium. The village doctor—the only one around the lake—was away. Armando
and Rosa nursed me, sitting patiently by my bed for hours, telling
stories and sharing confidences. During this period, I learned that
both of them were estranged from their spouses, who lived in
Guatemala City. I had often wondered why my two friends seldom seemed to see their mates but was too shy to ask. In a Catholic Latin country at that time, no one got divorced. A pair simply
split up, stayed married, but usually found a new hidden relationship in time. Now I thought I knew why Armando dropped by
Rosa's house so often and ate many a meal there. Perhaps he was
just lonesome. Perhaps he and she were lovers. That much they
didn't tell me.

After my fever went down, Armando warned me not to go out
in the sun for several days. He was right. Waves of faintness
washed over me, and my heart pounded at the slightest exertion.

Bright light made my head ache. I spent the time quietly reading and wishing for a decent library where I could look up the many facts I wanted to know about bass, grebes, and limnology (the study of fresh water) in general. I also did a lot thinking about the giant grebes. Daily I preached to Doña Rosa, Armando, and Don Emilio about how morally unjust it was for the grebes to be exterminated due to human blundering and mismanagement. I quoted Sir Peter Scott, a conservationist of international fame, who wrote eloquently, "Only natural cataclysmic forces have the right to take lives or force into extinction any wild creature."

It was Armando who finally said, "Well, why don't you start to save the poc?"

"Who, me?"

"Why not?" he shot back. "Think of a program which will help the birds and the reeds, and we'll go see the Minister of Agriculture in Guatemala City and propose it to him. I have a cousin who is married to a relative of his."

Armando's questions spurred me to conceive of a conservation campaign. Aldo Leopold, father of game management in the States and Canada, had written that wildlife could be restored by the creative use of the same tools which heretofore destroyed it. He believed that land and water could be managed to produce continuous crops of wild animals. He advocated some controls— over hunting, predators, disease, and the habitat—and also thought wildlife refuges were important.

I dreamed up a name—"Operation Protection of the Poc"— in which enforcement, education, habitat management, and a new refuge were combined to try and save the grebes. Maybe we could stop the downward slide and bring the birds back to their original numbers.

After I discussed it with Armando, he called his cousin and arranged a meeting with the Minister of Agriculture, who was in charge not only of ranching and farming for the whole country but also of wildlife, fisheries, and forestry. Since he owned a vaca-

tion home at Lake Atitlán, I hoped he would take an active interest in the pocs. Armando drove me to the city and accompanied
me to the National Palace. In passionate but halting Spanish, I
described the giant grebes, their lovely courtship and huge nests.
Then I explained the census figures, reed cutting, lack of enforcement of the grebe law, and bad effects of the largemouth bass. I
ended with my idea for a conservation campaign. I was so excited
that I used a few of Don Emilio's swear words.

"La lobina negra es muy jodida" (The black bass has fucked
up the lake), I exclaimed, not knowing the exact translation. The
word certainly had a galvanizing effect. The Minister stared at
me. Armando turned beet red. There was complete silence in that
elegant office, and then the Minister burst out laughing.

"So, señorita," he said when he'd calmed down. "What is it
you want me to do?"

"We need a game warden, even part time," I answered, "with
a boat, gas, and oil, to patrol."

The Minister picked up the phone, called his Division of
Fauna, and ordered a *vigilante* to be hired and go to Lake Atitlán.
Armando and I exchanged triumphant glances. As far as we knew,
this was the first official conservation officer ever to be appointed
in Guatemala. The man would bring a motorboat and stay at
Santiago Atitlán. He would begin next week.

"What else?" asked the Minister graciously.

"I can't really think of anything now," I said. "But I'm going
to try to get more grant money when I go back to the States.
Perhaps we can start a broad conservation campaign when I return to Guatemala next fall."

"I shall be waiting at your service, señorita," the Minister
assured me.

At the car, Armando and I broke up laughing. "See what's
possible?" said Armando. "By having that sunstroke and using
that swear word, you found a way to start saving the pocs."

5
More Black Magic

A s soon as I felt better, I went back to the Bay of Santiago Atitlán, heady with anticipation. What would I find in the nest of the Organ Grinders, my favorite pair? Armando was eager to see this marvel of poc construction, so he came, too. Also, he worried I might have a relapse of sunstroke or not be strong enough to plow through the reeds. We both wore wet suits to avoid the mud rash, as well as gloves and bandannas against the sun. As we approached the nest, I spotted four small eggs, stained a mottled brown from the damp vegetation. They lay in the nest depression, only inches from the water surface. The frightened female had just deserted her home and covered her treasures with a light blanket of pondweed and roots of water hyacinth. To one side, peeking out from this protective camouflage, was a chick!

I let out a hoot of exultation. At last! Unwrapping my camera from several plastic bags, I snapped the first portrait ever taken of a baby Atitlán grebe. From nearby, the mother made a low, reassuring sound to her youngster—"poc-poc-poc." Now I knew where the Indian name came from. The tiny puffball stared boldly at Armando and me. It was striped in black and white from beak to tail like a little zebra, with touches of scarlet-orange at the lores and base of the bill. It looked only hours old, yet it was dry, fluffy, and cheeping constantly. Again, its mother called, "poc-poc." Abruptly, the little creature waddled to the nest edge and dived. Astonished, Armando and I watched it swim under water a few inches, pop to the surface like a cork, and start swimming toward its parent.

She, meanwhile, hurried through the reeds to meet it. I glimpsed her making a half turn, depressing her rear in the water, and waiting. The precocious baby scrambled onto her back and cuddled down out of sight between her wings! Slowly she disappeared. I took a few more pictures of the nest but didn't want to disturb the grebes further. Quietly, we maneuvered our way back to the boat.

Armando and I heaved ourselves in and stripped off our wet suits. Joyfully, we exchanged a hug. What a glorious discovery. Now that I'd found my first nest, and knew how to handle the reeds, I was wild to search for more. Yet over that spring and the next two years, I only found twenty new nests, each with from two to five eggs, never more. This is roughly half the number laid by the common pied-billed grebe, its closest relative.

I discovered that both parents care for their young. The chicks' insistent cheeping and begging wins them a steady supply of water insects, hellgrammites, crustaceans, and tiny fish. After they become stronger and larger, the youngsters venture forth with the adults to learn to fish and dive in the open water. At this time, the mated pair divide the brood in two. The father takes one or two babies; the mother, one or two. They no longer carry the youngsters on their backs for safety. Fish caught by the parents are either torn to pieces on the surface and offered to the chicks or are given to them whole.

However, I once saw a parent present a small bass to a fledgling twenty-five times! Struggle as it might, the little bird could not swallow the thick, spiny fish. Certainly, young bass are different in shape from the native minnows and cyprinids that adult grebes were accustomed to catching and feeding their youngsters.

Young grebes, I found, go off on their own at ten to twelve weeks of age. Until then, their plumage changes from zebra striping, to striped necks and heads, to all-over dull coffee brown. The lores fade to ivory and the beak is dingy gray. Once independent, juveniles skulk along the shoreline hiding from other pocs and strange objects. Their drab color is the perfect camouflage during this critical period in their lives. Now they have no protection, no home range, no sure food supply. I calculated that chick survival during these first twelve weeks was roughly half the brood, or 47 percent. Thereafter, mortality probably increased greatly.

During this time, I found two female juveniles which seemed so weak and emaciated that I caught them to examine and resusci-

During David Allen's photo assignment, I was kept busy searching for nests, eggs, and chicks. Photo by David G. Allen

Here I have discovered a makeshift breeding platform used by the giant grebes.

The first picture taken of a giant grebe chick. Barely two hours old, it huddles atop the huge floating nest constructed by its parents.

Photo by David G. Allen

tate. I tried to feed them little fishes and hard-boiled eggs in a
bathtub, but they did not take to captivity. I was sure they'd have
died in the wild anyway. (The two young birds, pickled in formalin, ended up in the museum at the University of Michigan.) I
wondered if these somewhat older birds were also experiencing
trouble catching and swallowing the exotic bass.

Meanwhile, the new game warden had arrived at Santiago. I
spent several hours trying to explain the lake and its moods and
train him for patrol work. One morning, Armando had gone with
me to start measuring the reed beds. There was a norther blowing,
but he thought the calm water along the north shore would give
us a chance to try out the stopwatch method on reeds. For two
hours we cruised and timed ourselves, until we got the technique
down smoothly. We were reveling in the bright sunshine and
sparkling blustery day when Armando suggested we try to find the
warden and see how he was doing. As we were passing the village
of San Pedro de la Laguna, he stared hard at the reeds and made a
run toward them. Gunning the motor, he crashed right into the
bed. As we careened through the thick vegetation, I saw what had
caught his eye. The game warden's boat was tied up snugly and he
was rocking gently inside fast asleep.

"Jodida!" muttered Armando, his face flushed with anger.
"Qué pasa, hombre?" he shouted. The poor fellow started awake
and almost jumped overboard.

"Ah, Don Armando, qué tal?" he gasped.

It was all too evident. The *norte* had scared the man and he
had hidden out. Shamefaced, he confided that he barely knew
how to swim and had never been out in such wind and waves. I
felt sorry for him, remembering my own initial fears. But not
Armando. He was furious. "Imagine sending such a coward to
Atitlán for this job," he fumed.

That warden's job was short-lived. Not only did he shirk his
patrols except on the calmest mornings, but we heard that he was
selling off the unused gas and oil for extra profit in the village.

Such shenanigans appalled me, but Armando merely shrugged and said, *"Típico."*

After the warden left in disgrace, there was no one to watch the lake. I worried about this constantly for soon it would be time to go back to the States. However, a strange new problem was growing daily. All during the spring months I had found odd bits of debris on or around my boat, *Xelaju.* Sometimes it was a circle of stones, or a burned out candle stub. Other times it was sticks set in a peculiar pattern, or bird feathers. I figured that Don Emilio's kids were playing on the beach. They were very fond of me and full of mischief. Once they had brought a glass jar full of black widow spiders to "show me." Appalled, I asked where they got them. "Oh, in the stone wall of our house," they answered. "Lots live in there. They don't ever bite us."

Then one morning it became obvious that the signs were not being left by children. A pile of human feces sat right on the bow with burned matches sticking in it! Someone clearly did not like me.

I ran to look for Armando. I could think of no one I'd harmed or insulted, but maybe he'd have an idea. He was painting a car, and as soon as I had babbled out the story, he closed his paint can and accompanied me to the beach. With a strong oath, he picked up the foul mess and flung it into the bushes. "This is the work of a bruja." he said. "Someone has asked for a spell to be brought against you."

"But *who* can it be?" I wailed.

"I don't know. You must think carefully," counseled Armando. "Think of anyone you might have spoken to unkindly, or perhaps not paid enough money, or something like that. Could it be one of the fishermen you interviewed, Anita? Or one who sold you a big bass?"

I shook my head.

"Don't worry," he soothed me. "I will take you to a very good shaman who lives up in the hills beyond Sololá. Jesús will tell you what to do." He patted my shoulder. "Come to me if anything else happens, but don't tell another soul. Not even Doña Rosa."

A chill crept up my back. I just could not believe in black magic; yet, having no alternative, I decided to fight fire with fire. For the next few days I slept fitfully and jumped at the slightest sound. Doña Rosa said I looked overworked. But nothing more showed up at the boat.

Then one cloudy afternoon Armando came for me in his Land Rover. "Let's go, Anita," he said. "I got word to Jesús by telegraph and runner. He's expecting us. He'll get to the bottom of this mess."

For two hours we wound our way higher and higher into the pine-clad mountains north of the lake. The air became colder and my breath shorter. Unlike the powerful young volcanoes rimming the southern edge of the lake, these hills were old and rounded limestone. Deep valleys slashed through them, and their geological origins were completely different. Close to 9,000 feet of elevation, Armando nosed his Land Rover onto a narrow dirt track and headed down into a canyon. Dust billowed up under the floorboards, and I tried not to look out at the sheer drop-off beside us. We reached the valley floor just before sunset. A colonial Catholic church dominated the landscape like a huge mother hen. Scattered like chicks out around the valley and up the slopes were small Indian huts. No matter which direction they went, every inhabitant had to pass by the church door in this *aldea* (tiny town).

Armando parked in front of the steps and pulled out a cigarette. "Jesús will be here soon," he said comfortingly. As the sun set, golden shafts slipped through the banks of clouds and gilded the church and pine forests. A few Indian men plodded by, bent and weary, bound for home after a hard day in the fields. One man came striding toward us, tall, erect, confident. Bronze skin was taut over high cheekbones and a narrow aquiline nose. The firmly chiseled mouth and deep-set black eyes gave me the impression of Maya royalty. More than the perfection of features was the look of calm and kindness. I'd never seen such bearing in my life. Here was a man with power and compassion. Regardless of how I felt about witch doctors, this person looked as though he could offer wisdom and good advice.

Armando introduced me to the shaman. He bowed ever so slightly, then beckoned us up a footpath leading to two adobe huts. The Indian stopped briefly at the first one to get something, then led us into the second. He produced three little straight-backed chairs and invited us to sit down. In the gloomy room I could see a statue of the Virgin Mary and the Christ child on a small table surrounded with candles and fake flowers. Strings of herbs hung from the rafters. Hand-carved wooden masks were nailed to the walls. The whole room seemed to be a mixture of Catholicism and paganism.

The shaman said nothing as he tied a square of heavy red cotton cloth around his head. Its black tassels hung over his shoulders, and he looked more regal than ever. Now he produced three cloth bags. He lit one candle and placed it in the center of the unoccupied chair. Lighting it, he crossed himself, then lit the others and prayed to the Virgin Mary. I was bemused. How could all this ritual help me?

Turning back to us, the shaman knelt by the empty chair and fixed me with his penetrating eyes. "Tell me about your trouble."

Hesitantly, I described what I'd found around my boat and what I was doing at the lake. Armando helped out with his colorful Spanish. The shaman listened gravely. He began to recite the Lord's Prayer, mixed up with Latin and Indian (Cakchiquel) words. Then he switched wholly to the Maya dialect and continued his prayerlike recitation, swaying slightly. Gradually, a curious sensation of peace stole through my body. I also had the sense of a force in that room—something vibrant and harmonious. My scientific training was making me coolly observe, classify, analyze the entire ceremony; at the same time, my emotional being was thrilling to what was happening. For the first time since being in Guatemala, I suspended judgment, let go, gave myself up to a different culture. I slipped into a trancelike lethargy.

Jesús opened the three bags, which held polished stones, and divided them into three piles. He began mixing the pebbles into three heaps. As he kneaded the stones with strong brown hands, he chanted an Indian invocation. Three times he formed three piles. Then he shoved them all into one group, blew out the candle, and sat back on his heels. Except for the flickering lights around the Virgin, we were in deep shadow.

A long silence passed before he spoke softly. "There is a work-man who does not like you. He works for you, but you do not pay him. He wants money. Also, he does not understand the strange objects you carry back and forth to your boat. He is afraid of them, thinks they're black magic. However, he is not dangerous. He will not harm you. He only wants to scare you away from there. Far away from there. You must go back and act as if nothing has happened. Go on with your work. Pay him nothing. It will pass."

Another long silence. My trance deepened. Then Jesús suddenly stood up and started chatting with Armando in Spanish. The atmosphere changed immediately. The force was gone. I glanced at my watch. An hour had flown by. It was pitch dark. Armando laid a few cigarettes, coins, and fresh candles on the ceremonial chair and got up. "Come, Anita," he murmured. "We must go now."

As we bounced back out of the valley, Armando neatly cleared up the problem. "It's Doña Rosa's houseboy," he said with certainty. "He's the only person you know who could possibly expect payment for anything. He probably thinks you should give him money for mopping your floor and bringing in firewood. He doesn't realize that you pay rent to Rosa; however, she no doubt gives him nothing more than his usual salary despite the extra work."

"How much does he earn a month?" I asked.

"About thirty-five quetzals."

I gasped. It was slightly more than a dollar a day. Immediately I offered to pay him more on the side.

"No," Armando said firmly. "Remember what Jesús told you! I'll speak to Rosa, but you can't interfere with the way she runs her house. Just don't do anything, Anita. Please."

Jesús was right. The black magic stopped, though I'm sure the houseboy never got a raise.

Once again, I could put all my energies into field research, trying to fathom Lake Atitlán's complicated ecosystem. The reed and cattail measuring paid off with the first figures ever available on shoreline habitat. Of the seventy-five miles of lakeshore, only fifteen miles had vegetation. Most of it was in reed beds, with cattails and *Phragmites* accounting for a mere 10 percent. This meant that the grebes had a very limited area for nesting and roosting. It also clarified how critical this edging of aquatic plants was to the health of the lake. The vegetation not only provided wildlife sanctuaries and fish nurseries but filtered out sediments and absorbed nutrients, keeping the water clear and clean. Life depended on this fragile fringe of reeds and cattails. Destroy it and Lake Atitlán's ecological diversity and water quality would be severely affected.

The rainy season announced its coming with a few violent thunderstorms which raged around the volcanoes at night. It was mid-May and time for me to go home. Armando assured me I couldn't do much on the lake from late May to early October. Besides I wanted to start looking for new grants from conservation organizations in the States and to make plans for Operation Protection of the Poc. Also, with all the data I was gathering, it might be sensible to apply for a Ph.D. program in wildlife ecology at my alma mater, Cornell University. The giant grebes could be my thesis topic. Most importantly, I wanted to finalize my divorce and get that behind me. The Adirondacks and my little log cabin beckoned. The one or two months I'd planned to be away had stretched into almost seven.

On my last night in Panajachel, I walked down to the beach, just as I had on arrival. Don Emilio and Armando were sitting there watching a spectacular display of lightning above the Pacific coast. They asked me to join them. Spikes of lightning struck the volcanoes repeatedly, and chains lashed horizontally over the coast. The lake was quiet and reflected the sporadic glow. We could hear distant thunder even as we sat dry on the warm sand. A far different set of emotions surged through me now than on my first night in the village. I would say goodbye with real regret to Doña Rosa, Don Emilio, his dogs and kids, Edgar, Armando, and my beloved pocs—all of whom I'd come to love.

Next day Armando drove me to the airport. "You'll come back, Anita?" he asked, his blue eyes sad and a little misty.

"Of course, Armando, of course," I promised, grasping his calloused, capable hands. "I can't thank you enough for all you've done. But I have to go back home and try to straighten out my life. You've helped me set some new goals and shown me a beautiful country. Yes, I'll be back."

6

Operation Poc and a "Pinabeta"

T HE FOLLOWING NOVEMBER I returned to Lake Atitlán. My time away had been profitable. New grant money had come in from the World Wildlife Fund, Smithsonian Institution, and National Geographic Society. With my divorce final, I would be receiving small, but steady, alimony payments over the next three years. *National Geographic* magazine had given me free film and a good telephoto lens on loan to see if I could get better photos. If not, Mary Smith told me, they might send a free-lance photographer. Best of all, I'd gone to Cornell and been accepted in a doctoral program. The graduate committee of professors seemed enthusiastic about my research and agreed that I could stay "in absentia" during the first year. They suggested many useful techniques and approaches for my fieldwork.

While I was at Cornell getting enrolled, I spent several days at its marvelous libraries. All the questions which had bothered me in Panajachel should find answers here. Once again, as with my bachelor's and master's work, I thrilled to the accumulation of human knowledge in just a few buildings and the intricate system worked out for its retrieval. If my new degree taught me nothing more, it would show me how to use libraries.

I read everything I could find on grebe behavior, especially the classic work by Sir Julian Huxley on the great crested grebes in England. His descriptions and sketches were enormously helpful toward my giant grebe observations. Then I delved into the natural history of Guatemala, particularly its highlands and lakes. I found several very old references to the limnology and geology of Lake Atitlán. One book especially interested me. It described the ancient life of the Tzutujiles around Lake Atitlán. Not only was Santiago Atitlán a village over 1,000 years old, but the surrounding lands had harbored small rectangular stone huts where Indian farmers lived. Some ruins, wrote Samuel Lothrop, could still be found on the southern shore, as well as pottery shards and small stelae (stone slabs carved to commemorate a priest or god) on the once-sacred hill called 'Chuitinamit', across from Santiago. In the back of my mind, I resolved to search for these artifacts whenever I had free time in my fieldwork.

What a happy day when I gazed again at the immense sapphire lake with its backdrop of volcanoes; when I received bear hugs of welcome from Armando and his father; when I saw my boat, *Xelaju,* freshly painted blue and white and another red and white one beside it. "Now," exclaimed Armando, "I can help you more on the lake. If one boat breaks down, we'll have another. If you get sick again, I can still go out. Even Rosa could learn to run the motor and be of assistance."

Apart from the new boat, there were other changes in my life at Panajachel. Because of the incident with Doña Rosa's houseboy and the turmoil I caused her staff with my strange hours, I had decided to rent my own small house. That way I could come and go at will and not inconvenience anyone. Moreover, since all houses have houseboys in Guatemala, I would have someone to clean, garden, bring in firewood, and even do some marketing.

"Casita Feliz" (The Happy House) and its houseboy cost $60 a month. It was indeed a happy place with its cheerful fireplace, high hedges of hibiscus and poinsettias, cozy living room, and minuscule kitchen. I didn't care about the kitchen. Cooking was the last thing on my mind these days. My houseboy was Juan, a courteous, capable man about my age with a sweet wife and five children. Every day she sent me hot tortillas straight from her fireplace.

I also had a new dog. Don Emilio's bitch had had puppies over the summer, and he had saved a male for me. The young dog was handsome and very unruly. I named him Jessie, and at six months of age he started going with me in the boat when I wasn't sitting quietly to make observations. He was a great companion and never afraid of the heavy winds or waves. On the other hand, Jessie's erect ears, large size, and glistening canines had a terrifying effect on the local Indians. Whenever I stopped my boat to try and ask questions of a fisherman, crabman, or reed cutter they would paddle furiously away in the opposite direction. The reason was, I soon learned, that German shepherds are used exclusively as guard dogs around well-to-do homes and shops in Guatemala and have a fearsome reputation. They are about the only breed one sees there that is purebred, fat, and healthy. Most Indian dogs are pitifully undernourished, scrawny, and full of worms. Whereas Jessie and his ilk thrived on meat and dog chow; village mongrels survived with scraps of tortillas, rice, and roadside kills.

Soon I picked up where I'd left off on the lake. A new census showed that grebe numbers were still depressed. All my nest sites were inactive and no chicks or juveniles appeared. That was a bad sign. I decided that if the wild population of pocs was doomed, we should at least keep a small nucleus alive in a sanctuary. A refuge might save the genetic pool until such time as we might manage to release birds back into the main lake, or try captive breeding somewhere else.

But in order to have a safe refuge, and a safe lake, a game warden was vital. I had been impressed by the interest Edgar was

showing in my work. He showed up almost every day in his old
wooden boat, offering to help or to tell me of an observation he'd
made on the pocs at his farm. Why not ask Edgar to be the new
official, year-round warden? I thought. He had lived at the lake
most of his adult life. He had a boat and did not fear the *chocomil*
or *norte*. He drove to Santiago daily for his mail and supplies, so
could receive telegrams from me. And he knew the Mayor and
Secretary. Moreover, since he employed a dozen Indians as laborers on his farm, he spoke Tzutujil. Armando agreed that he'd be a
fine choice.

One morning, Jessie and I paid a visit to his farm. Very tactfully, I proposed the idea to Edgar and his mother. I was actually
afraid of insulting him because in Guatemala, as in other Central
American countries, a conservation officer earned only about
$100 a month. In addition, the boats and motors supplied by
government agencies were not always reliable. Shipments of gas
and oil often arrived late, or not at all. There were no fringe
benefits. I mentally compared what the government would be
offering Edgar to what a conservation officer would receive in
New York State. The salary in New York began at about $8,000–
10,000 in 1965, and equipment might include a boat and motor,
snowmobile, snowshoes, patrol car or jeep, revolver, uniforms, and
boots. Fringe benefits would cover sick leave, medical payments,
and retirement, not to mention vacation pay. I feared Edgar
would never consider the job. And who could blame him?

Edgar and his mother listened impassively while we sipped
small cups of essence of coffee. They exchanged a flurry of Spanish too fast for me to understand. The wind began rustling the
eucalyptus trees outside. I nibbled a tortilla. Jessie thumped the
floor with his tail. Then Edgar accepted with a broad smile, twirling his mustache. His mother was proud. Her son would be important. The job was prestigious, and more interesting than just
planting avocado trees and picking coffee beans. I was thrilled.

Armando drove me to Guatemala City again to see the Minister of Agriculture. This time he was very attentive and I was much

surer of myself. I explained the format of Operation Protection of
the Poc: enforcement, habitat management, education and ap-
preciation, and finally, a refuge. Most important, I told him, was
the need for a full-time official warden at the lake. Someone who
was brave, trustworthy, and interested in the program. Then I
proposed Edgar.

"I quite agree with you," said the Minister. "I will appoint
him and make sure he gets fifty gallons of gas a month delivered to
his farm." He made a note on his pad.

Now Armando suggested that he and I be appointed honorary
game wardens. "One of us is always near or on the lake," he
explained, "and we both have boats and motors. Anita pays for
the gas and oil with her grant funds. We could help your warden
at no extra cost by covering the north shore since he lives so far
away."

"Excellent idea," said the Minister, jotting down more notes.
"I'll see to official papers for the three of you."

"Why don't I provide uniforms and design an emblem for our
shirts?" I offered. "We'll have more authority that way, and it's
good publicity. In fact, we should have our own stationary and
print up big poc posters to put around the lake villages."

"Very good," said the Minister, still scribbling.

"Is there any way that reed cutting could be controlled?" I
ventured. "At least during the grebe nesting season?"

"I'm not sure," answered the official, "it might be quite involved. But I'll have the Division of Fauna call a meeting of
Indian reed cutters and yourselves in Santiago Atitlán. Perhaps
you can come to some agreement, but I warn you the Tzutujiles
are tough negotiators. If it works, the Ministry of Agriculture
might propose a law."

Next I outlined my thoughts for a refuge—how it might be
the final resort for saving the pocs if the wild population disappeared. "I will try to get more grant money to build it," I said,
"and I wonder if the government could put up matching funds in
the form of salaries for workmen and materials?

I had always wanted to be an honorary game warden. Here, with my work partners and my boat, *Xelajú*.

"After all," I heard myself saying artfully, "this rare bird is found only in your beautiful country. Guatemalans should be proud to have it. People will come from all over the world to see and photograph this unique species." I described my experiences with both National Audubon Society and my later wildlife tours. "There are hundreds and thousands of birdwatchers who love to travel to see new species. If you increase tourism from birdwatchers and nature lovers, you'll get more money into Guatemala."

Unwittingly, I had hit on the two points most persuasive to Latin mentality—national pride and economics. If I'd used more esoteric arguments about aesthetics, morals, or genetics, I would have failed.

There and then the Minister committed himself to our program. Armando and I left his office giddy with success. I could never have imagined getting such ready results with an important official in the United States. I was becoming aware of two things: being a blond, female scientist from a foreign country helped more than it hindered. I was not considered a threat, whereas a male professional from abroad, unless most diplomatic, might

Edgar Bauer in his Operation Protection Poc uniform.

have aroused feelings of competition or inadequacy on the part of less educated or experienced colleagues. Also, I sensed that by treating the Guatemalan officials with utmost courtesy, humility, and respect, they always treated me the same. Unfortunately, I had occasion to meet a few visiting foreign scientists during my stay at Lake Atitlán and was always disturbed by their conde-scending ways. Few remembered to send back copies of their research reports, photographs, or published papers. It's not sur-prising that, with time, such behavior has led to the concept of "scientific imperialism." It has forced some countries today to demand letters of intent from visiting scientists and contracts which promise to share any data or publications resulting from their visits.

Before we left Guatemala City, Armando and I stopped to see Jorge Ibarra at the Museum of Natural History. We invited him to come to the lake and talk to schoolchildren in each of the twelve villages ringing the shore and the eight hamlets higher up on the slopes of its watershed. Jorge was the lone voice of conser-vation at the time, and none of the kids had even heard the word "conservation." I hoped that by telling them about our poc cam-paign and explaining the good that would come from it, the chil-dren would share this with their parents and word would spread. Luckily, Mr. Ibarra was most willing. Since he spoke some Indian dialect, he would not need an interpreter. Over the next two years, he would make three such conservation education trips to Atitlán.

In order to have some posters for Jorge to distribute in the schools and for the game warden to give each Secretary, I visited the leading printer in Guatemala City, who also published the popular daily paper, *El Imparcial.* When he heard about our pro-gram, he refused to take any payment for his work. Instead, he graciously gave me stationary and envelopes, both with the poc emblem, and several sets of cardboard posters. One type showed the birds and urged people to protect them: *"Sea Buen Guatemal-teco"* (Be a Good Guatemalan). Another stated the law protecting water birds at the lake and the fine for killing or molesting pocs.

He also arranged for the colored emblems. "Operation Protection Poc" on a yellow background with a black and white bird in front of a volcano. As soon as the emblems were ready, I sewed them on the left sleeve of the khaki shirts I'd bought for uniforms.

It was a proud day when Edgar, Armando, and I set out with our new uniforms and arm patches. We planned to stop at each village to speak to its Mayor and Secretary and distribute posters. We would ask that a town crier announce the new program and the law. This way we hoped to ensure compliance from the estimated 50,000 Indians living in Atitlán's hamlets. And I very much wanted to involve them.

All my life I'd wanted to be a game warden. Perhaps it was the pride of wearing a uniform and having the authority to protect wildlife. Perhaps it was the challenge of an all-male profession where women were the exception. Perhaps it was the romance associated with working in the field and under rugged conditions. Whatever. . . . As I gunned the motor and maneuvered my boat side by side with Edgar's and Armando's crafts, I felt this dream had come true. Indeed, I was probably the only female conservation officer in the Western Hemisphere, albeit an honorary one. It was not usual for women to work professionally outdoors and shoulder to shoulder with men in law enforcement. My head was high, pigtails flying in the wind, as we crossed to the tiny fishing village of Santa Catarina.

There, to our great surprise, we were met with stares of horror. We tied up our three boats and hurried to the mayor's office. Children and women scurried away in fright. No one spoke to us. Finally, we learned from the Secretary that the color I'd chosen for the uniforms of Operation Protection Poc was the same as that worn by insurgent guerrillas! A band of them was terrorizing local inhabitants in the faraway Sierra de las Minas mountains, and word of their activity had spread like wildfire throughout Guatemala. These illiterate natives, living without radio, TV,

phones, or newspapers, imagined that the rebels had arrived at
Lake Atitlán! In those days, I was completely naive about politics
so had no idea that this distant localized rebellion was part of
larger leftist insurgency which was to smolder and flare intermit-
tently for the next twenty-five years in Guatemala. Possibly in-
spired by the Cuban example, it is the longest-running revolution
in Central America. I simply dismissed this guerrilla rumor as an
isolated, homegrown uprising having no bearing on my poc project or future, except for changing the color of our uniforms.

After carefully explaining our positions and program to the
Secretary and Mayor, we nailed a few posters to the walls of their
office and the school house. Then we rushed back to Panajachel.
Armando saved the day by driving us to market and encouraging
me to buy wide colorful Indian sashes and new sombreros. We
ripped the poc emblems off our sleeves and pinned them to the
front of our shirts. Surely, no hard-fighting guerrillas would look
like this.

Before we started out to the villages again, Armando took us
up to Sololá to meet the Governor of this district. "It's better we
start at the top," he explained, "and get his cooperation. If he's
behind Operation Poc, then the whole population of the lake will
know and help you."

The Governor was a kindly man with a portly figure. He was a
retired Army colonel, but looked more like a huggable grandfa-
ther. I liked him at once. He became very interested in our campaign, and before the afternoon was over he had composed and
sent telegrams to each of the twenty hamlets within the watershed. One slender wire, crossing mountain ranges and dipping
into canyons, was the main link, the only link, with this higher
authority. The Governor ordered each Mayor and Secretary to
cooperate with us and obey the poc law. He also dictated official
letters for each of us to carry, declaring our mission, complete
with impressive seals.

I offered the Governor poc posters for his office, and he nailed
them up himself with relish. I was so grateful to this man that

when he said goodbye, shook my hand, and asked why I wore such a huge, handsome watch, I promptly took it off and gave it to him. "It's for snorkeling and scuba-diving," I explained. "Completely waterproof. My watch is your watch. You must have it, Governor."

He was enchanted. For the first time, I had performed a truly Guatemalan act of hospitality: "My house is your house." While I doubted very much that the portly colonel would ever dive with it, I was happy to think of him wearing it in his office perched 2,000 feet above that mighty lake.

Now our trip around Atitlán went off without a hitch.

Shortly after this, Jorge Ibarra came up and we could begin to

Jorge Ibarra explains the goals of conservation to schoolchildren. Note the poster for Operation Protection Poc.

lecture to the school kids. Barefoot tykes in colorful Indian clothing sat awestruck as the Museum director told them about conservation and showed them his crazy stuffed grebe. Most of them
knew what the poc was but had no idea that the birds only lived
here. None of them had ever been away from their homes, and
none went to school beyond fourth grade. They were needed to
work with their parents.

Soon it was time for the reed cutters' meeting. While *I* was
adamant that we stop all harvesting of reeds, to protect habitat,
Edgar disagreed with me tactfully. *He* felt that the reeds and
cattails could be cut and cared for in the same way that he
managed his coffee and avocado crops. The reed cutters, for their
part, declared that any change would cause economic hardship for
their families and spoil their cottage industry. The representatives
from the Division of Fauna didn't know *what* to do. For three
days, brightly clad Indians with machetes, government officials in
suits and ties, Armando, Edgar, and I in our uniforms stubbornly
and loudly debated. The Minister was correct—the Tzutujiles
were tough.

At this meeting, Edgar showed himself something of a states-
man. He and one official cleverly devised the solution that was
finally accepted. The proposal was that reed cutting be curtailed
annually between May 1 and August 15, in order to protect the
endangered grebe families. No eggs or nests could be taken or
destroyed at *any* time. The rest of the year was open for reed and
cattail cutting; however, every man must cut only *half* his plot
each year. That way, we were assured of having 50 percent of the
habitat standing at any given time.

This compromise satisfied everyone. Foremost, the prohibited
period fell partly during rainy season, so few reeds could be cut
and dried anyway. Secondly, it became apparent with time that
the vegetation grew better and taller under this regime. Edgar was
right. Sleeping mats and little seats would still be produced, perhaps more than ever. The pocs were fairly safe (I would have

preferred a March 1st start, but the Indians flatly opposed this)
during most of the critical time with their chicks. The whole
experience taught me a lot about the need for compromise in
conservation work and the art of balancing wildlife *and* human
needs. In 1968, this astute plan became presidential law.

When I wasn't engaged with all these new activities, I carried
out field observations. Doña Rosa and Jessie occasionally joined
me. She had sharp eyes and was uncomplaining about spending
hours in the boat. In fact, she had the idea one day as we were
passing San Pedro de la Laguna to suggest that the Indians incorporate the poc motif into their arts and crafts.

"Right here in San Pedro," she said, "there's a small rug cooperative where village girls weave woolen rugs. Mostly they use the
quetzal in their designs since it's the national bird. But you could
show them how to draw a grebe."

Rosa was right. The factory head accepted her suggestion
with enthusiasm, and I sketched out a grebe. Some weeks later, I
had the pleasure of buying the first such rug, in bright red with a
black and beige poc, for $25. The lobed feet of the bird hung
below it, as large as steamship propellers, its eye as big as a horse's.
Yet the overall effect was striking. I felt it looked appropriate to
initiate this boost in the local economy. Jessie received stern orders to leave it alone.

Indian artisans must have carried the idea from one to another
because not long after, a primitive painter offered me a charming
oil painting showing a mother poc with three chicks swimming
down the Bay of Santiago Atitlán. She was the size of a battleship,
whereas the Indian boy hiding in the reeds with a slingshot was
dwarf-like. I bought the painting from him and later hung it in my
bedroom. Not the least of "grebe" Indian crafts was an enormous
poc which suddenly materialized out of a cypress bush. The owner
of the garden in Panajachel had the bush cut in the shape of a
grebe!

How many rugs, paintings, textiles, and other "objects d'art" were actually created with giant grebe designs, I never knew. Indians have habitually viewed animals either as sources of food or labor. The only exception is the quetzal, which has been honored and revered for centuries in Maya culture and art and now is the name of the currency and the national symbol (like our bald eagle). If the Indians would accept the poc as a worthy motif for their crafts, it seemed our conservation efforts might succeed locally.

Meanwhile, it was almost Christmas. Operation Poc was going into full swing, but I stayed home to buy gifts and help Doña Rosa decorate her house. Once again, I would accompany her family to Midnight Mass and then go to her party. We were busy fixing deviled eggs and eggnog in her kitchen when she sighed and said, "Ah, if only we had a *pinabeta* (balsam fir) for a Christmas tree. Nothing smells so good or looks so nice with candles on it."

"Can't I get you one at the market?" I asked.

"I doubt it. They only come from high, high up in the mountains."

"I'll bet Armando would know where to find one," I said teasingly. He had just appeared in the doorway, laden with gifts.

Armando volunteered at once to look for a tree. "If I leave now," he estimated, "and drive up toward Quetzaltenango, I can be back by nine or ten and still go to Mass."

Doña Rosa broke into a smile. "Take my axe, Armando. I'll find some rope. I wish I could go, too, but there's so much to be done for the party."

"Come on, Anita," coaxed Armando. "You come help me."

Moments later we were in his Land Rover headed for the mountains above 9,000 feet. Twilight was falling when we reached the first pine, fir, and oak forests. A norther was blowing

Poc rug created by the weavers' cooperative.

BIENVENIDOS
COOPERATIVA DE TEJEDORAS
SAN PEDRO·LA LAGUNA R.L.
Fundada el 10 de Noviembre de 1964 con el·auspicio·de
S. F. E. I.

A painting by Rafael Gonzalez G. shows a boy with a slingshot aiming at a battleship-sized poc and her chicks.

here, and its deep roaring filled our ears as the wind soughed through the trees. A thousand stars seemed strung along the black branches, and an almost full moon was rising over the wild mountain crests. I shivered as I got out of the jeep. Armando grabbed the extra jacket he always carried and held it out for me. "Here, Anita," he said gently, "put this on." Then he took the axe and big flashlight and started into the forest. As he probed with the beam, this way and that, looking at individual trees, I followed blindly. The only sense of direction I had was the cold wind on my left cheek. Yet, I felt no fear or unease. If I'd been alone in the Adirondack woods, I'd have all my feelers out and be marking my way. But with this man, I always felt safe, always cared for.

"Here's a beauty," he exclaimed, shining the light on a symmetrical fir. Then I remembered. Hadn't the Secretary in Santiago told me there might be a law to protect *pinabetas,* and pocs, but not birds?

"Armando," I said hesitantly. "Do you think we should take a fir? Isn't that prohibited in Guatemala since so few of them grow here?"

One fanciful gardener who joined the conservation effort fashioned a poc from a cypress tree.

He stopped with the axe held high and turned toward me.
What would he say? Would he feel I was interfering? Especially
when his dear Rosa had asked for a fir. After all, what was one less
tree in all these wild mountains?

"Who told you that?" he asked.

"The Secretary at Santiago. The day my things were stolen.
When I first went there."

"I think you're right, Anita," Armando said. "Well, if we
protect pocs, we have to protect firs. You are a great conservationist. Rosa will be mad, but perhaps she'll be tipsy and won't notice.
After all, I think a pine looks just as nice."

I relaxed instantly, my heart went out to this good-natured,
supportive man who'd been such a great help and field companion
over the past year. My work would never have gotten very far
without him.

Armando soon found a bushy young pine, chopped it down,
and trimmed the base. Together we dragged it back to the jeep
and tied it to the top. Once our shoulders touched, and I felt my
heart lurch. Back in the jeep, I told myself to stop acting like a
romantic. I was imagining things. At the same time I recalled how
attracted to Armand I'd felt when we swam to the hot springs.
But, Armando had teen-age children, and I was fifteen years his
junior. Besides, he probably loved Rosa since he spent so much
time at her house.

Rosa was delighted with her tree, even though it was not a fir.
When she heard the reason, she nodded her approval. Dexter-
ously, she propped the bushy pine in a corner by the fireplace and
decorated it. Then we all set off to church. This time when I
walked down the aisle, Armando was beside me, like last year. But
this time he turned his head, smiled, and took my hand in his
strong one. He gave it a soft squeeze and murmured, "You came
back, Anita. I'm so glad." Suddenly, I knew that what I'd felt in
the forest had been mutual.

Rosa's party was even jollier than the year before. Armando

and I darted quick looks at each other across the room while guests cavorted. As the pink flush of Christmas Day filled the sky, Doña Rosa was asleep on the sofa, snoring, the victim of too many *ron popos* (rum eggnogs). Armando gathered me passionately in his arms. At first I held back. After my divorce, I had vowed never to fall in love again. Yet a longing for companionship and affection had stayed alive, now welling up strongly. On my second Christmas in Guatemala, I allowed myself to love, and be loved, again.

7

Ancient Ruins
and a New Love

NEW YEAR'S 1966 was for me a year of new life. I had a new
house, a new dog, and a new boat. There were new goals
to work for. Most of all, I had a new love. I'd never felt
more pleased with life. The contrast to my previous year was
incredible. The only thing not working out was my photography
of pocs for *National Geographic*.

Armando and I worked together almost every day, taking time
to talk and get to know each other as we had not done before. We
spent days patrolling, checking reeds, working on Don Emilio's
beach fixing the boats, chatting with the old man, and trying to
train Jessie. Our outward demeanor was as it always had been—
discreet, respectful, attentive. Yet inwardly we were a whirl of
emotions. Needs long suppressed by both of us boiled to the surface.

Still my professional commitment to work and a new career
was equally strong. I could combine them now, but I wasn't sure
how things would work in the long run. After all, we were two

different nationalities, two distinct ages, and I had committed myself to a degree at a major university. Armando, too, had obligations to his family, even though separated, and to his work.

One evening he told me he was running behind on delivery of orders with his trucking service. At once I felt guilty because he spent so much time with me. "I need to drive to several remote villages, both here at the lake and in the highlands," he explained "and give my staff some time off during these holidays." (Unlike our country, Latins usually celebrate the first six days of January as part of the Christmas Season). "I'll be gone four or five days."

Even though it meant I could get back to solo observations, waiting hours in the reeds at my three best sites, I hated to be without Armando. He, being so active and energetic, disliked sitting for any length of time in the boat. He was a typical Aries, I thought, always on the go, full of courage and vigor.

"Would you like to go with me?" he asked, catching me by surprise.

"Well," I began, "it's been a long time since I checked on the grebes . . . and my pictures are still . . ." Then I stopped. "Of course, I'll go, Armando."

That settled it. Two days later we left in a large truck loaded to the tops of the racks with bottled soft drinks, cases of beer, boxes of canned milk, roofing, wire, nails, and more. Armando had rolled up two sets of sleeping blankets, cooking pots, and bottled water. Two young boys accompanied us to unload items and help Armando if the truck got stuck. They rode in the back, enduring dust, wind, cold, and bumps as if it were an everyday matter. We took off around the eastern shore of the lake, climbing high along a paved, then dirt road, at the crest of the watershed. At every crossroads of a trail with the road there stood a tiny general store. We would stop and leave several bottles of soft drinks, a case of beer, and whatever else the owner had ordered. Empty bottles were neatly loaded back on the truck, counted over and over, and the deposit paid by Armando to the owner. An empty bottle was worth more than a full one, it seemed. Each brought ten cents—an enormous amount for a poor shopkeeper, whereas the full bottle sold for fifteen cents. I was witnessing a penny economy at work. Armando carried a huge leather bag full of change to make these negotiations. He never lost his patience, although the owner might insist on counting his deposit three times over.

By noontime, we had dropped back down to the lake at San Lucas Tolimán, the second largest village. Armando had several stops to make here, and I marveled at how pleased people were to see him. He had a cheerful word or joke for everyone. After a while I got bored with bottles and pennies, so wandered off to look for textiles. When I returned, it was almost dusk.

"We'll sleep here," Armando said. "The road is too rough to Santiago Atitlán to take a chance in the dark. This way we can get an early start tomorrow." He sent one of the helpers for tortillas and beans and parked near the open shore. Then he unrolled our sleeping blankets under the truck. "We're going to sleep there?" I gasped. *"Under* the truck?"

"Yes, Anita. Where else?" he said. "There are no hotels or pensions anywhere along these shores. I don't own a tent, nor do you. The cab is too crowded. And the boys use hammocks."

"Hammocks? Here? There's not a tree in sight."

He chuckled and knelt beside the truck to show me how hammocks could be tied to the springs and axles and allow a person to swing comfortably below. "Who could ask for a better shelter? The rain and wind can't reach under here. Actually, our sleeping rolls are considered a luxury."

That night I looked out over Atitlán from a totally new perspective. Huddled next to Armando on the ground with a greasy transmission eighteen inches above my head, I could see the lights twinkling in Panajachel fifteen miles away. The wind moaned down from the mighty shoulders of Tolimán and Atitlán behind us and penetrated even the thick wool of a Momostenango blanket. Armando held me in his arms to warm me and whispered romantic words in my ear. Even so, I shivered all night. How those two boys stood it in their string hammocks with old wraps, I'll never know. But they snored peacefully.

Next morning after boiling up coffee on a campfire and eating some sweet bread, we went to Santiago Atitlán. The road was truly horrible. The truck rocked and creaked so much that I was sure we'd break an axle. The glass bottles clinked and rattled behind us until I was certain they'd shatter and spill everything. Then I remembered this was the area Sam Lothrop had written about in his book about Lake Atitlán.

"Armando, when we come back this way, could we stop and look for old ruins of the ancient Mayas?" I asked.

He was instantly interested and promised we would. After we delivered in Santiago, the road became smooth and level along the bay shore. We rolled under lush groves of coffee trees. All at once I saw a familiar sight: two lines of tall eucalyptus trees and several small huts beside the roadway. "Isn't this Edgar's farm?" I asked.

"Yes, it is," Armando said. "He has the best soil and rain conditions on the lake, being so close to the Pacific coast. The volcanoes made rich earth over the centuries, and there's seldom a day it doesn't rain here when the clouds drift up from the lowlands."

"But his workers certainly live in awful places," I observed. "Can't he give them better houses?"

"*Típico,*" Armando said. "No better or worse than on most farms. Also, the landowner is responsible to provide all the corn, beans, rice, and firewood that a worker's family needs every month. As well as a house, farm tools, and water."

I was still wondering about the fairness of such a system when we arrived in San Pedro de la Laguna at the end of the dirt road. Like all the other towns we'd stopped at, i was amazed how different they seemed when one was on land, not water. I had an idyllic vision from my boat, of peaceful Indian hamlets framed by reed beds; whereas in reality they were bustling, struggling centers of commerce. Indians walked miles to attend markets, or bring produce, or seek medical help in these places. A few lived in concrete or adobe houses with rudimentary plumbing, but most had only one- or two-room huts with no toilets or water.

The truck was half empty by the time Armando finished in San Pedro. As we came to the roughest stretch of road, Armando stopped beside a fruiting tree covered with small yellow balls. "Let's eat our lunch here, Anita," he suggested, "and pick some of these *jocotes* for dessert."

The yellow fruits were dead ripe and I ate several. Then we left the two boys to take a siesta while Armando and I walked into the cornfields and rocky hills to look for ruins. "The book I read at Cornell said the early Indians lived in long, narrow, low huts looking over their fields and the lake. They usually had two or three rooms, so we should look for rectangular rock walls, a few feet high," I said.

We scuffed along, dust covering our shoes, jumping over boulders. There were few trees, only cornfields or abandoned cornfields filled with weeds. When we'd walked about half a mile toward the lake from the truck, I got my first glimpse of the aquamarine water. The northern mountains looked bluish and cold. There sat Sololá on the edge of the cliff above Atitlán. I wondered what the Governor and his watch were doing today. The town looked so minuscule from here. Almost directly below it lay Panajachel, 2,000 feet lower, with the white gash of canyon where the Rio Panajachel feeds into the lake. I now knew from my reading that there are only *two* small rivers which enter Atitlán, and *no* rivers going out. For a lake that size, this was truly remarkable. It meant that the lake received and kept most of its water from rainfall and huge underground springs—all three cubic miles of water! Its annual fluctuation was a mere three feet between the dry and rainy seasons.

I lifted my eyes above Sololá and imagined how Armando and

I had driven back into those high forests to see Jesús, the shaman, and to cut our Christmas tree. I smiled. How lucky I'd been to see this side of Guatemala. Just then, I stumbled over a stone and fell on to my knees. Armando helped me up, then knelt down again. "Look here, Anita. This stone has been cut. It's almost square."

Thus we found our first ruin on the shores of Atitlán. It was easy to picture the low stone hut with its thatch roof, long since rotted away. This home was situated looking over a round yard fenced with huge boulders. Cacti grew on top of these, making entry or exit impossible. I wondered if this could have been the family's "yard" or nursery. No child could crawl off from here. Then we found a break in the circular barrier with worn steps which faced the lake. "I'll bet this is where they walked down for water," I said excitedly. "Maybe things haven't changed that much in a thousand years." I pictured the young girls with their clay jugs in Santiago.

Just then, I felt a peculiar stab of pain in my stomach. I stopped a moment, but it passed. We kept on walking, looking for more ruins. Another cramp came and went. But within twenty minutes I was doubled over with the worst stomach pains I could recall. Armando picked me up in his strong arms and carried me back to the truck. He tried not to grin. When the boys saw me scuttle off into the weeds, they burst out laughing. Jocotes!

When I reappeared, weak and pale, Armando explained that jocotes can be a powerful emetic on some people. "Why didn't you warn me?" I sulked.

"How was I to know?" replied that intractable man. "Look *amorcita* (little love), we're heading back to Panajachel now. You'll be fine again before we get there, but let's stay there tonight so you can shower and get cleaned up. Then tomorrow we'll head into the highlands and finish our deliveries."

The way I felt, I'd never go anywhere again. Yet Armando was right. When we reached Panajachel at dusk, I'd recovered. Moreover, there was a wonderful telegram waiting for me. It was from

Mary Smith and announced that a photographer, David G. Allen, would be available in March to photograph the nesting season of the grebes. He was the son of Dr. Arthur A. Allen, the noted ornithologist and bird photographer, and ran a business, Bird Photos, Inc. If anyone could obtain good pictures, he would.

I quickly realized I had to get back to the lake and be sure of where mated pairs of pocs lived and what their cycle was. I also needed to find a site for the refuge and start work there. The more I had to show Mr. Allen, the better. But it meant being apart from Armando at least half a week. Sadly I told him I would go with him another time.

Next day I set out with only Jessie to comb the lakeshore for a sanctuary site. The entire north, east, and west shores were unsuitable because of their precipitous slopes, sparse reed beds, and unprotected location. I concentrated on the south side of the lake and found two or three coves which might be partially enclosed and protected. When I asked Edgar to look over the sites, he pointed out that one place, Xecamuc, had been a colonial Spanish fish hatchery two or three centuries earlier. Spanish priests had run it. A low rock wall had once separated the tiny bay from the lake. Now it lay in ruins underwater, but I could still see the foundation. Edgar thought it might provide a ready-made base for construction of a new refuge enclosure.

I was so excited about this find that I could barely wait for Armando to return. As soon as he had, we set off to see the place. It was a windy afternoon and late. He tied up the boat in some reeds and we waded ashore. Quickly, we skirted the cove and then stuck a stick in the water to see how deep the old rock base lay.

"This shouldn't be so hard to rebuild, Anita," Armando said thoughtfully. "The wall should come up three feet or more above lake level and attach into boulders on both shores. "We'll leave a mouth for fresh-water exchange with the lake. And maybe . . ." His voice trailed off as he looked westward. "How about building a little visitors center on that knoll?" He pointed upward.

As the sun set, we scrambled on to the rise and looked about.
The view toward Panajachel was lovely, and one could also see
right down into the bay. "I can picture birdwatchers setting up
their telephoto lens right here," I said enthusiastically, "and we
could put up a display about the birds."

Armando was now staring further up the hill and shaking his
head. "Anita, I think those ruins that we discovered last week are
right up there. See where the shadow meets the sun?"

He was right. The long light of sunset had brought out the
relief of those ancient stone walls. We rushed up to the site and

**Jessie and I at the grebe refuge site. It was one of the few bays that was
shallow enough to support reeds and permit the building of a stone wall. -**
Photo by George Holton

gazed around. The sun was slipping between burgundy and gold
clouds as it set behind Volcano San Pedro. The wind had whipped
the lake into purple. "No wonder those people choose to live here
and not in Santiago," I exclaimed. Not a light, not a house, not a
road, not a boat broke the spectacular scenery. "What I wouldn't
give to have a hut here myself."

Shortly after, I began discussions with the Division of Fauna,
through the Minister, about constructing the refuge. I put up
several hundred dollars from my grants, and the government
reciprocated by hiring local workmen to rebuild the wall and start
a visitors center. I understood the Ministry would purchase or
lease the two or three acres of land around the cove from the
native owner(s) so I did not get involved in that aspect.

Now the advantage of having Edgar nearby came into play.
He came daily to oversee the workmen and make sure that government supplies of mortar, boards, nails, and tools were delivered
to the site. However, it was Armando who took charge of the
actual plans and construction. He would boat over with me once
or twice a week to lay out the work and measurements.

"Where did you ever learn to do so many things?" I asked him
one day. "Did you go to college and study engineering?"

"No. I never even went to high school."

Little by little the wall rose again and was connected to the
sides. A twelve-foot opening was left in the center. On hot mid-
days, I would often stop at the refuge after observations and help
the workmen set a few stones. They never ceased to wonder at a
woman carrying cement and rocks, or running a boat. One day it
was time to line the bottom of the opening with freshly cut rocks
to prevent erosion from the waves. The mouth held eight feet of
water. None of the Indian lads swam. Edgar was not there. So I
volunteered to dive down and do the job. The foreman of the
workers cautioned me to be careful as I put on my snorkel and
fins. "These stones are very rough," he said.

The men formed a line and passed rock by rock down to me,
while I dove and set them in place. At that altitude, I had to rest

often to catch my breath. We were almost finished, and I was four feet under water, when an outer corner of the upper wall suddenly tumbled down. The rocks narrowly missed my head but scraped over my right shoulder and arm. I surfaced at once. As soon as my body hit the air, the blood began coursing down my arm and back. I pulled off my face mask and fins while the men watched in alarm. They whispered rapidly to each other in Tzutujil. "The 'Mama Poc' has been hurt!"

Wrapping my beach towel around my arm, I told the foreman not to worry and left for Panajachel. When Armando saw me that night, he was furious. Doña Rosa had patched me up. There was no infection. Still he ordered me to stay away from the refuge unless he or Edgar was there. "Supposing those rocks had hit your head?" he kept repeating. "You could be drowned. No one there could run the boat and take you for help. Oh, Anita . . ." He held me very gently and I felt tears running down his cheeks, though he never cried.

From then on I followed Armando's instructions. The refuge continued to move along slowly. The *abaniles* (masons) did beautiful rustic work with the volcanic rock, cutting true straight blocks and cementing them carefully together. They would walk to the refuge site from Santiago each morning, a distance of three miles, break rocks all day in the sun, walk home again—all for a dollar a day!

Armando designed the visitors center and work started on that, too. Other Indians were hired to fence in the cove, top off the stone wall, and erect a large sign. I painted a sheet of 4 × 8 foot marine plywood with the words "Giant Grebe Refuge" in three languages. I figured that way Guatemalans and other Spanish-speaking tourists, Americans, and Germans could read the message. The sign showed grebes, reeds, and their nests and outlined the law protecting them.

Another cable arrived in which Mr. Allen advised me of his arrival dates. He planned to stay a month and wanted accommodations in Panajachel. Armando and I went to the airport to pick

The Giant Grebe Refuge
is supported in part by the
WORLD WILDLIFE FUND, Smithsonian
Institution, Pan American Section ICBP.

Este es el Refugio del Pok
apoyado en parte por la FUNDACION de la
VIDA SILVESTRE del MUNDO, el Instituto
Smithsonian, Sección Pan Americana de ICBP.
Operación Protección del Pok.

him up and marveled at the load of photographic gear he'd
brought along.

David was taciturn at first, only asking questions about the
grebes, their nesting areas, length of daylight, logistics of travel.
He was a no-nonsense type of person. Our first night together for
dinner, he made it clear that my job was to locate grebes and as
many active nests as possible for him. He hired Armando for a
month on the spot and rented his red and white boat. "I'll need a
tower," he said during dessert. "About twelve feet above the
water surface."

The Visitors Center, in 1967, with "Giant Grebe Refuge" on the sign in two languages. Note normal lake level near top of retaining wall.

Armando stared at him in surprise. Here was an intriguing new challenge. "The reeds often grow eighteen feet from lake bottom to their tops," he explained to David, "especially in the bay where Anita's been working. That would mean a tower thirty feet tall."

"Yes, that's about right," David said, as if there was nothing strange about his request. "Then I'll need a platform with a ladder going to it on which to set my tripod, cameras, batteries, and strobe lights."

"Are you going to carry all that equipment up and down from

a boat or leave it in the open overnight?" Armando asked, then added, "It's not safe to do so."

I knew he was thinking of my stolen knapsack and nodded my head in agreement.

"I have a stout canvas blind that sits on the platform," David said, "and I can padlock the zipper shut at night. A thief would have to slash the canvas to get in."

"No one will do that," Armando assured him, "because they'll be too frightened by that strange object in the air. It'll be a first for Atitlán."

I could tell that David and Armando would get along, but I wasn't sure I could deliver everything David wanted of me. The next morning it was clear we had our work cut out for us. Armando took David out to see the lake and reeds, while I was dispatched to look for bamboo. Lake Atitlán's climate is barely warm enough for this tropical plant, but there were several clumps at the southern edge of town. Armando feared that he would never find lumber long enough for the tower. Indeed, he was correct. We finally rigged up its legs out of spliced wood with long bamboo supports. Everyone pitched in to help. Rosa went for nails and bolts. Juan, my houseboy, helped carry the leggy object down to the beach along with David, Armando, and me. Don Emilio gave copious orders and opinions. His children all hung around peering at the mounds of equipment, and Jessie barked at the tower, after which he "christened" it with a lift of his leg.

It took both boats to transport everything to Edgar's farm. Then he and all the rest of us worked three days to install the tower. The entire project was dependent on *my* say-so that a pair of grebes had just built a nest there and laid eggs. If the pair were disturbed too badly, they might desert. Birds are poorly bonded to their nests before and just after eggs are laid; strongly so after the chicks hatch. Then, the tower might have to be taken down and repositioned. Needless to say, we kept quiet as owls.

Once the tower, platform, and blind were installed, we saw

very little of David. Armando took him across the lake by boat
each dawn, escorted him right *into* the blind, and left. That way,
if the pocs were watching, they thought both intruders had de-
parted. Birds cannot count. The only way we knew whether
David was alive or dead was the thin trickle of cigarette smoke
issuing from the top of the blind. He was seldom without a cigarette in his mouth. In the late afternoon, Armando picked him up
again and took him back to the hotel. I had never seen a photographer work as hard as David Allen, and he gained my total respect.

Then, too, I'd never worked as hard myself. Usually I spent
the days searching for nests, breeding platforms, or families of
pocs. I became adept at knowing just what part of a reed bed a
pair would pick and build in. Sometimes Armando stayed with
me; sometimes he worked at the refuge. At night I was so exhausted that I could not stay and eat with David but fell into bed.
This constant crossing and searching was costing me a lot of
money for gas and oil for the boat, not to mention energy.

One day, Armando came early to Casita Feliz to say the roof
over the visitors center had just been finished. "Come and see it,
Anita," he urged. "Leave your birds for a while and relax."

The minute I saw the building, even though it had no windows (so that photographers could shoot from within), an idea
came to me. "Why don't I camp here at night with Jessie?" I said.
"That would save a lot of boating time and I could get more work
done."

He was hesitant to leave me alone there but realized I was safe
with that hefty, alert dog. The workers came early, left late, and
one now stayed as a refuge guardian. No one wanted the materials
stolen. So it was decided that I would spend a few nights each
week in the newly finished visitors center.

Since the afternoon was sunny and mild, we walked up to the
old ruins and sat on a boulder to admire the view. Jessie bounded
away after a road runner. "Do you possibly think, Armando," I
began, "that I might buy this piece of land with the ruins? Visi-

tors who came to the refuge might like to walk up here, as an added attraction."

He thought for a moment, then said, "It probably belongs to an Indian in Santiago who grows corn. But clearly nothing's been planted here for a long time. If we asked the Secretary, he could tell us who owns it. Then I'll talk to him for you. It's better that way. If an Indian thinks a *gringa* wants to buy it, the price will go sky high."

We poked around the walls and yard again. The volcanoes made a mighty backdrop. I wondered how long since they had spewed lava down their slopes. It wouldn't take long for a wave of molten rock to reach the shore. Just then, I looked down at a small stone and saw it had been roughly cut in the shape of a duck. "Look! Armando." I shrieked. "It's a little poc. What luck! This is a symbol, a good luck piece. Now I know I have to buy this land."

He smiled and brushed off the stone bird. "Imagine some Indian child playing with this here a thousand years ago, Anita." Carefully, he put it in his woven shoulder bag. "Let's wash it off down by the lake."

We clambered over huge white rocks to the water and sloshed the stone bird around. Now we could see it even had eyes cut in.

"Let's take a swim, as long as we're here, Anita," Armando suggested.

"My suit's back in the boat," I said "and I'm too lazy to walk way back there."

"No one can see us from the refuge, and there are no canoes out on the water. We'll just go bare."

I was hesitant. Even though I went skinny-dipping every morning in the Adirondacks, the situation was far different in Guatemala. Maya people are extremely modest, and women *never* expose themselves above the knees or upper arms, and even then, only when washing clothes in the lake. Men are sometimes seen without a shirt, and little boys may splash in the shallows naked as jay birds. But a naked adult is taboo. Our workmen would have been appalled to see me that way. In fact, when the first hippies began coming to Lake Atitlán, they caused great consternation with their nude sunbathing.

But Armando had already stripped and dove in. He swam exuberantly along the shore. "It's wonderful. Come on in."

I looked all around me. No one in sight. Just then Jessie scrambled over the rocks and flung himself into the lake, splashing water all over me. So the decision was made for me. I took off my drenched outer clothes, then slipped into the water and removed my bra and panties. The transparent, cool water was a balm on my suntanned skin. "Remember the night we sat in the hot springs, *amorcita?*" Armando had suddenly emerged next to me. He gave me a wet kiss. "Even then I wanted to hold you."

Only then did I realize how long this sturdy, kind, and adventurous man had been attracted to me. Gently, I kissed him back.

After our swim we took the boat across the Bay of Santiago Atitlán, almost to the place where I'd first seen an Indian reed cutter and hauled it up on a little beach. Then we slowly climbed up Chuitinamit, looking for pottery shards. I found several incised and fluted pieces which must have been lips to water jugs or bowls.

At the top there appeared to be the faint indentation of a temple—a square sort of mound—Chuitinamit looked due east toward Cerro d'Oro and the rising sun. Whoever had stood here a thousand years ago looked out at a fabulous view and could salute the gods of sun, wind, rain, and moon. Suddenly, Armando tugged at my arm. "There's a small stela lying face down in the grass!"

We poked around and tried to lift it up, but the stone weighed far too much. "I wonder what's carved on the front?" he mused. "We should come back with the workmen and set it right."

"Better than that, Armando," I said. "Why don't we take it to the refuge and set it up there as another exhibit?"

"Of course, Anita," he agreed. "It'll be much safer there. But

we'll have to get special permission from the Museum of Ar-
cheology since all Guatemalan antiquities are protected. We can
try."

Just then I remembered David, probably broiling in his blind.
"We better get back to work, Armando," I said. And we scrambled down the hill like two kids who'd been playing hooky.

David Allen at the tower blind from which he could photograph nesting pocs.

In his month at Atitlán, David obtained superb photos of grebes—males, females, chicks, nests, and various displays. He set out mirrors, decoys, fake chicks—anything to elicit a behavioral response without harming the birds. He even had me put on scuba gear, rent a tank, and try to herd a wild poc toward him, hidden in a boat. I learned a great deal about dedication and bird behavior from David.

Eventually my story and David's pictures appeared in both National Geographic Society's *School Bulletin* (now called *World*) and in *Audubon* magazine. But we did not make it into *National Geographic* itself. That opportunity was preempted by another Guatemalan bird—the legendary quetzal—which David, Armando, and I tracked two years later!

Locally, I was receiving a lot of publicity, too. The owner of *Prensa Libre,* one of the leading newspapers, sent a reporter to Atitlán and ran a story about the conservation campaign and the new refuge. Then other city papers picked up on it and gave us more coverage. I hated having my picture taken (always have), yet Armando encouraged me to cooperate. "It's good to let people in the city know about all the work we're doing up here. They need to understand conservation, too."

My priest friend in the city sent me the clippings and I put them in a scrapbook. One afternoon I took them to show Doña Rosa. She scanned through the stories, then sat back and grinned. "And I remember when you arrived at Lake Atitlán, Anna. You knew no one but *me.* Now everyone knows *you.*"

8
Pixibaj

AFTER DAVID LEFT, we slacked off work on Operation Poc. Armando and I were worn out, and the refuge was close to being finished. Grebe breeding season was slowing down, too, so I felt justified in taking some personal time.

The first thing we did was go see about the land with the ruins. While I waited at the refuge, Armando boated over to Santiago Atitlán and spoke with the Secretary. He produced the Indian owner's name, and Armando went to see him. The man no longer went there to plant corn, but he couldn't figure out why Armando wanted his old fields inland instead of waterfront property. It was useless to explain to him about the ancient ruins and people. Modern-day Maya believe old pots and artifacts may bring bad luck and often shatter them. So Armando simply said he was working at the refuge and it would be useful to have a place to stay nearby. It was an honest explanation. Moreover, since no foreigner is allowed to own land within two hundred meters of any water body in Guatemala—for national security, the reason for which became clear to me much later—Armando would in all likelihood put the property in his name, although I would be the rightful owner.

The Indian was indecisive. Rather than seem too interested, Armando left. He suggested to me that we go to the city and see about obtaining permission to move the little stela down from the top of Chuitinamit to the refuge. We explained to the proper authorities about the purpose of our visitors center and how we would like to show some of the artifacts of the region, not just giant grebes and their habitat. Armando mentioned that a full-time guardian would live near the refuge and that the stone slab would probably be safer and better off standing there than lying upside down at the top of the uninhabited hill.

Permission was granted. And that led to more construction. A smooth stone terrace with steps leading down from the open-air center was built close to shore. The stela would stand by the water and visitors could stroll down to admire it. Edgar then said that a small office with windows and a door would be very useful to him. It could be attached to the open exhibit room and would give him a place to write reports for the government, pay the workmen, and store materials. "As it is now," he said, "all the cement, lime, and tools are being stored in the guardian's hut. He barely has room for his bed. Besides"—he gave me a warm smile—"if Anna keeps camping here, she could sleep in the office and be warmer and drier when the rains start."

It sounded like such a good idea that we immediately started scouting for the right site. I was walking around when I saw a boulder about four feet high whose top had been carved into a tiny square temple.

"Look at this!" I exclaimed. "I'll bet this is a replica of the temple we *think* stood on top of Chuitinamit. See? The steps to the west face directly toward the holy hill; the steps to the east, toward Cerro d'Oro. Didn't you tell me, Edgar, that hill is also supposed to have old ruins, hidden treasure, and be holy?"

I was amazed by the signs of early occupation we were finding and anxious to preserve and incorporate them into our sanctuary. "Armando, please be sure the workmen realize this is a rarity.

Under no circumstances should they break up this boulder for
building rocks. Tell them it's sacred!"

Armando chuckled. "The way things are going, Anita, you'll
have an archeological museum here before you have a poc refuge.
Remember there's still a lot to do—set up an exhibit, get the bass
out of the bay, restock native fishes for food, put the pocs in,
and—"

"Stop, stop, Armando," I pleaded. "We'll do all that soon.
But for now, let's go get the stela. Then we'll have this temple
rock, the ruins on the hill, the stela, oh, yes, and my little stone
poc to show." (It was safely back at Casita Feliz in my living
room.)

Next morning, Armando and I got to the refuge early, carrying two ten-foot lengths of heavy iron pipe in his boat and ropes
and tackle in mine. He advised the stonecutters that they could
have a break that day and help bring the stela down the mountain.
"However," Armando said wisely, "if any of you don't want to go
in the boats, you can stay here." He knew how fearful the Indians
are of deep water. Some would have never boarded a motorboat
before.

None of the eight men declined, so we divided them up between us and headed for Chuitinamit. Those in Armando's boat
eyed the heavy pipes nervously, knowing they could sink the boat
if it hit a shoal. Those in mine stared apprehensively every which
way, trying to ignore the fact that a woman was driving them
across Lake Atitlán. After a brisk climb uphill, hauling all that
gear, Armando supervised as the men pried the slab into a standing position.

There, clear as an etching, was a stylized face. "What do you
think it is?" I asked Armando. "It looks like a bird to me."

"Well, it's not a poc, if that's what you're thinking," he said.
"Could be a hawk, or eagle, or even a monkey."

The workmen were watching it warily. They made no com-
ments. I wondered if they considered it bad luck. Ever since my

experience with the shaman, Jesús, I was much more open to believe in spirits, white and black magic, and consider the world in a different context.

No one hesitated when Armando slid the two pipes in front like railroad tracks and tied ropes around the slab. Soon the men had it positioned on the pipes. "Now hold tight," Armando advised. "When the stela starts sliding downhill, you'll have to grab hard. It must weigh at least 800 pounds."

I simply stood by in admiration. I sensed that Armando had all the talents of a mechanical engineer and had missed out on a rewarding career. But maybe he was happier living at this magnificent lake and taking care of his trucks, cars, and boats.

The trip downhill was arduous, but no one got hurt and the stela didn't crack. Getting it into Armando's boat was the most difficult task. Once inside, the water reached within four inches of the gunwales.

"You take the boys in your boat, Anita. Make two trips," Armando said. "There are waves now from the *chocomil,* and we mustn't take chances with the men. There are no life jackets."

It was almost twilight when the heavy stone was finally in place on the terrace. It blended beautifully with the gray volcanic rock base. We ferried the workmen back to Santiago, saving them that weary walk, and paid them an extra day's wage for their hard labor.

The next day, at the refuge, we were admiring our handiwork when the Indian owner of the ruins came by. He went into a huddle with Armando, and the two of them disappeared up the hill. Later, when the man had gone, Armando said to me, "He'll sell." My heart leaped with joy. "It measures 100 by 200 *varas.*"

"What is a *vara?*" I asked.

"Come. I'll show you, *cariña.*" He led the way up to the ruins. "See this *izote* (yucca plant)?" Armando pointed to a tall, cactus-like plant growing from a rock pile. "That's a corner marker. Now sight down toward the lake. There's another *izote* about 200 yards

away. A *vara* is one of your yards, more or less, or maybe a meter."
He tweaked my nose playfully and grabbed my fingertips. "The
standard way to measure a *vara* is from the tip of your nose to the
end of your hand. The man and I just did that. The markers are
correct."

"You mean no one uses a tapemeasure?"

"No one *has* a tapemeasure," Armando said dryly.

We walked the boundary of the rectangular plot. Translated
into yards, I figured it contained almost three acres. The ruins lay
well back on the land toward the volcanoes. The part near the lake
had two large trees—unusual on this dry rocky shore—an avocado
and a jocote. They gave pleasant shade and were just the right
distance apart to string a hammock.

"Armando," I pointed out, "we can put up two hammocks,
take a siesta here, and munch jocotes all afternoon."

"The day you take a siesta, I'll eat the hammock."

"How much does he want for the land?" I asked, dreading the
answer.

"Around $400. That's a little high, but I didn't start to bar-
gain yet."

"High? High? With this view and the ruins?"

"Anita, you cannot eat the view and the ruins are of no earthly
use to anyone. The soil is rocky and the site is a long way from
town. I think it's overpriced, and I can get it for less."

I decided to keep quiet. Even though $400 seemed very little
for three acres, it was still a lot for me to scrape together. As it
turned out, Armando bought it for $300. I went with him to the
Secretary to witness the elaborate paperwork. Special lined and
stamped paper was needed on which the official wrote, in his
feathery handwriting, a description of the land and who the past
owners were. These owners, plus other witnesses, had to put their
thumbprints at the bottom of the paper. Since these Indians did
not read or write, a thumbprint was considered a signature. Armando and I sighed with relief when it was all done.

My first act as a landowner was to spend a day clearing around the ruins and putting up a sign. I had the workmen open a trail down to the refuge so tourists could walk up here. Then I sat down to rest by the big avocado tree. As I was admiring the site and my handiwork, the thought came—why not build myself an Indian hut right here? A home exactly like those of the Tzutujiles? A square structure of stone and cornstalk walls with a thatch roof and a clay pot at its peak? I was so excited that I ran down to the refuge and almost collided with Edgar coming out of the new office.

When I'd finished chattering, he asked, "Do you want a dirt floor, Anna? That's what the Indians usually have. Will you sleep on a *petate?* And cook over three stones and a fire?"

"Edgar, I want to live just as the Tzutujiles do," I said. "I really admire the simplicity of their living style. But I think it would be cleaner and neater if there was a cement floor and a bed. It could be set up on four posts in the corner, with boards for a bottom and a *petate* for a mattress."

"What about the windows? Do you want any? Will you put in glass?"

"Heavens, yes, with a view like this. Do the Indians use glass?"

"No," he replied. "It's too expensive. They just close the shutters if it rains or blows too much."

"Then that's what I'll use. Shutters. Painted green to match the avocado. And a door. I'll have a lock, Edgar, because I'd like to leave my field gear inside when I'm away."

"I can do this for you, Anna," Edgar said generously. "I've built several huts for my workmen at the farm. It's not hard. But you realize how small a house it will be?"

"No. How small? You know my cabin in the Adirondacks is only twelve by twelve feet. I like compact places."

"Then you should feel right at home," laughed Edgar, "because the typical hut is about ten by ten feet."

And that's how my backcountry home in Guatemala started. "La Casita con Ventanas Verdes" (The Little House with Green Shutters) was the name I chose. Edgar offered this extra work to the men at the refuge, explaining carefully that it was *not* part of the refuge and *not* to be paid by the government or my grants. This was strictly a house for the "Mama Poc." What they thought of an American woman wanting to live like them, I never heard. But it made sense to me. These Mayas had evolved a sensible way of life over many more centuries than had Americans. I wanted to try living like these beautiful people while I was in Guatemala.

With everything done by hand, the tiny structure seemed to take ages. The cement, nails, cornstalks, cornhusks for tying together the walls, wooden boards for bed, shutters, and door, all came on human backs and heads. The stone walls went up to three feet high, then the cornstalk sides rose to the eaves. Three window openings were made. Shutters and door were hung. Stout branches for supporting the four-sided roof were cut and carried down from the volcano sides, where mountain forest still grew. Last of all was the roof.

Edgar came to me one day and said, "Anna, the bunch grass which the Indians use for roofs grows very high on the volcano. It takes a man half a day to walk that far. Then he must cut and bundle it. Usually he has to sleep overnight in the forest and walk back down with the load and a tumpline around his forehead next day. The men say they want more money to do this, or else they will use *laminas* (tin sheets). It's cheaper."

"Horrors, no," I exclaimed. "That would look awful in this beautiful setting and sound dreadful when the rain pounds on it. How much has the hut cost so far, Edgar?"

He consulted the notebook he always carried in a small leather briefcase with his meticulous records of farm crops, refuge materials, workmen's wages, and my new venture. He produced the current running costs. "$32.76 so far," he said. "The usual hut runs around $45, but with your special floor and roof, and the extra windows, I estimate it will be closer to $60."

"Well, please tell the men to go for the bunch grass," I said. "Oh, and could you have them carry up those two big cardboard drums that I brought in my boat? I want to put them under the bed to store my clothes and field gear in eventually." I had gotten the drums free from the Lab of Ornithology at Cornell and had shipped my things in those instead of suitcases. They were stout and had metal lids which clipped on. Formerly they'd have been used to hold quantities of birdseed.

"By the way," said Edgar, "my mother sent you this little gift for your new house." He reached in the briefcase and pulled out a wicker basket with a bright red woven cotton cloth lining. "This is for your tortillas, to keep them warm." He handed me the basket and gave me a pat on the shoulder. I hugged him back, thankful that this dependable man and his mother were so caring.

Although I would stay in Guatemala until almost September this time, much had to be done for Operation Protection Poc before rainy season. I made a mental checklist. The refuge was almost complete—just landscaping and walkways and a dock to be built. Edgar was bringing small trees and flowering plants from his farm to put around the visitors center. The display was coming along. Using some of David's pictures and my own black and white photos, I was having them framed in the city. Then I would attach clean fresh *petates* to the walls for a backdrop and nail the pictures and captions to them. Rosa was helping me with the Spanish translation from my English text. I needed to go to the city and talk to the Fishery people about poisoning out the bass from the refuge. And to arrange for the reintroduction of small fishes. The pocs were holding their own. My last census showed a few more than eighty birds, some juveniles.

My trip to the city did not go well. Edgar drove me down because he had to buy certain parts for his motor. Not only could he not find them, but the Fishery people told us they had no

funds and no way to poison the bass. Fingerlings of native fishes
they could send us anytime, but I'd have to find another way to rid
the refuge of bass. Also, Edgar found that there'd been a change
of officials in the Ministry. The Minister who'd been so easy to
work with was gone. The new man was not aware of our program
and would have to be met and informed. This happened about
five or six times in my years in Guatemala. Unfortunately, at times
there was little continuity from leader to leader. Entire programs
might be eliminated and new ones set up. This made me apprehensive, but I figured as long as I kept bringing money in, Operation Protection Poc would continue. Once again I wrote away for
new grants and made a special plea to World Wildlife Fund for a
new boat and motor for Edgar. It wasn't fair that he had to use his
own boat to do his patrols, *and* pay for his own parts and repairs. I
didn't know what to do about the bass, and started brooding.

When we got back to Panajachel, Edgar dropped me off at
Casita Feliz and went to ask Armando if *he* had any spare parts
for the motor. Luckily he did, so enforcement work continued
(until the next breakdown). That night Armando arrived at my
place bearing flowers, some ripe mangoes, and an invitation. "I
heard from Edgar that you had a tough trip," he began as he
kneaded my shoulders to relax me. "Why don't you come away
with me again, *paloma* (dove), into the highlands? I have to take
another long truck trip."

I thought of my promise to him. The rains would soon turn
backcountry roads to mud, and before they ended I'd have to go
back to Cornell. This seemed as good a time as any.

"It would be super, Armando," I said. "Just to be alone together again and on the road. Who knows," I added. "Maybe it'll
clear my mind for the next step."

"Bring your warmest clothes, Anita," he cautioned me. "The
nights are much colder in the highlands than beside the lake."

A couple of days later we left at dawn with the same two boys
in the back and the same incredible load. This time we headed

north toward Quetzaltenango but frequently turned off the Pan
American Highway to take dirt roads into Indian towns. The first
two days we managed to be out on the paved highway by dusk and
found restaurants and motels for overnighting. I sat at fly-specked
tables with truck drivers and cargo boys from all over Central
America passing through on the Pan American. Steaming plates
of soup were served with tortillas, and there was no etiquette
about slurping it up. Great chunks of gristly beef mixed with
potatoes and cabbage made the main course. Men ate as if it were
their last meal. Then they pushed on, making time even though
bone-tired.

I gained a tremendous respect for these long-distance haulers
operating between Mexico and Panama. They dealt with land-
slides, washouts, chuckholes big enough to break all axles on an
eighteen-wheeler, mountains where speeds slowed to 10 m.p.h.
for an hour's drive uphill, isolated gas stations, and poor food.

Our last drop on Armando's route lay back in the hills toward
Chichicastenango. The tiny hamlet nestled in the shadows of a
deep canyon, and the road was a one-way goat track that barely
accommodated the truck. Since this was the end of dry season,
the dust lay four inches thick and billowed into our windows.
When we reached the bottom and pulled up to the little shop, the
storekeeper was at his home, a twenty-minute walk up the valley.
Armando sent a runner and began to unload cases and supplies.
The only other buildings were the Mayor's room, a small schoolhouse, and the church.

Finally the shopkeeper arrived, out of breath, and began
bringing out his empty bottles. Apparently, Armando's trucking
service only came in here twice a year due to its isolated location.
There were hundreds of bottles stored up. Moreover, this owner
would not accept paper bills, only coins. The people had no paper
money in this valley, he told us. He was extra suspicious about the
deposits being paid. Over and over he sorted out piles of pennies,
nickels, dimes, and quarters on the hood of Armando's truck.

Shadows lengthened. A cold wind began blowing down the canyon. I stood up from where I'd been reading, got into the cab, and
rolled up the window.

Armando shot me a look of pure exasperation, then said in a
loud voice, "We'll be leaving soon, Anita. We must get out before
dark to see the road." The store owner paid no attention.

The first candles were glowing in the huts up the valley when
all was finally settled. Armando motioned his boys into the back
and leaped into the cab. *"Sin vergueñza* (scoundrel)," he muttered
under his breath as he turned the key and gunned the engine.
"That man was driving me nuts." The truck shifted into first and
began rolling forward with a peculiar lurching motion. *"Caramba!"*
shouted Armando. "Lucas, look at the tires."

One of the boys leaped off the bed of the truck and squatted
underneath. *"Sí,* Armando, one is flat," he called out.

My good-natured man let out an awesome string of swear
words and pushed open the door. "We'll never get out of here,"
he stormed. He brought out a jack and told one of the boys to set
it in place. Meanwhile he found a big flashlight and shone its
beam on the rear axle. "Okay, Lucas, be quick now. We can still
see enough to drive out if we hurry."

The cold wind was strengthening and the pines tossing their
branches. The first night star twinkled. I saw Lucas crawl out from
under the truck and approach Armando. "I can't find the handle," he said sheepishly. "I think it was left at the Texaco station
to be welded and I forgot to pick it up."

Armando gave him a scathing look, but he was never one for
recrimination. He looked up and down the valley, then spied a
telegraph line. "We'll send a telegraph to the station and tell
them to bring it tomorrow with my jeep." Once again, this thin
line of communication was all there was between us and the outside world.

"Come on out, Anita," he said. "We've got to find someone

to send the message. You'll freeze in there. No heaters in Central
American trucks."

We began walking toward the nearest light, which turned out
to be the shopkeeper's home. He, in turn, sent his son as a runner
to the Mayor, who was the only person capable of sending Morse
code. Then he sold us some stale crackers, warm beer (from Armando's load), and two large cans of sardines from the shop.
There was nothing to do but wait. The four of us found a spot out
of the wind on the Mayor's steps and ate supper. It was pitch-
black now.

An hour later a dim flashlight came wobbling toward us, and
the Mayor arrived. This was clearly a big event in his day. He
opened up his office, spread gunny sacks on the benches for us to
sit on, and activated his telegraph machine. I was shivering hard
now as I listened to the staccato tap-tap-tap. Was the line open?
Would anyone be at the telegraph office in Panajachel to receive
the code? Was the handle repaired? Would someone dare drive in
here to bring it next morning and rescue us?

But more importantly, where would we sleep tonight? As if
reading my thoughts, Armando squeezed my hand reassuringly
and asked the Mayor if we might stay in his office.

"But, of course," was the response. "Only I have no blankets
or *petates* or *anything.*"

"Please do not worry," Armando said. "We have warm jackets. As long as we are out of the wind."

The two boys decided to curl up in the cab, conserving their
warmth like puppies. Armando and I were left with one guttering
candle and fifteen gunny sacks in the frigid office. It looked to me
like a choice between the cement floor or the stone benches. But
Armando ingeniously shoved the Mayor's big wooden table
against the far wall, stomped flat some empty cardboard boxes in
the back of the truck, and laid them down for a "mattress." Our
blankets were the gunny sacks. If I had thought sleeping under a

truck was roughing it, this new adventure gave me better insights into comfort. The temperature must have dropped close to freezing that night, so deep in the highlands, and none of us slept much.

By morning we were all ravenous. Dozens of little children appeared and began clustering around the schoolhouse. At length, a stout teacher arrived and opened the door. I watched the classes line up as the Guatemalan flag was raised and the national anthem sung. Armando waited till the students were all settled inside, then went to speak to the teacher. Taking pity on us, she sent messages in all directions, and within an hour we had scrambled eggs, refried beans, tortillas, and strong black coffee. Afterward, the teacher introduced us to her students. Some had never seen blond hair and shyly pointed at me.

Then Armando made their day by introducing me as the Mama Poc of Lake Atitlán and telling them all about our conservation work. He soon had them giggling and asking questions despite his outrageous mixture of Spanish, Cakchiquel, and Tzutujil words. This clearly was the most exciting event around here in a long time. We more than paid for our breakfast.

Armando's driver and jeep miraculously drove down into the hamlet at ten o'clock that morning. The flat tire was quickly changed, and we were home by midafternoon. "What was the name of that village?" I asked Armando as I sat brushing dust from my hair and scratching my legs.

"Pixibaj," Armando said. "Little Flea."

9

The Little House
with Green Shutters

THE LITTLE FLEA INTERLUDE had certainly cleared my mind.
I now saw that the whole fish poisoning and restocking
program would have to wait until I could get advice from
fishery biologists at Cornell. I also did not know enough to attempt catching pocs and transferring them. That meant at least a
half year's delay. Also, even though the exhibit was largely complete for the visitors center, Edgar advised me not to hang the
photos and other materials up during the five-month rainy season.
Moisture and wind moving through the open windows might
damage them. So all this exhibit material was stored at his farm.
In addition, I was scheduled for another half-year delay while I
began course work at the university in September for two semesters.

Since we couldn't put pocs inside their sanctuary until it was
safe from bass and contained food, I went back to studying the
wild birds. Never having been at the lake in June, July, and August, I was able to learn more of grebe life history. But compared
to breeding season, pocs took life in the slow lane now.

In June it rained every day. We had a *temporal* (long stormy period), when the lake rose a foot in one week and the surface was covered with white pieces of pumice, which had been washed down from the volcano slopes and, being full of air, floated, even though they were rocks. Armando told me to gather several round pieces and put them in a can with kerosene. "You can keep these at your *ranchito* and use them to start fires. The kerosene soaks in and will burn, but the pumice will not. You can use each piece over and over. You could even take some home with you to your cabin," he said finally. It was a subject we generally avoided—my eventual return to the Adirondacks and school.

My back-country home and base of operations at Lake Atitlán. I called my hut The Little House with Green Shutters.

Luckily, the workmen had gotten the bunch grass down the mountain and finished my roof before the rains came in full force. My hut was safe and dry, but I did not feel like camping there in this weather and having to snuggle up to a wet dog. Rainy season in Central America reminded me of winter up north. No one went out much, except when the mornings were clear. Life was lazy. People slept a lot, read a lot, talked a lot. When the afternoon thunderstorms boomed overhead, they just sat and listened. Jessie disappeared under the bed.

In the middle of July and into August came a delightful time called the *canicula*, or little dry season. Rain showers were brief, the days were warm, everything was green and fresh. Cornfields were high. I decided it was time to fix up the inside of my little Tzutujil hut and spend a few days there. So after explaining to Armando, my houseboy, and Don Emilio where I was going, Jessie and I headed across the lake. I brought all my field notes with me for it seemed a perfect time to bring them up to date. I wasn't able to explain fully how much I needed some quiet and contemplative time alone.

I arrived in the morning and tied *Xelaju* safely to the new dock. At least I wouldn't have to wrestle the boat into the reed beds and worry about wind and waves damaging it now. Then I found the refuge guardian, Salvador, and asked him to help me carry my gear to the hut. At the last moment Armando had given me the top of a fifty-five-gallon oil drum. "Use this for cooking on top of the three stones," he explained. "You can toast tortillas, too. Many Indian women have nothing but this, a coffee pot, and a soup caldron in their 'kitchens.'" He also pressed upon me several empty jugs that radiator coolant and motor oil had come in. "I washed these out so you can carry water to your hut, Anita. You haven't learned to balance a *tinaja* (clay jug) on your head yet."

Salvador and I made three trips before everything was in the *ranchito*. I fluffed out my sleeping bag atop the new *petate* on the board bed and slipped some extra khaki shirts and pants and old sneakers into the cardboard drums underneath it. They worked better than a dresser. Then I set a tin plate, coffee pot, cup, and spoon that I'd bought in the market for a few cents beside the fireplace. It sat in the southeast corner, where the least wind would blow in, and was simply three volcanic rocks on the cement floor. Salvador went out to find some firewood. I could see that would be a problem with so few trees around. Too bad that all this land had been cleared for so long.

There was no table and chair, but I planned to build them with the leftover boards from the shutters and door. Luckily, I'd remembered to bring nails and a hammer, plus matches and some newspaper. For the time being, I lit two candles and dripped wax onto the floor to hold them. That would be my source of light, except for a flashlight in an emergency. I unpacked my food—cans of sardines, coffee and sugar, canned milk, a few avocados, bananas, and potatoes—and set it by the fireplace. Salvador assured me his wife would bring extra tortillas when she walked from Santiago Atitlán with his food, so I would have them three times a week. The dog's concentrated food I also set on the floor under the bed along with the jugs of water. By noon, these simple tasks were done.

I spent the afternoon with Salvador exploring the property and making plans for a front lawn, a small terrace around the hut, and a shed for firewood. Toward evening, billowing silver thunderheads rose above the two volcanoes behind my hut. Jessie and I hurried down to the lake to fetch fresh water in the same place Armando and I had gone skinny-dipping. There was an aching loneliness in my chest, and I wondered if this time alone had been a good idea. I gazed off across the water to Panajachel and wondered what Armando was doing. Was he going for supper with Rosa? Had he headed off for Guatemala City to check on his family while I was away? Or was he catching up on the bookkeeping and bill paying, which he hated? A twinge of remorse and jealousy crept through me.

Back at the hut I said good night to Salvador and closed the three shutters and door. Thunder rumbled nearby. As it grew dark, the enormity of my situation hit. Here I was miles from any English-speaking people, in a hut with no electricity, phone, lights, stove, or furniture (to speak of). Half of me was scared, half was thrilled. Jessie whined softly and I came out of my thoughts to fix his supper. But first I needed hot water to mix with his chow. I started a little fire and lit the two candles, then filled the coffee pot and put it on the oil drum top. The fire made a cheerful flickering against the rough-hewn stone and golden cornstalk walls. I opened some sardines and an avocado for supper and prepared a cup of tea. A few raindrops splattered on the grass roof. I scanned the construction, hoping there were no holes or leaks. But the storm passed on to the north and the night grew quiet. I relaxed.

After we'd eaten, Jessie and I sat by the fire. Rhythmically I stroked his belly, so glad he was with me. There was nothing to do and little light to do it in. I didn't feel like tackling those field notes now. Thinking of the Indians living in similar huts in Santiago, I suddenly yearned for a family. How cozy it would be with kids tumbling on the floor, a mongrel dog yipping, the smell of hot tortillas in the air, and perhaps a grandmother weaving textiles. No wonder the Maya had large families. They kept away the loneliness.

During the night, something rustled up in the grass roof. Something else gnawed under the bed. Jessie snored. The wind picked up and shook the shutters. Breezes passed right through the cornstalk walls. Tomorrow I'd have to get Salvador to double up on the stalks and tie them tighter. Remembering the children with their black widow spiders, I worried about spiders in the stone walls. I was glad when dawn finally came.

With the coffee bubbling and the sun streaming through the open windows, I felt much better. I had made my initiation to living like a Maya Indian. Outside in the jocote tree, doves cooed softly. Boat-tailed grackles gave their clanging call down by the shoreline. Dozens of little birds chirped and sang around the avocado tree. The lake lay satin-smooth and azure blue out of my doorway. I heard a soft cough and a *"Buenos dias."* Salvador stood discreetly outside the door with a stack of hot tortillas and a jug of fresh water. How good it was to see him.

"Come in, Salvador," I said. "Have some coffee with me."

He entered shyly and placed the tortillas on the bed away from the dog. Then he looked down. *"Ay Dios,"* he muttered. *"Una rata. Mira, Doña Anna."*

I looked where he was pointing and saw signs of how an animal had eaten a large hole in Jessie's food bag and devoured the rest of the avocados and bananas. There went my food supply. It must be a wild wood rat, I thought, to take so much food.

According to Salvador, the animal was probably living up in the roof. As soon as the grass was well smoked from my fire, he would move away. Salvador offered to have his wife buy fresh food at the market in Santiago that morning. One of his sons could bring it out that afternoon. Quickly I agreed, gave Salvador some money, and walked down to meet his wife and decide on the produce. She spoke very little Spanish and would not look me in the eye. Well, I thought, that would change when she saw I was not a fancy tourist or dangerous foreigner.

Back up at the *ranchito,* I swept out the mess left by the wood rat and brought in more firewood. How little one really needed to live. I was down to real basics: fuel wood and a place to cook, a surface to sleep on, water, shelter, a few clothes, candles. It satisfied some deep need in me to do this.

Suddenly, I heard a boat coming. Peering out the window, I saw Edgar cruising up to the dock. I ran down to greet him and invited him up for coffee. This was hardly turning out to be a solitary experience! He admired my little abode and gave me some pointers on how to make the walls more windproof. "Here is some of my best coffee," he offered. "And my mother sent you these fried plantains and a caramel flan for dessert. She's so worried about you. I told her you were safer here than anywhere else in Guatemala."

Edgar and I strolled outside after coffee so I could show him my plans for the terrace and grass strip. "Would you like some bougainvilleas and poinsettias from my farm?" he asked.

"Wonderful!" I exclaimed. "They would look beautiful out in front among the rocks."

We walked back toward the ruins. "What I'd really like to have, Edgar, are more trees. I don't feel right without them after the Adirondacks. Also, they'd be good for the soil and provide firewood eventually."

"That's easy," replied my neatly dressed friend. "I have a small *vivero* (nursery) at the farm for growing shade trees for the coffee. My variety of bean won't stand much sun. I can bring you jacaranda, silk, oak, Montezuma pine, and eucalyptus."

At once I accepted his offer. "When can you bring them, Edgar? I am staying a week here and could plant any time."

"I'll bring them in two or three days. Just as soon as my workmen finish the job they're doing right now."

Visions of a green forest in place of these weedy, dusty, rocky fields danced in my head all day. I couldn't wait. But for now, I had more serious work to do. With all the obligations to David Allen and Operation Poc, my field notes were in disarray. I stretched out in the sun in my bathing suit and set to work on bringing them into order. That afternoon, I strung a hammock I'd borrowed from Rosa between the two trees and lay down awhile, facing the two volcanoes. Clouds streamed over their tops, building up for another storm. Sunlight played over the high mountain cloud forest, where supposedly quetzals, monkeys, and even the rare horned guans (a turkey-size black and white bird with a bare red "horn" atop its head) still existed. Lower down, the forest met cornfields. I marveled that men would grow crops on such steep slopes and at such heights. Armando had told me that sometimes farmers had to tie themselves to trees in order to till their fields on the mountains. Some woodcutters walked all day up the volcanoes to find pine trees for firewood. Then they carried the split sticks downhill on their backs with tumplines to market. Compared to the virgin forest and ready supply of fuelwood around my cabin, this seemed like sheer drudgery.

I lazed away the afternoon and prepared for night with less apprehension than the day before. All my food and dog provisions were safely stored in one of the cardboard drums. I had plenty of small sticks for my fire. The storms were far away this evening, and the lake lay calm under a blazing orange sunset. I was finding this backcountry life very satisfying.

I was rolling up the hammock when I spied a tiny speck moving across the lake. Who would be out at this time, I wondered? I stowed the hammock inside, then stepped out again to see where the boat was going. It was headed for the refuge. My heart skipped a beat. Could it be Armando?

Grabbing my flashlight, I scrambled down to the dock and waited. I didn't dare hope my man was coming, yet my heart pounded wildly. The drone of a motor got louder and louder, and suddenly a red and white boat zoomed around the island protecting this cove and sped to where I was waiting. My dear love cut the motor and lithely leapt out with a rope in his hands. He snubbed it quickly around a post and hurried to meet me—arms wide open. "Anita, Anita, how are you, *cariña?*" he murmured, crushing me against him. Then he held me at arm's length. "Ah, you look fine. You look *beautiful!*"

Indeed, I felt so. The morning in the sun had given me a golden glow. My hair was soft and glistening after a shampoo in the clean lake water. The afternoon in a hammock had rested me, and there must have been a flush on my cheeks from seeing Armando so unexpectedly.

"I couldn't leave for the city with you all alone over here and missing you so much." He grabbed my hand and pulled me toward the boat. Was he going to make me go back with him? But instead Armando pulled out a large *canasta* full of fruit and vegetables and a *morral.* Handing me the shoulder bag, he hefted the basket and started for the *ranchito.*

Inside the hut I lit the two candles and helped him put the basket down. "Oh, Armando," I said. "What gorgeous fruit.

Thank you." And I told him about the wood rat. He laughed and said, "We'll get rid of him tomorrow."

He started the fire so we'd have more light, then motioned me to sit down on the bed. There was no place else but the cement floor for I'd been too busy that day to build the chair and table. "Anita," he said softly. "I brought you a little present." He reached inside his *morral* and brought out a tiny packet. Inside was a pair of earrings with flashing red stones hanging on delicate golden chains.

"Oh, Armando, I love them." It was the first outright gift he'd given me, apart from his constant care and concern. I put them on and moved my head back and forth to catch the winking, dancing firelight.

Gently he laid me down on the *petate*, stroking my hair, my face, and then my entire body. Thus, while the fire burned down and the candles guttered to stubs, I experienced my first night of lovemaking in an Indian hut.

Later, while we ate a midnight supper, Armando said very simply, "I don't know what I shall do when you go back to the States. How long must you stay at the college?"

"At least one semester, better two. But I can fly down for a month's vacation at Christmas, and maybe again at Easter. And"—I paused considering the new idea—"you could always fly up to see me."

He watched me with fascination.

"Have you ever seen snow, Armando?"

"No. I've never even flown anywhere."

"Well, if you came in the winter, we could drive to my cabin and you'd see all the snow you *ever* want to see." Suddenly, the separation didn't seem so horrible to me.

"Let's see what happens," he murmured. "We still have some time together."

The next morning we built the table and *two* chairs, then we went for a swim at our favorite rocks. After that, Armando had to go back to Panajachel. "Can't you stay another night?" I begged. But his work was calling, and he knew I'd be back in another four days. I watched from the windows of La Casita con Ventanas Verdes until his boat merged with the waves.

Next day, Edgar brought a boatload of small trees and flowering plants. We spent a pleasant day digging round holes with little moats around them. Edgar explained that when these were filled with water, the moats would keep the *sanpopos* (large ants) from eating up the tender young stems and leaves. By nightfall we had planted about fifty trees on the back part of my land and around the ruins. Edgar showed me where to put the flowers near the hut and told Salvador to help me carry water next day.

"It's important you keep them watered well in the beginning and watch for the *sanpopos*. They can completely destroy these trees in a couple of days if you don't keep the moats full. After a week or so," Edgar explained, "the seedlings will have taken hold and will be strong enough to grow. You'll see how quickly you'll have a woods here."

By the time I left my hut, it had been transformed from an empty shack to a cozy home. Salvador had hoed out a flat space in front of the windows where I could sunbathe and helped me plant the flowers. He would work on the terrace and watering the trees part time, and I paid him an extra wage for this. Lastly, I gave him permission to plant some corn on my land down toward the lake. It was silly to let the soil lie fallow, and it would help him feed his family. It was the least I could do to reciprocate for all the tortillas his wife had brought.

Back in Panajachel, my departure for the States loomed even larger. I made inquiries about bringing Jessie home with me, but the airline wanted him to travel in a special crate and the fare would be over $150. I simply did not have enough money. I was not even sure whether dogs were allowed in the dormitory where I'd reserved a room. It would cost even more if I had to board him while I went to school. I knew that dogs were a big part of the scene at Cornell and often attended classes with their owners, but that might not extend to college sleeping quarters. With real regret, I asked Doña Rosa if she would care for the dog while I was away. I knew she fed her dogs well and that Jessie would be in good hands.

Before I left, Don Emilio paid me a great honor by giving me a piece of jade from his Nestlé can collection. It was a small face of polished light green stone. Perfect for a ring. I resolved to have it made back in the States and wear it as a talisman toward my eventual return to Lake Atitlán. Meanwhile, my idyllic scientific sojourn in Guatemala was coming to an end. I'd now spent another ten months at Atitlán, or a total of over a year and a half working with the pocs. How could I not leave to pursue the degree this work lent itself to, and the career I'd decided upon? Yet how could I leave my friends, my hut, my pocs, and Armando?

In the end, fate made the decision easy. Don Emilio took sick up at his farm, and Armando was called into the hills to help him. He was gone for weeks. It was a good thing. I might never have boarded the plane in Guatemala City if I'd had to say goodbye to him at the airport. As it was, I cried all the way back to New York.

10
Night Monster

AFTER A YEAR IN Guatemala, I did not adapt easily to campus life. I was used to controlling my own schedule and work. I had little patience with academic regulations, graduate student games of one-upmanship, amassing a stack of credits. I had grown accustomed to brilliant sun, not the endless cloudy days of central New York. I had thrilled to speeding across that splendid lake and climbing volcanoes instead of walking across quads and trudging up stairs to classrooms.

What I wanted was sound, pragmatic advice, knowledge, and library references to help accomplish my goal of saving the grebes. Moreover, I now realized my plan had to include saving the lake, especially its reeds and cattails, and watershed. My professors—many of them men my own age and some even younger, but no women—insisted on course work which I felt had no practical application. How could General Physiology 504 or Russian 101 possibly help me save an endangered species or promote conservation of a lake in Central America? I knew that Cornell was especially flexible and open to students constructing much of their own course work. It had been one of the early colleges to encour-

age women students. Nevertheless, I began to question seriously
my decision to return to college and the value of a Ph.D.

As Christmas approached, I could see that a trip to Guatemala would be untimely. There was too much course work and
library research, too many seminars. My grades were not that
good, as I found concentrated studying difficult after the freedom
of fieldwork. Moreover, I wanted to spend a little time at my
cabin over the holidays. As it was, I raced up there every weekend,
laden with books and papers, 200 miles of driving. Then I raced
back for Monday morning classes. It was the only thing that kept
me sane.

Most of the time I was depressed. The dormitory room was a
mere ten by twelve feet, scarcely bigger than my Indian hut, and a
tad smaller than my cabin. Yet, it had none of the charm or views
of the others. I looked out at a brick wall. The hot water pipes and
radiators clattered at night. Other residents came and went at all
hours, their heels and boots hammering the drab linoleum hall
floors. Every evening I thought of Casita Feliz with its crackling
fireplace, or of my hut with its windows looking out over the
turquoise lake.

As late January and spring semester approached, I fell ill with
the flu. Insomnia struck. My mood darkened. In desperation, I
tried going to the Student Counseling Service. The psychologist
asked kindly, "What's wrong with your life?"

I replied, "Everything." Listing all the trials and adjustments
necessary to pursue this degree, I ended with the major hardship.
"Besides, I'm in love with a man 2,000 miles away. And it doesn't
look like I can see him again until June."

The psychologist didn't have any magical formula. Then one
morning I burst into tears in the office of one of my professors.
"I'm quitting," I declared. "It's too hard. I'm too lonesome. I
can't go on."

This sympathetic man canceled appointments and spent the

next hour reassuring me. "You *must* go on," he insisted. "That degree will open doors you never dreamed of. It will be your credit card in conservation work for years to come. You can move on to larger and better ecological work with the credentials of a Ph.D., not to mention getting grant money more easily."

I shook my head doubtfully.

"Then why not take a leave of absence right now," he suggested, "before spring semester gets underway and you spend all that money on tuition and books?"

I raised my head and wiped at the tears.

"Go back to Guatemala and gather more information for your thesis. Get your campaign reactivated. After all, you have seven years to complete requirements for a degree."

His words were like a sudden bright light. Why not? I broke out smiling and thanked the professor. He had seen me past a critical point. If he had not been so understanding, I would have dropped the degree then and there. After persuading the rest of my committee of the need to leave and tending to paperwork at the Registrar's Office, I flew back to my beloved Armando and Guatemala.

How "right" it felt once again to speed across that mighty lake at dawn with Jessie in *Xelaju,* to huddle for hours in the reeds watching those jaunty grebes; and to snuggle by the fire after supper with Armando at Casita Feliz again. We talked for hours about what had happened while we were apart, for in truth, Armando was not a good letter writer. And we discussed Operation Protection Poc and its future. The entire ecological picture at the lake was clearer and my conservation goals were better defined, thanks to that semester at Cornell. I now knew the techniques needed to stock the refuge with new fishes and then pocs.

Furthermore, in one of my classes—International Conservation—we had explored the idea of "selling" conservation to the general public. The professor had explained how vital it is to win public sympathy and support for campaigns. I looked up my printer patron in Guatemala City and gave more newspaper interviews explaining about this rare and endangered bird and about Operation Protection Poc. I even attempted a few small lectures in Spanish to city groups.

One idea which had particularly appealed to me was Sir Peter Scott's scheme of using postage stamps to convey a conservation message. Almost everyone in the world gets mail, so what better way to broadcast an appeal than with attractive nature stamps?

Through the aid of my colleague, the former Minister of Agriculture, I obtained an audience with the head of the National Postal Service. In my naive way, I was slowly learning that the best way to get things done, at least in a Latin country, is to go right to the top and ask for what you want. However, grass-roots support was also crucial. If we hadn't tried to work with both Ministers and Indians, Operation Poc might never have succeeded.

The National Postal Director agreed on a poc stamp; in fact, not one but three. *National Geographic* helpfully sent duplicate slides of David's work and a Guatemalan artist rendered faithful reproductions. To my delight, the stamps—4¢ for local, 9¢ for Central America and Panama, and 21¢ for worldwide airmail— were printed in full color. One depicted Lake Atitlán, home of the grebes. The next was a scene with a pair of birds in the reeds. The last was a nest with the same little zebra-striped chick that I had first found! I smiled at the airmail stamp, for at last my giant grebes could fly.

The stamps turned out to be the most attractive ever issued in Guatemala. The first-day commemorative cover was stunning. It featured grebes and lake and read: "Let us conserve the grebe or poc." Underneath was written the scientific name, the scientist who had discovered the birds (Griscom), and Lake Atitlán. The stamp was featured in an article in the *New York Times*. Within two and a half years, the series was sold out and the Postal Service had grossed $123,000!

CONSERVEMOS AL ZAMBULLIDOR O POC
PODILYMBUS GIGAS GRISCOM — LAGO DE ATITLAN

The pocs were featured on three stamps, printed in three denominations. Above, a first-day cover with text that reads: "Let us conserve the diving duck or poc—*Podilymbus gigas* Griscom—Lake Atitlán."

Pictured were lake and volcanoes, swimming pocs, and a poc chick on a nest.

How I wish I'd gotten my hands on some of that money. But it went back into a general government fund, not to Operation Poc. If I had not been so new to this type of work, I would have certainly struck a deal to channel a percentage of the sales into our work.

Meanwhile, the Ministry of Agriculture continued to support construction, laborers, Edgar's salary as game warden, plus his gas and oil. It was talking about putting a rough road into the refuge. I received word from World Wildlife Fund International that a grant of $5,000 had been approved for a boat and motor. When I went to tell Edgar, he was very happy. His own old boat kept breaking down, and his work at patrolling and catching any violators was impossible with a 25 h.p. engine.

We went to every marine dealer and priced various models. I soon saw that new American fiberglass boats and engines like Evinrude and Johnson were double in cost in Guatemala because of the duty charged. As it was, the $5,000 grant would only allow us to buy a used boat. We were both apprehensive about buying an off-brand name in a country other than the States or Canada. Edgar kept a list and jotted down every boat he liked. Finally, when we had exhausted all possibilities, Edgar precisely narrowed the choice down to three.

"Anna, that blue boat is beautiful but the shape does not look safe to me for crossing in the *chocomil.* The yellow one is much better constructed, but it only has a 50 h.p. used motor. That will not be fast enough to catch someone with a 100 h.p. Mercury. The one we saw last, the white one, has a 70 h.p. But the fiberglass hull was made in Salvador. I'm not sure they use good epoxy or cure it as well as the American models."

We decided on the yellow boat. I advised Edgar that if hunters or poachers really wanted to get away, they would. And that his most important service was educating people who broke the law, not apprehending them. We bargained for the best price we could get, and the manager promised to deliver the boat to Panajachel next day. Edgar would cross over to get it and tow it back to his farm.

Everything was moving along so well that a problem seemed inevitable. When it did occur, it was the most outlandish and perilous to the project imaginable.

Through my professors at Cornell, I had learned that the Wisconsin Alumni Research Foundation, a reputable research group, was testing a new fish toxicant called Antimycin. It worked much faster than rotenone, and had no effects on warm-blooded animals. They needed a place to try out its effectiveness in warm, tropical waters. I wrote the Foundation at once and requested that they consider carrying out their experiment at the new grebe refuge. The test could be carefully controlled here by sealing off the mouth of the little cove from the main lake. Furthermore, I explained, it would solve our problem of getting rid of the intro-

Thanks to a grant from World Wildlife Fund, International, we had a safer, faster patrol boat.

duced bass before restocking the water with native fishes. They agreed. A technician, Mr. James Powers, was flown down with twenty pounds of the new "miracle" chemical. Supposedly, Antimycin affected cold-blooded vertebrates only by interfering with the respiratory mechanism in their gills. In warm waters, the lab had predicted the chemical would lose its effectiveness within forty-eight hours. (Rotenone, on the other hand, often took weeks, or even months, to detoxify depending on water temperature.) This meant we could safely stock the refuge in a week's time.

Nevertheless, Antimycin was still in its experimental stage. We resolved to let *no one* touch or eat any of the fish poisoned within the refuge. In addition, we hung a stout sheet of canvas from one of Armando's trucks over the screened entrance of the reserve. That way, the lake could not be contaminated, for no toxicant could leak out.

I invited personnel from the Division of Fauna, and two of their Fishery people arrived. Together with Mr. Powers, we scattered the harmless-looking white powder over the two acres of water in the refuge. Indian canoers waited to collect every stunned fish that floated to the surface so we could weigh, measure, identify, and record the data. This way, the Foundation could obtain a clear picture of which species and sizes succumbed first to the chemical, and I could see what the composition of Atitlán's resident fish population was now.

Within an hour, the first bass started floating to the top, gasping. Then came mojarras, crappies, guapotes, and a few small cyprinids. At least some of the native fishes were still alive. However, the experiment definitely showed that the majority of fish were the introduced bass and crappies. Every fish was collected and laid out on shore. We worked for three days cataloguing them. Then we wrapped up all the fish and buried them. As far as Mr. Powers and I could tell, none of the Indians had taken any away for a free meal.

We made no effort to hide the fact that we were "poisoning" the refuge. Actually, "reclaiming" is a much better word, but had no direct Spanish equivalent. The Spanish word for poison is a scary one. *Veneno.* Everyone fears it. The Indian canoers talked about the experiment. Rumors spread and grew into weird distortions.

By sheerest coincidence, a die-off of crappies had been going on for the past few weeks. I had found many dead fish washed up on the shores with yellow goo covering their gills. The Fishery technicians thought it was a slime-mold infection. Now the die-off worsened. Piles of crappies lay decaying among the reeds and rocks. Inevitably, the dead crappies got linked up to our experiment with Antimycin.

One morning Armando burst into my living room at Casita Feliz and thrust the front page of Guatemala's leading newspaper in my face.

"¿Lago Atitlán Evenenado?" (Lake Atitlán Poisoned?), it read. The letters were three inches high.

The story went on to say that fish were dying around the lake, and it raised some ugly implications. Fortunately, it also left a little room for doubt. It mentioned Operation Protection Poc and our campaign to put pocs in the refuge for safety. I could not figure how, if the reporter had come to the lake, he had managed to write an article with such a biased viewpoint. Given the Latin flair for emotionalism, however, this story might balloon and jeopardize our campaign.

"Don't go out today!" Armando ordered. "And get ready for a trip to the city. We have to see that the fishery people with Division of Fauna make their report and publish it to present a balanced picture. Good thing they came to the refuge and that you took photos."

I spent an uneasy day with Jessie indoors, compounded by more bad news when Juan, my houseboy, came to work. "Some of the Indian fishermen are grumbling about the *gringa* and her 'poison pills,' " he warned me. "They are upset because it's their livelihood to catch and sell fish. Some of them are carrying their machetes."

Now I was really worried. I sent a message to Armando that we should go at once to see the Governor. He had been a constant source of support. Perhaps he could send telegrams to all the villages, advising them there was no danger. We whizzed up to Sololá and explained exactly what had happened. I showed the Governor the correspondence with the Wisconsin Alumni Research Foundation and our data sheets of the dead fishes.* I was learning the importance of documenting *everything*.

The Governor of Sololá immediately sent out word to the Secretaries of all villages within Atitlán's watershed that the water of the lake was safe to drink and the fish to eat. Then we journeyed to Guatemala City and I gave interviews to the major papers. Both the Division of Fauna and Mr. Ibarra at the Museum backed me up. They explained the scientific procedures and goals of our campaign.

Suddenly, I was a celebrity, albeit a notorious one. As I walked down the busy city streets, several people came up to me and asked, "Aren't you 'Doña Anna de los Pocs' (Lady Anne of the Pocs)?"

Luckily, the crappie die-off stopped, and in a few weeks so did the furor over the poisoning. I reflected that if it was publicity I'd wanted, I'd gotten enough, both good and bad. It also showed how much people cared about this queen of Guatemalan lakes. I only hoped the old adage that any publicity is better than no publicity was true.

A week after the poisoning, the lake water was safe for new fingerlings. The Division of Fauna trucked up 6,000 small native fishes in plastic bags filled with oxygen and water. Armando and I

*Later with Mr. Powers as co-author I wrote a paper for the American Fishery Society's *Transactions*, "Elimination of the Fish in the Giant Grebe Refuge Using the Fish Toxicant, Antimycin" (vol. 96, no. 2 [1967]: 210–13).

Fishery biologist Mario Saavedra distributes Antimycin powder in the grebe refuge. It was used on an experimental basis to eliminate large-mouth bass.

Jim Powers, from Wisconsin Alumni Research Foundation, points to the results. Almost all the toxified fish were the introduced bass.

Later, 6,000 fingerlings of small native species were released inside the refuge as food for the pocs. They arrived in large plastic bags pumped full of oxygen.

released them gently into the refuge, then stood back with a prayer that they all live to make food for the grebes.

I had small indications at this time that the grebe population might be increasing slightly. Also, that the bass population might have peaked and be dropping. Fishermen were catching smaller fish and some were stunted. Bluegills, which Edgar and I had stocked in the refuge along with the government fishes, had taken hold. They were multiplying rapidly and moving out into the lake. They are a good buffer fish for bass, and I hoped they might take the pressure off the small native fish and crabs. Moreover, bluegills could provide nice pan fish for the Indians. I resolved to keep tabs on the fish situation, for the natural trend of introduction, explosion, peak, crash, and decline is a usual pattern among introduced species. No one knew if and when this phenomenon would occur at Lake Atitlán.

Edgar, Armando, and I had a planning session. It was time to catch pocs and place them in their new sanctuary. We needed this captive population of breeding birds to assure the species' survival, but none of us was sure how to catch them. I had tried the usual approach alone with my boat, herding them toward shore or chasing them until tired. With the exception of the two young and emaciated juveniles I'd found months before, no grebe ever let itself get anywhere near my boat. Now we tried with *three* boats. We spent hours following pocs, but they always slipped away. We tried baiting them with decoys, mirrors, and special traps in the reeds, but they invariably detected them in time. Again, I donned scuba gear and approached stealthily underwater, planning to grab their legs, but the air bubbles gave me away.

Edgar thought we should try from land, not water. So the three of us spent hours wading and crawling through countless reed and cattail beds where mated birds lived, hoping to drive them out into nets encircling the vegetation. The rascals calmly executed their accordion alarm dive and then periscope-surveyed us until we gave up. Those diving birds were absolutely uncanny in their ability to outwit our schemes and ploys.

"Let's ask the Indians for help," I said, thoroughly frustrated. "They know the lake and pocs better than we do."

Edgar arranged for thirty Tzutujil canoeists to meet us near Santiago Atitlán one weekend. The plan was for them to spend the day trying to catch live grebes near the reeds in the big bay. There was a lot of shouting and splashing, but all returned empty-handed that afternoon. I paid them the agreed upon 50¢ each and asked the Indians to try again. Next day—same results. I lost confidence in this tactic.

Edgar offered to erect a special spring trap over the poc nests in front of his farm. But since the birds were nest building and incubating, it seemed too dangerous to take a chance. Unless the most delicate maneuvering were done in the reeds, the pocs would desert.

Catching grebes was proving to be the most difficult part of Operation Poc. And the most embarrassing. The government and I had spent a total of $10,000 so far, counting labor and supplies—much of it for the sanctuary. We had built, reclaimed, stocked this bay, and made a visitors center and exhibit—all for the pocs. But none were in it!

I was spending every waking moment on the lake, concentrating on this vital task. My skin was burned walnut brown, my hair bleached strawberry blond. I ate wherever hunger found me: sometimes a packed lunch, sometimes at Edgar's farm, and even in Indian huts with Armando when he saw someone he knew.

One evening I had stomach pains and a fever. Could it be another sunstroke, I wondered? I always wore a hat but had spent a lot of time in bathing suits recently. In the morning I was better and managed to eat a small breakfast. But by night my temperature was up to 102° F. And so it went for several days. Spiking fever, stomachaches, diarrhea. Armando prescribed Indian teas. Juan brought me strange-looking brews. Finally, I decided to go to the city for professional help. Armando was away on a business trip, so I took the bus, hoping nothing would embarrass me en route. At the hotel where I usually stayed, the owner recommended a well-known internist. By now I was weak and thin. Sitting in his office, I didn't even care if I caught those grebes or not.

A tall, proud, blue-eyed Spanish man was the only other patient waiting. He soon engaged me in conversation. We shared our symptoms. Then I told him what I was doing in Guatemala. At once, a radiant smile spread across the man's face. "Why, my wife, Isabela, and I are so impressed by what you are doing for Guatemala," he said warmly. "I'm Don Carlos and I want to know if I can help." He handed me his card. "Call us," he said, as the nurse signaled him into the examining room.

This man's genuine concern made me feel better, and the doctor completed the job. Within an hour I was taking strong drugs to combat the amoebas I had picked up, probably from one of the Indian huts where I'd eaten lunch. I was ordered to rest for a week and eat bland foods. The whole regime of pills had to be repeated in ten days because amoebas are so hard to eliminate from one's digestive system.

During this enforced convalescence, I wrote frantic letters to the New York Zoological Society at the Bronx Zoo and to my professors about the problem of catching pocs. My professor of wildlife ecology, Dr. Daniel Q. Thompson, wrote back promptly. He described a technique of night-lighting used at Montezuma National Wildlife Refuge in upstate New York. An airboat or light motorboat goes out at night with an extremely powerful light mounted on the bow. Waterfowl of all kinds are literally "hypnotized" and can be scooped up in a large net on a long pole. This technique is used on many refuges to capture, band, and release large numbers of geese and ducks.

It sounded like a good possibility, but in order to run the light, I needed a generator. Armando didn't have one and there were none in Panajachel. Edgar had a large one at his farm, but it was too massive for a boat. The situation seemed hopeless, short of renting one in the city. Then I suddenly thought of Don Carlos. He said he wanted to help. Maybe he could. I sent a telegram to the address he'd given me and explained the situation. Within twenty-four hours I had a reply. "Generator, Isabela, and I arriving Saturday noon." Taken by surprise, all I could think of was what to serve them for lunch. Armando, always more practical, started looking for an extra-bright bulb and mount for the boat.

As it turned out, I needn't have worried about lunch. My newly met friends arrived at Casita Feliz with baskets of tropical fruit, fresh tortillas, homemade cheeses, a casserole, and a bottle of wine. Doña Isabela was as petite as Carlos was robust. She had short curly hair and a trim figure from her days as an Olympic diver. She gave me a gay ceramic wreath made in Antigua for my door. Don Carlos proudly pointed to the generator in back of his station wagon. I could not believe such generosity, yet was learning it is typical of most Guatemalans, rich or poor. Of course, it helped that my friends owned two hotels and several businesses. Doña Isabela and I hit it off at once. Armando dropped in and at once captivated Don Carlos with his plans for installing the generator on the boat. We spent a wonderful afternoon and parted fast friends. As they were about to leave, I impulsively hugged Isabela and said, "Just think, if it hadn't have been for my *animalitos* (little animals, meaning my amoebas), we never would have met." She laughed and invited me to stay at their farm near the city on my next trip.

After the generator and bulb were rigged up on the boat, Armando and I spent three nights cruising the shoreline of Lake Atitlán. I sat in front with the net ready, and he steered standing up behind. The generator made an awful noise and a fiendishly bright light, but it worked. We saw hundreds of coots, gallinules, ducks, frogs, grackles, and even fishes. As soon as that spotlight hit them, they froze until we passed. Each species had eyes that glowed in different colors. Once when we stopped to refuel, I heard a great horned owl hooting and a chuck will's widow crying plaintively up on the hills. This experience was giving me a whole new insight into night life at Atitlán.

Nevertheless, in all those seventy-five miles of shoreline, we saw only one lone male grebe outside the reeds. He was not mesmerized at all. After a look, he merely dived back in toward shore and disappeared. So much for night-lighting to catch pocs.

The Indians, however, were deeply impressed by our scientific experiment. Rumors began spreading around the lake that a man-eating monster was roaming the shores and would devour anyone who happened to be out canoeing or crabbing alone! Armando and I roared with laughter when we heard this story. Yet, in more serious moments, I sometimes compared myself to the large-mouth bass. *Their* introduction into the finely balanced aquatic ecosystem of Lake Atitlán had had unexpected repercussions and had deranged the food chain. *My* coming to the lake, as well-meaning and simplistic as it was at first, was also having far-reaching effects. In a sincere effort to save some of the nation's wildlife, I had, at *worst,* worried the public with "poison pills" and frightened the Maya with "man-eating monsters." At *best,* I reflected, my activities might enrich the local folklore of those colorful people. If pocs could stay underwater half an hour, and travel half a mile, why couldn't I turn into a monster at night?

11
Snares and Success

AFTER THE NIGHT-LIGHTING FIASCO, the weeks slipped by. There was no word from the New York Zoological Society, so I turned back to normal fieldwork. The reed beds along the shore at Edgar's farm were a veritable nursery this time of year. Fluffy black chicks of common gallinules trailed like flotillas behind their parents. Boat-tailed grackles guarded their bulky nests. Flocks of coots floated everywhere on the lake, though few of these birds raised young on Lake Atitlán. Like the ducks, sandpipers, least and eared grebes, coots would migrate north shortly and probably nest in the States. One morning a beautiful band of white pelicans bobbed in the center of the bay, but left soon after.

In my field observations, during which time Jessie had to stay home, I started out by carefully measuring and describing a set of five poc eggs which I found abandoned in a nest. Sniffing them gingerly, I noted they were odorless (not always the case in birds), and a chalky blue color beneath the brown stains from the rotted vegetation on which they lie. Eggs of pocs were slightly larger than those of common pied-billed grebes studied in Iowa.

Next, I set out the grebe decoy David Allen had used and hid

my boat in the reeds to see what might happen. I hoped an adult
male might attack the fake bird. Every few minutes I would play
the gulping cow call on my tape recorder. Finally, the male living
closest to my boat emerged and made a semicircular tour around
the styrofoam poc at a distance of forty to sixty feet. He did
several accordion alarm dives, peeked up like a periscope, and
swam on the surface in short spurts.

Not to be left out, his mate appeared, and the couple made a
semicircular inspection of this odd interloper. The male swam
directly at the decoy and gave a low danger grunt call. The female
did not react at all and finally sat quietly near the decoy. By then,
the pair seemed to have realized it was not a threat.

I set up the mirror David had used as another experiment.
The same male noticed it about an hour later. Again, he swam
aggressively right at it, diving when about fifteen feet away. He
surfaced next to the glass in the snakehead display but did not
peck or splash at the image. Instead, he pivoted and turned several
times, just like a street dog with a rival. Eventually, his feathers
sleeked down, and he swam back into the reeds, as if to say he
wasn't fooled by the bold new trespasser.

I was also busy with my recorder every day, trying to capture
new vocalizations. When the chicks were small (one to three
weeks), they kept up a constant peeping—high, lisping, melodi-
ous sounds that were difficult to record against the whisper of
reeds, and wavelets, and other waterfowl calling.

A new sound was a low, sweet, hoarse call given solely by
female pocs when their mates were away. Sir Huxley had noted it
in great crested grebes and said it was a type of "advertising."
These calls definitely served to maintain family contacts. Since
most grebes lack striking plumage colors and look alike as males
and females, they need a means of identification, especially in
dense reeds. Vocalizations are their chief means of communication.

I became aware of important differences in diving behavior

between male and female birds. The average time of dives for males in self-maintenance feeding was thirty-five seconds underwater, but for females was twenty-seven seconds. When feeding chicks, diving time shortened to twenty and twenty-four seconds, respectively. Moreover, the total time it took males to catch some food was eleven minutes; whereas females spent twenty minutes. This meant that males almost *doubled* their performance time as parents. This meant they had a secondary sexual advantage over females in obtaining food for their young. This data indicated that males have greater success at foraging due to their larger size and weight. They have evidently adapted to deeper dives and can stay submerged longer.

Pocs were not above stealing food from each other. When a bird saw that one of his fellows had caught a fish, it swam rapidly toward the lucky grebe with its head down, neck swollen, and body low in the water. It might chase the fish-bearing bird up to 300 feet across the lake, forcing it to patter-fly and plunge-dive to escape. There could be several chases before the grebe with the fish outdistanced the would-be thief and found time to gulp its meal. Or the fish snatcher might catch up and rob the other bird.

If a fish was larger than two to three inches, a grebe had a hard time juggling it until the head lay toward its throat. I saw a lot of neck wriggling and head shaking when pocs tried to swallow small bass. I also watched various pocs pluck feathers from their breasts and eat them. In the stomach contents of the four adults I collected as specimens, they each had feathers or balls of feathers inside. These probably help to strain out fish bones and hold indigestible materials.

One of my biggest constraints was not being able to mark my birds. Normally, biologists can use ear tags or wing tags, ribbons, painted spots, or bleach marks to identify individuals. But since I could not even *catch* a grebe, there was no way to mark them. However, my general impression (gleaned from subtle markings) was that poc pairs bonded for long periods—possibly for life.

Definitely for an entire breeding season. I never witnessed signs of
promiscuous mating among pocs.

One morning a grebe with six chicks appeared at the edge of
the reeds. At once I sat upright. *Six* chicks? I had never seen more
than five; usually two or three. I looked intently through my
binoculars. The parent began shoveling for food on the surface,
presumably picking up small insects. Then it dove. But it stayed
close to shore and made very short pauses on the surface. Something about it was different. A gut feeling told me this was not a
poc. But it looked like one. Slowly, I poled closer for a better look.

I mentally compared the bird before me with an average giant
grebe, which had a broad, deep white bill with a distinctive black
mark, a striking white eye ring, a tiny tuft of a rudimentary white
tail, and an extremely black throat patch. Those features plus its
overall sooty charcoal appearance and alert stance were what
spelled "poc" to me. This bird, by contrast, was nervous, not alert.
Its bill and tail were smaller, the body less robust, and overall color
more yellowish-gray. It had to be a common pied-billed grebe
with chicks!

I thanked my lucky stars to find a breeding bird so close to my
mated pocs. In the past, commons had migrated north in spring
and never bred here to my knowledge. This observation would
give me great behavioral comparisons between the two types and
strong support to the theory that they *are* separate and distinct
species.

Next day I moved my gear over to Casita con Ventanas
Verdes and stayed there for ten days while observing the two
species in close proximity. The pocs always fed farther out from
shore and dove longer, deeper, and more powerfully. The timed
dives I'd taken before came in very handy to verify this distinc-
tion. Also, pocs didn't seem to mind rough water, whereas the
commons avoided it. Undoubtedly, the smaller species couldn't
catch larger food and compensated by eating other things closer
to land. I found three nests of commons, and all were in shallower

water and closer to shore than pocs' nests. The chicks looked the same but seemed to grow up faster and leave the parents sooner. I also noted that the commons laid their eggs earlier, perhaps to be ready for the spring migration later.

I never saw any aggression between the two species, or any other kind of interaction. They seemed to be separated by subtle ecological factors, like food choice and water depth, and to live compatibly in winter on the lake.

When I returned to Panajachel, two letters were waiting for me. One was a bulky, battered, dirty envelope postmarked Cochabamba, Bolivia, of all places! The writer was Charles Cordier, an expert animal trapper who worked part time for the Bronx Zoo. Happily, my letter had been forwarded to him. I read his instructions carefully: Buy fourteen-pound test monofilament fish line. Make several *hundred* snares with slip knots from this line. Tie them onto a long line set between poles at the edge of the reed beds. Hide and be ready to rescue the birds when they swim in or out and lasso themselves. This line, he went on to say, is almost invisible, yet strong enough to hold birds of that size. They cannot choke to death because of the slipknots.

Even though Mr. Cordier had enclosed a sample snare, I could not see how I'd ever be able to manage this. But Armando soon cheered me up. "We'll use the poles left over from David's blind and tower. One of my drivers can buy the line in Guatemala City next time a truck goes in. You'll have to hire Juan, or someone else, to work with you. It'll take time, but think of the reward, Anita."

Armando was right. It *did* take time. Juan and I spent three days patiently tying knots. Edgar and I spent two days erecting the poles in front of two separate reed beds where I knew mated birds lived. Another morning I worked alone simply transporting those fragile slip knots across the lake and keeping them from tangling. When the big day came, I hired Juan to come with me and set up the lines. Painstakingly, we tied 500 snares on one line between poles. (The other 500 we set aside for the other line.) I became touchy with impatience. If the *chocomil* began early, it would hopelessly entangle all the snares. If the boat bumped the main line, it could snap it. As soon as everything was in place, we hid in the reeds and sat down to wait.

Thirty-five minutes later we heard a thrashing, and there was our first lassoed grebe! I scooped it up before it could harm itself. Then, holding the bird (a female) triumphantly, we sped to the refuge and released it gently into the water. I didn't even measure or weigh it so as to keep its stress level down.

We hurried back to the same spot. If we were lucky, we'd catch her mate, too. But the wind had begun, and we were thwarted until next morning. By then, Juan and I had to unravel and reset most of the 500 snares because the wind and waves had turned them into a rat's nest. By noon, however, we had captured the male and reunited him with his mate in the refuge.

It took the rest of the week to catch the other pocs, but at last we ended up with two mated pairs and one lone male in the grebe reserve. No eggs or chicks had been sacrificed in the process. Finally, the last step of Operation Poc was complete.

Best of all, the numbers were encouraging that spring of 1968. I actually counted 116 pocs and estimated there could be 125 with young of the year. That meant a goodly increase since the low of 80 in 1964–65. I also worked out a rough estimate of the carrying capacity for the lake at that time, given the length of shoreline vegetation and the present fish populations. Assuming the birds had sufficient habitat and enough food, Atitlán could support a bit over 250 giant grebes. We were almost at the half-way mark! My overall job was done.

The second letter in my mail, however, led to unexpected work and a bizarre trip. It was from a prisoner in the national jail at Quetzaltenango! He'd seen pocs in a small pond high on the slopes of a volcano near that city a few years ago. The man professed to be a great outdoors lover and sure of his information.

We had to make hundreds of snares to capture the pocs safely.

The first poc caught by the snare method is released in the refuge.

I consulted Armando. "What should I do? Believe him and go see, or just ignore him?"

Armando thought I should follow every lead. "Supposing there are pocs there and you tell everyone they only exist in Lake Atitlán. Then no one would believe in you as a scientist. And if there *are* pocs there," he continued logically, "we might be able to use the pond as a second kind of refuge."

He was right, of course, but I wanted to go slowly. "Why don't we see the prisoner first, get more details, and be sure," I said. "There's no sense wasting time in the bush. Not now, anyway. We should be making plans for an inauguration of the refuge before the rains begin."

During these two years of fieldwork, I had developed a conservation ethic which basically said, "Help others to help themselves." I didn't want to be a babysitter for this project. I just wanted to be the catalyst. That had succeeded with the grant funds, the new boat, and the foreign support. So, psychologically, it was time to turn over Operation Protection Poc, which was running smoothly, to the Guatemalans, whose obligation it really was anyway. I could still do fieldwork on the pocs, for there was more to learn, and branch out into other endangered species research in Guatemala. By inaugurating the refuge in the best Latin style and tradition, this transfer could be accomplished joyfully.

In the end, Armando and I compromised. We set out to question the prisoner, yet we also took along backpacking equipment so we could explore the volcano pond if it seemed worthwhile. I had never been to a prison before, and the sight of the drab, gray building surrounded with barbed wire fences chilled me. Armando spoke to the guard in charge and showed him the letter. We also had brought along the elegant epistle with seals and the Governor's signature requesting that our program be given every assistance. After a long delay in a cold cement waiting room, the guard motioned us down a hall to a gate. Several prisoners stood behind it, dressed in tattered clothing. The wind whistled through the building and there was a nip in the air even at noon. Quetzaltenango (Guatemala's second largest city) lies close to 8,000 feet, and the weather is always brisk.

One man with a pocked, moon face separated himself from the others and came close to the gate. "I'm the one who wrote you," he said hoarsely, coughed, and smiled. Then, while the guards looked on, he described the birds and drew a map of how to reach the pond. He seemed like an educated man, well-spoken and intelligent. I wondered what his crime had been.

The prisoner's descriptions were not really detailed enough for us to be sure whether pocs or common grebes lived on the volcano, so we decided to go see.

"Come back and tell me," the prisoner said. *"Please* come back."

Armando and I walked back down the hall and out the gate, and I could feel the prisoners' eyes riveted to my back. As we said goodbye to the chief guard, I asked hesitantly, "Can you tell us what crime that man is here for?"

"He's a political prisoner," was the terse reply.

I was silent for many miles as Armando skillfully negotiated along the base of the volcano and started up its slopes. The road got worse. We passed isolated farms surrounded by tiny workers' huts and sheds and hemmed in by gigantic forest trees. Coffee and quinine were the crops. Compared to Edgar's neat farm, these holdings were shabby and ill kept. The owners were mostly absentee, coming to their country places only for holidays or occasional checkups with their administrators. From what I could see, the workers never left the area for there were no cars or buses. The few I saw were wide-eyed and wary.

"Why so quiet, *amorcita?*" Armando asked.

"Oh, I feel so sad for that man in jail," I said. "He didn't look dangerous, and he is trying to help us. When we go back, Armando, let's take him some candies and cookies. And maybe some medicine for that cough."

Armando shook his head. "Anita, Anita, you have too soft a heart. You don't know anything about him or what he did."

"No, I don't," I admitted, "but what can be so bad about being a political prisoner?"

"You just don't *know*," Armando said firmly.

By now we were standing in the yard of a large, unpainted farmhouse. Everything was dilapidated. Chickens ran through the long grass and an old rusty jeep stood by the back door, which hung ajar. There was no schoolhouse or small workers' homes. Only a warehouse and a couple of large *galerías* (open-sided, barn-like buildings where workers and their families can sleep on a cement floor).

"This is the last farm," Armando said, "and the prisoner said we must walk from here." The slopes of the volcano, covered with dense green forest, rose before us.

"How far did he say the pond was?"

"About two miles."

I glanced at my watch. Three o'clock. The sun was already edging toward the flanks of the mountain and would soon slide behind, turning this south-facing slope into shadow. "Let's stay here," I suggested, "and get an early start tomorrow."

"I think you're right," said Armando. "I'll try the house, but it looks empty."

Not only were the owners away, but the workers must have been out in the coffee groves. No one showed up until 5 P.M., and then several skinny, ragged men approached us nervously, as if they hadn't seen outsiders for a long, long time. Armando grinned and spoke to them warmly, but it took a while till they relaxed. No one had heard of the pocs and only one or two men had been to the pond. They gave us skimpy directions.

"We would be happy to pay for a place to sleep tonight, and a chicken to cook for supper," Armando said.

The leader of the workmen looked blank. "There is no place," he said. "You have to speak to the women about a chicken."

"What happened to that wonderful Guatemalan hospitality?" I whispered to my love.

If anything, the women were even more apprehensive. Some were sitting in the late sun picking lice from their clothing, and they looked startled to see us. We finally spied an old chicken coop filled with musty straw and asked if we could sleep there. It seemed safer than sleeping next to the Land Rover in that rough-looking yard. Eventually, one woman offered to kill and cook a chicken for us. Given all the setbacks, it was pitch dark when Armando and I were at last settled in our sleeping bags in the shed with a boiled chicken and tortillas in front of us. My mouth was watering. We hadn't eaten since Quetzaltenango.

Armando sliced off a thigh for me with his pocket knife and I bit into the meat. Hopeless. It was the toughest old bird in the flock and impossible to eat. "Thank goodness I brought some peanut butter," I muttered as I spread it on the cold tortillas.

"Here, sweetheart." Armando handed me a small glass bottle, with a label of a buck deer and the name "Venado." "This will make you feel better."

I took a sip and the fiery liquid slid to my stomach like a fire bolt. Armando laughed and gulped a good-sized slug. "This is the local firewater," he explained. "Guaranteed to warm you up and turn a chicken coop into a castle."

Gradually, the coop did seem cozier, despite several missing boards in the roof. When a thunderstorm hit later that night, I didn't mind at all. As I nestled next to Armando, with the now empty bottle of Venado, the raindrops seemed to drum romantically on the roof. Some rain poured in, narrowly missing our sleeping bags, but we slept like drunken sailors, oblivious to it all.

At dawn, however, I accused Armando of giving me *veneno* not Venado. "There's no way I can hike two miles up the mountain like this," I groaned, holding my head.

He handed me a mug of steaming coffee and two aspirins, then started stuffing the sleeping bags into their sacks. "A walk is

just what we need," he said (a little glumly I thought). By noon,
the exercise had cured us and we emerged from an overgrown trail
on the shore of a jade green pond secreted into the folds of the
volcano. A few reeds edged it and huge trees cast shade on the
pebbly beach.

I unpacked my binoculars and searched the water. Nothing.
Could we have come on a wild grebe chase? We decided to wait a
while. Armando stretched out on the warm pebbles and was soon
fast asleep while I kept half an eye on the pond. An hour later, a
ripple spread across its still surface, and then a small water bird
emerged from the reeds and swam toward me. Motionless, I tightened my grip on the binoculars and stared at the bird. At last, I
had to admit it was only a common pied-billed grebe.

Disappointed, I lay down and dozed awhile, waking to afternoon shadows. Gently, I shook Armando awake. The grebe was
still feeding in the open, so I handed him the glasses. "It's not a
poc," I said sadly.

On the way back to Quetzaltenango, I said, "Even though we
didn't find pocs here, Armando, it might be a good idea to check
all the other lakes in Guatemala. There are not too many, but that
way, as you said, I can stand behind my own statement, and the
earlier scientists' reports, that giant grebes live only on Lake Atitlán."

That indomitable man was ready to take off then and there!
"Yes," he agreed, "we should check Lakes Ayarza, Petén Itza, El
Pino, Izabal (even though it's huge and near the Atlantic Ocean),
San Cristobal, and . . ." He rattled off a couple more.

So despite the failure of this trip, I went on to check every lake
in Guatemala that could possibly hold pocs. Some had no reeds or
cattails, some contained largemouth bass. Others were too shallow and hot, others had too many humans and cattle around the
shores. In summary, I could truthfully say that *only* Lake Atitlán
offered the unique set of ecological and geological features which

allowed pocs to survive. This knowledge made the existence of our small sanctuary doubly valuable. If the birds couldn't make it in the wild, this was the only hope they had left.

In Quetzaltenango I bought sweets and cough syrup for our prisoner and his comrades, and Armando distributed these. My conscience would not allow me to do otherwise. We told the prisoner of our findings. He was sorry to hear of our lack of success but glad he had written to me. "You'll hear from me again," he said enigmatically as we left.

On June 16, 1968, a large boat chugged away from the Panajachel dock carrying many dignitaries, Indians, Armando, and me. Despite rain earlier, the clouds had lifted and the lake was gray-blue and calm. At the refuge, I welcomed everyone in the name of Operation Protection Poc. The floor of the visitors center was strewn with fragrant pine needles. Armando, Edgar, and I served the champagne and little snacks. We wore special warden shirts made from the handsome green textile of San Lucas, with yellow trim and yellow poc emblems on the sleeves. The red poc rug and primitive painting hung on the wall, as did many photographs donated by *National Geographic.* The Governor of Sololá gave a stirring speech, as did Jorge Ibarra and the heads of the Guatemalan Institute of Tourism (INGUAT) and Institute of Forestry (INAFOR). The Ministry of Agriculture declared this small reserve Guatemala's first national wildlife refuge!

I glanced over at Edgar and Armando, my two best men friends in Guatemala, and my heart swelled with triumph at what we had accomplished.

Then the blue and white flag of Guatemala was raised on a tall pole that Edgar had installed only days before. At the close, a Catholic priest from Oklahoma who was working in Santiago Atitlán gave a prayer. He stood with his head bowed on the stone wall overlooking the sanctuary waters. Tall and blond, in black habit with white collar, Father Roberto said the perfect words.

"Dear God, we pray for the continued success of this conservation venture, and for the lives of all Guatemala's wild animals, and for this beautiful lake."

Almost as if in answer, the clouds parted and a thin watery rainbow arched over the southern shore between the assembled guests and the reed beds. One end seemed to touch the slopes of Volcano Atitlán and the other to dip into the refuge waters.

Walking back up to the visitors center to serve more champagne, I reflected that the proverbial pot of gold really was here.

12
A Rocky Road

CORNELL UNIVERSITY's doctoral requirements call for one year of residency to qualify for that degree. So far, I'd been away more than in class. If I wanted to get a Ph.D., I would have to go back for the fall *and* spring semester and earn it. The glow I felt after the refuge inauguration quickly faded as I contemplated living the life of a student again far from Armando and Lake Atitlán. To give myself enough time to fix up my cabin after its being empty all winter and find a rental apartment (no more dormitories for me), I had to fly home by the end of June. It was a heart-wrenching decision.

When I broke the news to Armando, he was stoical. We agreed that he would come for Christmas in New York State. That was the only tenuous lifeline our hearts had. However, we decided to devote every minute of the next two weeks to being together. It was well that we could for the refuge had to be cleaned up after the crowd of guests. I needed to put some finishing touches on my hut to secure it until I returned. Most importantly, I needed to formalize my estimate of carrying capacity of the lake for pocs. This figure would provide a basic benchmark against which past numbers and all future numbers

and trends could be compared. It would indicate how many
giant grebes could be supported in that ecosystem. It was critical
to my thesis.

Once again Armando and I circled the lake, remeasuring the
length and breadth of every reed and cattail bed. They were the
all-important factor because they formed the only existing habitat. To our surprise, we found less than fifteen miles of shoreline
vegetated. Down a little from our first estimate. Also, we found
ninety-two vacation homes. Up quite a bit from twenty-eight in
1960; thirty-two in 1965. Given that the usual grebe pair needed
300 feet or more of territorial width, I arrived at the maximum
number of birds which could comfortably survive at Lake Atitlán:
280.

I felt smug. This number corroborated my earlier rough estimate, as well as Griscom's and Wetmore's numbers of 200 or
more birds living here fifty years ago. It also verified Don Emilio's
vague guess of 300–400 pocs seventy years before. Of course, this
carrying capacity depended on two things. One was that there
were enough fish for food; and the other, that the lake level would
not change. Any drastic rise or fall would alter the shoreline vegetation growth. But I doubted that Atitlán *could* change since it
has no surface outlets and only two small surface inlets. Surely its
underground springs and the yearly rainfall cycle would stay constant. The minor drop of one meter in lake level at the end of dry
season seemed to be always compensated for by the end of the
rainy season.

For the moment, then, I felt complacent. Almost half the
possible numbers of pocs were alive and well. I could honestly say
that our modest cooperative conservation program had helped
reverse the birds' trend toward extinction and that Operation Poc
had so far been successful. More than this, I hoped that Guatemalans had been alerted to protection of their wildlife and guarding
against invasions of the ecosystem.

Two days before I had to leave for the States, Armando and I were tidying up the visitors center. It was foggy and raining lightly, but I volunteered to take the refuge guardian and his two children over to Santiago Atitlán by boat and also return the long overdue benches to the church. We piled the boat full, and the four of us crouched under plastic sheets to try and keep dry.

"I'll be back by five o'clock," I called to Armando.

When we rounded the island and started into the big bay by the Lions Rocks, the rain increased and blew into my face. Blinking to see, I looked up from time to time to make sure there were no other boats. But in that downpour and at that hour of the afternoon, who would be out? The guardian didn't even bother to look. He'd long since gotten over his fear of riding with me in a motorboat. I saw no one as we approached the docks of Santiago Atitlán.

Abruptly, I felt a heart-stopping jolt. A long gash appeared in the bow just above the waterline. We were too far past the Lions Rocks to have hit them. Leaping up, I saw an Indian canoe and its paddler topple over. His dugout had been coming dead on against us, and I had missed the knifelike silhouette against the gray lake.

A horrifying thought suddenly struck me: probably none of these people knew how to swim!

Acting purely on instinct, I shoved the motor gear into reverse and backed toward the Indian, who was going down. At the same time, I ripped off my jacket and flung it at the guardian. "Stuff it in the hole!" I shouted.

Wide-eyed with fright, he managed to close up the gushing hole and push his children toward me. I reached the young Indian and grabbed him by the shoulders. Flipping the motor into neutral, I hauled him over the transom. His bronze skin was ashen in color and his face held terror. I made a quick swipe for his paddle and *morral,* but his farm tools had already sunk. Now if we could just get to the dock without being inundated, we'd be all right. I kept the motor at half-speed and ordered everyone to stay at the back of the boat. That kept the gash as far as possible above water.

Gradually the shore crept closer. I began to breathe a little easier.

But then my blood turned cold. The entire village of Santiago Atitlán seemed to be rushing down to the lake. The speed with which news of our crash had traveled was incredible. The strongest, sturdiest men were crowded on the dock, carrying machetes. Women and girls were running down to the beach, long hair and shawls flying behind them. I could sense the angry mood even across the water. Not one friendly face watched me approach. I was caught between two dangers: risking drowning if I turned around or beaching my boat and facing the mob. I didn't know how violent these gentle people might become. My only experience had been when the press reported that I had poisoned the lake. But facing the crowd seemed the lesser of two evils.

I tried to act calm as I touched shore and matter-of-factly shut off the motor. Carefully, I helped the Indian out and told him we were going straight to the Catholic church clinic for an examination. His parents rushed up, berating me. Hundreds of Indians surrounded us and an angry murmur buzzed behind. Grabbing my equipment in one hand and holding the boy with the other, I started up those cobblestone streets toward the church. I tried not to think of the machetes. On the way, the green-eyed Secretary and the *aguaciles* arrived. A Spanish policeman ordered me to come to his office.

"Not until I'm sure this boy is all right," I said grimly. Again, murmurs rippled as the onlookers heard me defy authority. At the clinic, a nurse was waiting. She made a thorough examination and found nothing more than a bump on the head and a bad scare. She administered a tranquilizer with a hypodermic, which pleased the entire family. Maya have great faith in *los injecciones.* She laid the poor boy down to rest and told me to check back in an hour or two.

As I made my way toward the police office, a sudden hunch prompted me to step inside the telegraph office and send a message to Armando in Panajachel. Since we had come across the lake in two boats that day, he might have got tired of waiting and gone back. But mainly I was sending him thought messages: Help, Help, Help!

Two hours passed while the policeman interrogated me. I shivered from tension and wet clothes. The Secretary wrote down every detail of the accident in his fine script. Both men seemed astonished when I freely admitted my fault and offered to pay all expenses. Secretly, I was panic-stricken because I'd heard that Guatemalan law assumes everyone guilty until proven innocent. Might I be thrown in jail right now?

By now it was dark and suppertime. The crowds outside were lessening. I kept hoping Armando would come. The moment the policeman and the Secretary finished, I hurried back to the clinic and found the boy sleeping soundly. Both the nurse and Father Roberto assured me he'd be all right. Only then did I go over to the Mayor's office and beg him for an audience. I wanted to settle up at once. I sensed that if the matter waited overnight and into another day, the boy's parents and village rumor might cause the effect of the accident to escalate. I needed to act fairly, yet avoid exorbitant financial demands.

Just as the Mayor was agreeing to see me and the parents to negotiate a settlement, Armando rushed in. I resisted the urge to run into his arms and quickly whispered what had happened. He squeezed my hand approvingly and slipped some money into my pocket. Then he spoke to the Mayor and watched as that dignitary began writing out a list of items lost or damaged, with their estimated replacement costs.

1 dugout canoe, repairs	$25.00
1 hoe	5.00
1 machete	3.50
1 bottle filled with coffee	.15
1 pair sandals	1.50
1 plastic tarp	1.00
3 tortillas	.06
	$36.21

The Mayor left briefly to confirm this with a canoe maker and with the boy in the clinic. I fidgeted in my seat next to Armando, hoping the irate parents wouldn't start embellishing the list.

When the Mayor returned, the list was completed and the meeting began. A canoe builder presented his estimate for repairs. I paid that. The Secretary presented a bill for lost items. I took care of that. The boy's mother kept complaining and whining from the back of the room. "It's not enough, it's not enough."

I told the Mayor I was leaving three days' wages for the boy in case he needed to rest before going back to work. The mother and audience fell silent at this unexpected windfall. Armando said a few words to the Secretary, who nodded agreeably.

He came back to me and murmured, "I've asked for a document stating that you paid for all these things and gave the lad medical help and he is okay. Otherwise, someone might try to instigate further charges against you in the future. The boy has been taken care of, now you need your protection."

It was a wise move and one I'd not thought of. When the papers were ready, I signed several copies, with Armando and the Secretary as witnesses. The Mayor kept one, then gave one to me, Armando, the nurse, and the parents. I was free to go.

A few curiosity seekers still hung around the dock, muttering as we passed. Armando stuffed more old rags in the hole and tied my boat behind his for towing. He tucked a plastic sheet around my shoulders and draped a towel over my head. Finally, we were moving across the chilly surface of Lake Atitlán under a pitch-black, rainy sky. Only then, at midnight, with the near tragedy behind me and my near departure ahead, did I throw myself against Armando and start sobbing. The path to conservation and education was far rockier than I'd ever imagined.

13

Chuitinamit

FINALLY I COULD see that my four years of field and course work were joining and refining into a whole. I'd started out as a neophyte, picking up a thread here, a thread there, in the large ecological tapestry. I had not seen the overall design at first. Now I was weaving everything together into a doctoral thesis: field data, statistics, hypotheses, and my own intuitions.

I read the scientific literature on grebes, bass, lakes, and much more. I went through all my field notes, picking out key data and then subjecting it to statistical analysis. And finally, I started writing my thesis. It felt as much a form of art as a scientific treatise. There was no doubt I had more than the usual share of graduate student observations and data to work with. Best of all, the giant grebe project was all mine.

Meanwhile, I was taking some excellent classes both semesters. After judicial explanations to my graduate committee, I had gotten permission to drop the unessential courses. And through a special petition at the Graduate School, I was allowed to substitute Spanish for Russian or German. Without ever having taken a class in that language, and knowing dozens of awful swear words, I passed that language exam and requirement.

Armando wrote infrequently. His grammar, handwriting, and spelling were rudimentary, but his letters kept me going. I didn't need to go to Student Counseling this year. Soon it would be Christmas and we'd be together again. Edgar also wrote, far more regularly and by typewriter. He made a census on his own and told me the results. The grebe numbers were holding. He told me how the World Wildlife Fund boat was doing and how the refuge and my hut were weathering.

The snow started in Ithaca early and I was happy. It meant Armando would see plenty of it for his first time. I had my truck serviced and bought special food for Christmas at the cabin. Visions—not of sugarplums and snow angels—but of Armando and me cuddled by the wood stove, crept through my head. Our plan was to meet in Utica at the Greyhound bus station after his flight from Guatemala City to New York. I would drive from Ithaca, pick him up, and go right on to the Adirondacks. He was to wait at the station if I was late and not go *anywhere*, since he spoke no English.

It snowed heavily the night before he was due, and I was delayed in arrival. The day was overcast and chill with a north wind making it worse. The streets of Utica were full of slush and sooty snow. The buildings were dingy and rundown in that part of town. Upstate New York at its worst. I couldn't imagine a less romantic place to reunite with my love. Moreover, I'd lost all my tan and was pudgy from so much sitting at desks.

As I turned into the bus station, I stared at the few passengers waiting by the windows. Everyone was bundled in thick, dark winter wear. I didn't see Armando at first. Then I noticed a short, broad-shouldered man in a gray pork pie hat and ill-fitting brown overcoat, as drab as all the rest—except he had a deep tan. Screeching to a halt, I rushed into the building.

He looked woebegone and slightly apprehensive. I gave him a huge hug and saw that radiant smile start and a sparkle snap back into those twinkling blue eyes. "Anita, Anita," was all he said.

By the time we got to Black Bear Lake and parked, it was twilight. The temperature stood at zero and the wind-chill factor must have been about twenty below. The lake was completely empty. White snow-devils occasionally whirled down the expanse of ice. I took my axe out and cut a hole to see how deep the ice cover was. Already a foot thick. I wanted to feel completely safe walking up the lake a mile and a half to the cabin. I'd done it so many times in the past that I wasn't worried and knew where all the spring holes lay. But for Armando it would be a page from an adventure book.

I showed him how to strap on snowshoes and gave him a stout pole, extra mittens, wool sweater, a fur hat, and scarf. Then I put a box with all our food and drink in it and lashed it to the toboggan. Two pairs of snow goggles and big flashlights completed our outfits. Without them we would have been blinded by the cold wind in our eyes and the dark. "Are you warm enough, sweetheart?" I asked.

Yes, let's go, was his only reply.

We barely talked on the way up, saving our breath to tug the toboggan, lift our snowshoes, and stay warm against the north wind. The cabin was frigid. I went into a set routine to open up and warm the place. First, I checked that the stovepipe was intact and not blown off in a storm. Then, I lit a preset log fire in the Franklin stove. Opening the propane gas tanks, I moved from gaslight to gaslight, giving the air time to bleed out, then holding a match to the mantle. Grabbing an axe, I gave Armando two pails and took two myself. We wallowed down to the dock through snow over two feet deep. Kicking a spot of ice free from snow, I began chopping a hole for water. Armando soon caught on and took over. While he did this, I carried in the food and put it in the refrigerator. No need to light the gas for that, as it would stay below freezing inside the entire three days we planned to be here. Holding the flashlight in my mouth, I groped around for more wood and took several armloads inside. We'd have to get up two or three times that night to keep the fire roaring before the chill seeped out of the stout logs and we could be comfortable.

The last thing I did was open the door to the sleeping loft and turn down the heavy wool blankets so heat could penetrate the mattress. Armando would feel somewhat at home here, I reflected, for all my curtains, rugs, blankets, and pillow covers were from Guatemala.

By now he had broken through to the lake, and we carried up the four buckets of water. Two were simply for fire prevention. Armando's breath steamed and his bushy eyebrows were frosty as he lugged the pails and tried not to slop ice water on his feet. Finally, we were settled in and supper was cooking. He sat in my Boston rocker next to the fireplace, pulling off his boots. It was just as I had dreamed, but Armando was strangely silent.

"Is it anything like you imagined?" I asked.

"No, not at all."

"In what way, love?"

"I'm not sure. It's it's, well, it's smaller than I thought, and more rugged. The snow is really *cold*. Maybe I thought all Americans lived in big houses, or something, well, less like pioneers."

"But you saw my little Tzutujil hut. It's about the same size and just what I wanted." In some indefinable way I felt disappointed. I so wanted Armando to love my home and to want to come back again. Well, I thought, perhaps he'd enjoy it more in the morning when he could look around, and after he had had a good rest.

But rest was not easy to come by. I crept out of the loft twice during the night to restoke the Franklin. Armando tossed and turned and stole the blankets in his sleep. I shivered on my side of the bed.

Next morning was crystal clear with a fluffy mantle of snow over the firs and spruces. Trees cracked in the cold and the lake ice rumbled. We snowshoed around and had a snowball fight. Then we looked for tracks in the snow and I told him about the wildlife of the Adirondacks. The cabin got toasty warm and we had a much better evening snuggling in front of the fire after hot toddies and a steak dinner. It almost seemed as romantic as when he'd come to my hut near the refuge.

But I had to get back to the university. Much as I hated to leave the Adirondacks, I drove Armando to Ithaca and showed him around the campus. I introduced him to my major professors and was surprised when he acted so diffident and shy. He was definitely ill at ease with men in tweed jackets and horn-rimmed glasses and in this center of learning. Then I remembered he'd only gone through seventh grade in Guatemala.

We also went to see David Allen, Armando's only other link in this strange new world. Armando spent part of each day with David, looking at slides of Lake Atitlán while I wrote my thesis. Each time I drove off, I felt guilty about what I was making the poor man go through in this foreign and even hostile environment. He had trouble with English. He was unaccustomed to the penetrating cold. And he was alone much of the day.

When our two weeks were up, I saw Armando off at the bus station. We didn't have much to say during the drive. From his point of view the trip surely was a disappointment, although he was too polite to say so. He had lost most of his tan and looked like any other winter-weary commuter in upstate New York. After we had kissed goodbye, I promised I would fly down to Guatemala during spring break for a week. Then he was gone.

But somehow, some of the magic went with him. After a few days of grieving, I began to see that Armando could never fit into my life in the States. He *belonged* to Lake Atitlán, much as I belonged to the Adirondacks. If we were to stay together, I would have to adapt to a life down there—if he wanted me at all. I realized I was probably kidding myself that we could marry and be happy for our lifetime.

Our spring reunion didn't go much better. By good fortune, I had been able to persuade two of my professors to go to Guatemala with me and check out what I'd done. Moreover, through my contacts with INGUAT, I'd arranged for reduced fares and accommodations for them. It seemed important to take them there since most graduate students work far more closely with their committee than I had been able to so far.

We spent a busy week on the lake, reviewing all my work and watching pocs. I showed them the refuge and explained how we'd caught the birds. Most evenings I had to eat dinner with my professors, so as to discuss the day's events and to tell them more of Guatemala. That left me little time with Armando, and practically no privacy. He was sulky. I was remorseful. The only good things that happened were a report from Edgar that he'd counted 122 grebes and estimated 135; *and* the arrival of Pitzi.

I had stopped to pay my respects to Don Emilio. He was in fine fettle, despite his eighty-nine years, and took me into his kitchen to show me a litter of puppies. His small, pale gray, sweet-tempered German shepherd bitch had mated with my Jessie and produced five adorable young. They were just five and a half weeks old.

"Take a puppy," Don Emilio said, "as a remembrance of the lake and me."

"Oh, no," I began. "They are too young and I have to fly a long way." How could I manage a puppy on three airplanes, pass migration and Customs officials, carry my luggage and field gear, and travel 2,000 miles?

"If God so wills, you can do it," he said mystically. "Take him in your *morral.* "

On impulse I picked out the one puppy which had a white spot on its chin. A little male. Trustingly, he snuggled up to me. I opened the mouth of my *morral,* just to see if he really would fit in it. He did.

"See!" Dom Emilio exclaimed. "He's *pitzi* (a small puppy in the Maya Cakchiquel dialect). And in three days when you leave, he'll be six weeks old. Big enough to leave his mother."

But my first attempt as an animal smuggler almost failed. The puppy slept all the way to Miami, but as we stood in line at Customs he woke up. He poked his tiny head out of the *morral* and began nuzzling an American flag that hung by the entrance. No sooner did I stuff him frantically back in the bag than he peeked back out. Juggling passport, health card, *morral*, cameras, binoculars, and Pitzi, I managed to get past Customs officials during the few minutes the puppy stayed inside the bag. And so it went, in and out, in and out, the whole trip. The only time he was discovered was on the last leg of my flight to New York State. The precocious puppy crept out of my shoulder bag and went scampering up the aisle, almost colliding with a flight attendant. She grabbed him and came back to me with a frown.

"Do you know it's against the rules to carry a dog loose on a plane?" she began sternly. "He has to be in a dog carrier and his passage paid by weight. I'm supposed to report this to the captain."

I envisioned lengthy delays with the airlines and arguments with quarantine officials over the necessary papers and innoculations. I had not had time to take the puppy to a Guatemalan veterinary for clearance. His father had been my dog and I knew the female and her environment. Pitzi was as healthy as any American dog.

Pitzi saved himself. Giving a yawn which showed his tiny pink tongue curled above the pearly nubbins of teeth, he stretched out in the stewardess's arms and began sucking on her thumb. Charmed, she ticked his tummy, then passed him back to me. Minutes later, she brought a saucer of milk, scraps from chicken sandwiches, and a tiny bit of Dramamine to help him sleep the rest of the way.

Pitzi arrived at Cornell, and later Black Bear Lake, safe and sound. He grew up to be an enormous shepherd with clear amber eyes and one ear cocked rakishly to the side. He definitely was not a *little puppy*. And all about our twelve years together is written in *Woodswoman*.

Meanwhile, I was working feverishly to finish my thesis the

summer of 1969. I was uncertain what to do afterward, but I was sure that student life was not for me. Part of the time I dreamed of going back to Guatemala to be with Armando and do what I could in conservation there. I had been in love with Armando so long that not even the two disastrous visits could dissipate this dream. Yet, part of the time I fantasized about a good-paying job in the States. I'd been poor so long and deprived myself of so much that I really needed financial security. Armando wrote less often than before. He was still separated and living alone, but he did not propose any definite plan for us. Maybe there wasn't any, though he wanted to see me again. I constantly fretted how I could combine a career and a partner. In my confused state, I was not prepared for the bombshell that arrived in the mail.

It was a hot day in June when I opened a letter from Edgar, who had continued his detailed and loyal reports. I read that the National Institute of Electrification (INDE) had proposed a hydroelectric project for Lake Atitlán! The plan was to use the lake as a natural reservoir and bore through underwater tunnels along the southern shore between Volcanos Atitlán and San Pedro to allow a fall of water down the Pacific slope. Given the lake's elevation, the water would fall more than 3,000 feet down huge penstocks to the turbines. He wrote that engineers and geologists had been combing the land around his farm and even drilling test cores along the escarpment behind him.

The project was planned for development between 1970 and 1980, with Austrian consultants coming in to help the Guatemalan engineers. One field man had told Edgar that the project would result in a power capacity of almost 500 megawatts and an annual output of 1000 gigawatts. He didn't know what that meant, but it sounded like a lot. (I didn't know either, but resolved to find out at once.) Atitlán would provide 10–12 percent of the projected power demands of the entire country.

In order to compensate for the intentional lowering of the lake twenty-seven to thirty-seven feet temporarily (due to the outflow in the tunnels), and twenty-three feet *permanently*, four tunnels would be dug from the Rivers Madre Vieja, Nahualate, Samalá, and Yatzá. They would divert water into the lake. This would help bring the level back up a bit.

I had been past the Madre Vieja, Samalá, and Nahualate with Armando and remembered them all as being fairly muddy and probably contaminated since they passed various Indian villages. How could engineers possibly plan to mix those low-quality, turbid waters with the crystal clear, aquamarine water of Atitlán? The implications of what might happen to the grebes and their ecosystem started to dawn on me. The project had to be stopped. But I was a complete prisoner to the university and dedicated to finishing my thesis before August 31st. What could I do?

Racing down the worn steps of the Natural Resources Building, I searched for one of the professors on my committee who taught International Conservation. Breathless, I burst into his office and waved Edgar's letter in his face. "Look at this, Dr. Hamilton," I cried. "They are going to ruin Lake Atitlán!"

Since he was one of the two who'd gone there with me, he could visualize what was at stake. At once he offered to set up a meeting with professors from the Water Resources Department at Cornell's Engineering School and with other colleagues in Natural Resources. "You must try and get a copy of the engineering plan before we meet." he said. "Then we'll have a much better idea what's proposed."

I cabled Edgar that same day and within three weeks had the Verbund-Plan (1967), with modifications by INDE, on my desk. At our meeting, the professors showed deep concern and provided a wealth of information. What was evident was that most of the shoreline vegetation and submerged shallow aquatic plants would be reduced or eliminated if the water level dropped quickly. The proposed drawdown of three to four and a half feet *per year* initially would probably be more than reeds and cattails could adapt to. They would dry out and die. In many places it would be difficult for these plants to reestablish themselves because of the rocky, steep shoreline. Then, if the initial drop of twenty-seven feet was compounded by a dry season drop of three more, the die-off of habitat would be more severe.

A more insidious threat would be the loss of Atitlán's natural filtering-purifying system. Wetlands, at the edges of lakes and rivers, serve to slow down rain runoff so that suspended solids, silt, and pollutants settle to the bottom. There, chemical reactions occur to transform them to simple substances. Cattails and reeds absorb these nutrients, thus purifying and clarifying the water. What's left simply becomes deep wetland sediments.

One new thing I learned from the report was that Lake Atitlán is suspected of having occasional long-term natural fluctuations of around fifty to sixty feet over forty-year cycles. Indeed, I had once seen submerged standing giant willow trunks about ten feet under water and wondered how they got there. However, this natural drop and rise was gentle and slow. Plants could accommodate to these changing conditions. It was only a one and a half–foot drawdown per year maximum.

The water engineer who attended our meeting described how construction of tunnels forty feet below the surface, diversion ditches, sealing of subterranean filtration holes, and all the excavation rubble along the shores would definitely increase turbidity in the lake. Moreover, the four mountain rivers entering Atitlán could cause siltation and pollution. Deleterious effects might include bacterial contamination of drinking and domestic water for residents and vacationers; introduction of undesirable aquatic life or parasites; and the gradual eutrophication (enriching and aging) of Atitlán. One scientist predicted that it would take only *seventy-seven years* to replace completely the existing clear blue water in the lake with diverted brown river water! That meant a child born today who lived as long as Don Emilio would see a total change. Of course, fish, and other aquatic life, and my giant grebes could be endangered by the turbidity, silting, and pollution, or the introduction of competitive, predatory, or parasitic species. It didn't take me long to figure that one cost of this power project might be the extinction of the Atitlán grebes and the desecration of Lake Atitlán.

There was in addition a cost to humans and domestic animals living around the lake and downstream from the four diverted rivers. Tourism would be affected if the lake turned brown and dirty. Until now Atitlán had been considered one of the loveliest lakes on earth. The Indians along the shores would, no doubt, lose their cottage *petate* industry, and fishing and crabbing would probably diminish. People and domestic animals living along the rivers *below* the project would experience water shortages, which could affect crop production and their drinking supply. There could be flooding during peak power production hours. In the event of earthquakes, damage to the tunnels or retaining structures might release vast surges of water and even imperil life below on the Pacific slope.

One thing that the engineering professors drummed into my head that day was that power is badly needed in most developing nations. No matter what I did, my thrust must be to look for *alternative* sources of electricity, not simply to stop the Verbund-Plan.

After our meeting, I sat down with Dr. Hamilton and drew up a list of key conservation people to whom we might turn for help. Then he helped me draft a letter, balancing my almost hysterical fervor with calm reasoning. Juggling thesis editing with sending out those letters took every minute of my summer. But the conservation community rallied. Sir Peter Scott, Prince Philip of the United Kingdom, and Prince Bernhard of the Netherlands each sent letters to the President of Guatemala. Other less famous persons did, too. Key arguments were to point out the economic loss in tourist dollars to the region and the considerable potential danger to inhabitants around and below the lake. Major points were that Guatemala possesses abundant hydropower and geothermal sources which could be harnessed for electricity without imperiling this magnificent lake. Almost by common consent, few people mentioned the pocs. We did not want it to sound like a few flightless water birds were the *cause célèbre* behind our pleas. Of course, *I* did. But then I figured no one was more entitled to try and save them from this new potential extinction threat than me.

I never heard directly what happened at INDE. All I know is that the project was temporarily halted and other solutions were being looked into. Finally, Edgar mentioned in one of his letters that all the drilling equipment and field workers had left the lake.

By the time I read that good news I had my degree and was an assistant professor at Cornell. The offer had come over the summer and was too attractive financially to turn down. I had gone from one day to the next from being a wretched graduate student to being a paid academic! Part of my decision had been based on a letter from Armando. When I'd asked him what I should do, and if he ever thought he'd be free to marry, he said he could not change his present way of life. That meant I'd still have to live alone in Panajachel and we would use the same considerable discretion to see each other as we had in the past. Somehow I sensed that would not be enough for me. The signs were clear. I had to give up my obsession and start a career for myself.

Hard as it was, I did not go back to Guatemala during the two years I taught at Cornell. The despair I felt at not being with Armando gradually lessened, but it never left me. Life moved at such a fast pace. I was constantly caught up in committee meetings, teaching, seminars, helping graduate students, and then dashing off to my cabin on weekends. Still my heart was empty. Edgar continued sending his reports—all good. The pocs and the refuge were in capable hands and doing well.

Yet I never lost my taste for fieldwork and the freedom of planning my own work. I finally decided to leave Cornell and become a free-lance consultant and writer. I would base at my cabin and work wherever a job was offered. Fortunately, one of my first assignments was to work as a staff ecologist on the MS *Lindblad Explorer,* a natural history cruise ship which roamed the world experiencing unusual wildlife, archeological sites, and wilderness areas. The itinerary was down the coast of eastern Central America from Cancún, Mexico, to Corn Island, Nicaragua. Later, the ship would do the western coastline, from Panama's San Blas Islands, via the Canal, to the Pacific, and on up to San Diego, California. Both times, I would be able to spend three days en route in Guatemala. Excited, I wrote Armando and Edgar to see if they could meet me. I would leave the ship and suggested we make a quick census and reconnaissance of the lake.

I heard nothing from Armando. (I learned later that his father, Don Emilio, had died and he had had personal and financial problems.) Edgar did reply and offered to meet me at the ports of call, even though they were hours from the lake.

When we tied up to the huge dock at Puerto Barrios (now Mathias de Galvez), I spied Edgar—short, trim, clad in neatly pressed slacks and a white polo shirt. Immediately I asked our expedition leader if he could come aboard and tell the passengers about Operation Poc and his role as game warden. Since no one planned to go ashore in that dilapidated port, he agreed at once. Edgar captivated everyone with his broken English and precise explanations of our campaign. So much so that he was invited to join us next day on a flight to Tikal to see the ancient Maya ruins. I wanted so much to go to the lake, but Edgar had brought good news. His April census had revealed 157 grebes, with an estimated 185, including young.

"You needn't worry, Anna," he said. "The grebes are doing fine. The refuge is in order. I put in a flush toilet and a small patio out of the wind. If the government keeps its promise, I hope to add a dormitory for students, scientists, and photographers who want to stay. The Indian reed cutters are doing just as the law states."

I was reassured by his words. And I remembered how seldom he got away, how hard he worked, so I said, "Then let's go to Tikal with the group, Edgar."

After two wonderful days among jungle growth and hidden limestone temples, making rubbings and taking pictures, we were back at the port. I watched the ship slip away from the cement wall, roiling the oily water with mysterious patterns. Humidity made a halo around the dock lights and Edgar's headlights as he waved goodbye. Gradually the calm black water widened between us. I wished Armando had been able to come to the port and share the jungle ruins with me. But it looked as though I might not see or hear from him again—ever. I was deeply grateful for Edgar's friendship. I had begun to feel he was the brother I never had. Someone I could really count on.

On the western coast of Central America, a few months later, the ship put into Puerto San José, Guatemala. The Pacific was wild that day. We had to be off-loaded in small boxes strung to cables. The ship lurched beneath us and the jetty was wet with spray. Huge rollers crashed onto the black sand beaches. The horizon was jagged with white crests and the sea an ugly green. I was too scared to look at anything except where I would jump when the box touched down. I leaped away in case the wind would swing the heavy crate against me and found I had almost jumped into Edgar's arms. Again, he had come.

This time the passengers were to spend three days in Antigua and Guatemala City. Since I was well acquainted with these places, as was Edgar, we sped to the lake and made a quick census and tour. This time we counted 189 grebes, with an estimated 210. "If this keeps up," I crowed, "we may reach carrying capacity in two or three more years. This is a 20 per cent increase from your last count! 130 per cent from the low-low of 80 birds!"

On the way to the lake, Edgar had told me he had a surprise for me. "I don't think you should stay in your hut this time, Anna," he said. "We'll be working hard and long hours, and it's very difficult to cook there. So I thought you'd like to stay in a new place." But he would not tell me where it was.

We had arrived at his farm, said hello to Doña Carmela, and got right in the boat. Instead of heading for the refuge or the reeds, Edgar made straight for the holy hill, Chuitinamit. He cruised along the wild shoreline until we came opposite an attractive wooden weekend chalet perched on a promontory. A volcanic sand beach with a stand of reeds lay just below it. Edgar steered straight to the beach and jumped out without getting his shiny boots wet. Pulling the boat up, he helped me out and said, "Do you like it?"

"Like it? Why it's a super spot, Edgar. Whose is it?"

"Mine," he said simply.

"Yours?"

"Yes, I bought this piece of land and decided to build a getaway house that I could rent or use myself. It's the first one ever built on Chuitinamit. Come up and see the view."

We climbed several sets of stairs and entered the well-built but rustic building. A long veranda, shaded with young eucalypti, looked over the lake. But the spectacle was inside. Both walls facing out to the main lake were glass so I had the impression of being at the prow of a boat facing into the wind. There was a small stone fireplace, bright wool rugs, kitchen filled with gay ceramic dishes from Antigua, and two cozy bedrooms.

"It's absolutely charming, Edgar," I said after inspecting the whole house. "You are a very gifted architect."

"I love to build things, Anna," he said, "and this seemed like the perfect solution. I can get away from work and my mother, yet be close enough to the farm in case I'm needed. I can relax here, and now I can bring friends. Santiago Atitlán is only ten minutes by boat. And, most of all—if you need a place to stay—my house is your house."

That night as we were eating before the fire and listening to the wind rattle the windows, Edgar said, "Anna, do you think

World Wildlife Fund International might consider giving me another patrol boat? This one is getting faded, brittle, and worn, and the motor's been acting up lately. I'd still like a larger horse-power engine."

"Yes, Edgar," I said. "I can apply for another grant. There shouldn't be any problem. After all, you're crucial to the project, and no one wants you breaking down out on the lake."

Then he said a strange thing. "The Indians believe that this holy hill is haunted by the ancient Maya. They think there was a temple here and it is bad luck to stay overnight. The men come to work their fields, but no one sleeps here. That's why, I think, no one has ever built a weekend place on Chuitinamit, although there are more and more chalets going up around the rest of the lake."

"Yes, I've seen traces of an old temple on the top of the hill," I said, "when Armando and I went up to recover the stela and take it to the refuge, but I wonder if things that old and long ago can have any influence now. I think it's more likely that Pedro de Alvarado conquering the Tzutujiles right around here made this place kind of superstitious".

"Well"—Edgar looked thoughtful—"maybe it's really because there's no road on this side of the volcano and people can only come by boat. I don't know. Do *you* believe it could bring bad luck, Anna?"

"No, Edgar, I don't." I said emphatically. "How could any place this beautiful be bad luck?"

14
Out of Nothing—Hope

WHEN I RETURNED TO Guatemala I carried a check from World Wildlife Fund International (now World Wide Fund for Nature). Edgar met me at the airport and we went right out and got what he'd always wanted: a smart fiberglass craft with low, trim lines which would handle the waves and a 70 h.p. motor. We spent a day on the beach painting WWF on the sides. I did one side in English; Edgar did the other in Spanish. Two large panda decals went on the bow.

By now the government had completed a rough road into the refuge, and Edgar had arranged for a sign at the crossroads so that tourists could drive into the refuge. Lake Atitlán had been a national park since 1955 (at least on paper), but our sanctuary was as close as it came to providing rangers and a visitors center.

Other good news awaited me at the refuge. Two chicks had been hatched and reared by the captive birds. Edgar had released them from the sanctuary when they were able to fend for themselves. He also showed me the results of his last census. There were an estimated 232 pocs, adults and juveniles.

"The birds are back to where they were before the bass came into the picture!" I said. "Edgar, we've really done a great job and this is the proof. Young birds in the refuge and the wild population going up, up, up."

My friend's personal life had taken a different course too. After Doña Carmela's death, Edgar had taken a much firmer grip on his farm. For the past several years, he had won top awards for his excellent coffee. In addition, he had begun to raise avocados and certain ferns that were popular in the florist trade.

He now made many more business trips into the city. I noticed changes in his lifestyle. Hangers with neat shirts, jackets, and trousers from the dry cleaner hung on his porch. A huge TV sat in one corner. Edgar had built on a new kitchen and bathroom and abandoned the wood stove and rudimentary appliances of his mother. His office looked more organized and efficient than ever, and a new van was parked outside. I was happy for him and sensed

Edgar Bauer, government game warden at Lake Atitlán National Park for fourteen years, shares a snack with his cat.

a new vitality, maturity, and purpose in Edgar. There didn't seem to be any woman in his life. While he treated me with utmost courtesy, he was still very reticent about discussing his personal life.

Those were the stable, quiet years. The pocs stayed steady at 200 or more and tourists came to the refuge. No matter where my writing and consulting assignments took me—Panama, Costa Rica, Dominican Republic, the Amazon basin—I made it a practice to fly back by way of Guatemala. Usually I stayed a week, made a census, saw the government officials, and checked up on things with Edgar.

After such a trip, Pitzi and I were sitting in my Adirondack cabin one February evening in 1976 when a soft classical music program was interrupted for the following: "There has been an earthquake of major proportions in Guatemala, reaching 7.5 on the Richter scale. An estimated 10,000 persons are dead, thousands more are homeless, and 58,000 houses have been destroyed in Guatemala City alone."

I reached for the radio and turned up the volume.

"Hardest hit was the capital and outlying suburbs, with damage—"

Static obliterated the rest and I frantically shook the radio side to side, trying to catch any further remnants of information. My mind leaped—what about Isabela and Carlos? Edgar? Armando and Doña Rosa? My priest friend? Salvador, the refuge guardian? Jessie, my dog in Guatemala?

The next news announcement would not be for another hour. I knew I had to get out to a phone at first light. Grabbing my address book, extra clothes, some paperwork, I made up a knapsack and set it by the door. At dawn I would be ready to snowshoe down the lake. Meanwhile, the night dragged by. Each news report was worse as the death toll mounted. I learned that the epicenter had been near Chimaltenango, just twenty miles from the city, a center for brickmaking. The mortality rate there was 90 percent because heavy brick walls had fallen on sleeping people. Damage had been reported for seventy-five miles into the countryside.

Next morning when I tried to phone, all international lines were tied up. After countless calls, I realized it would be days before normal service was resumed. As it turned out, a local ham radio operator was the person who finally provided me with more information. The airport at Guatemala City was all but closed due to buckled runways. Roads were impassable. Relief help was slowly trickling into the country.

I decided to fly to Guatemala and tried to find out if I could join an emergency team. My only qualifications were that I spoke Spanish, knew the country, and was an emergency medical technician. No teams were going, so far as I could see. Then, I heard that do-gooders like me were being discouraged due to the lack of water, sanitary facilities, rooms, food, and difficulty of transportation. So I started packing boxes of clothes, blankets, and shoes and bullying my neighbors to donate to the earthquake victims. Frustrated and frightened about those I cared for, I mailed off boxes to the Guatemalan airline, Aviateca, who had offered to fly goods free to the country.

Three months later, I finally had an assignment in Central America which allowed me to visit Guatemala. The worst damage had been cleared, but in the city the National Cathedral's huge dome was cracked, and the central market where I had loved to shop for gifts was flattened. In Chimaltenango, most of the surviving populace were on crutches or wore casts. The country was battered. By now, 23,000 people were known dead.

News of my friends was better, however. Carlos and Isabela had spent three nights huddled in their car—the safest place around. Otherwise, the 400-year-old hacienda where they lived had received little damage. My priest friend had previously moved to a parish on the coast and escaped harm altogether. At the lake, I had news of Armando, Doña Rosa, and Jessie, though I did not see them. All were fine; Edgar, also, was well. His chalet at Chuitinamit was untouched, as were the buildings at the refuge. The force of the earthquake had dissipated by the time it reached Atitlán. Only one earth crack, perpendicular to the main crust slippage, had hit the lake.

At the time, this caused no alarm, but then, early in 1978, Edgar wrote me that the lake had gone down about four feet and had not risen again after the rains. Only four feet of water remained in the center of the refuge. "We may have to release the pocs inside if this keeps up," he predicted ominously. In the same letter, he pointed out that his last census had shown a drop in the number of birds and a decrease of reeds and cattails. "I think the shoreline vegetation is drying out due to the drop in lake level," he wrote, "so there's less habitat".

As soon as possible, I went back to Guatemala and saw with my own eyes how the earthquake of 1976 was affecting Lake Atitlán. There seemed to be nothing one could do, given its geology. One to two million years ago, Lake Atitlán had existed only as a shallow, small lake, or not at all. The two tiny rivers which comprise its only inlets today united higher up than the present lake site and flowed south via an uninterrupted canyon toward the Pacific Ocean. The present lake, however, owes its origin mainly to damming of this drainage pattern by lava flows from Volcanoes Atitlán and Tolimán, not far from where Edgar's farm now stood and at San Lucas. Thus, the basin is not a caldera, or a crater lake, nor is it a volcanic tectonic sink. The oval block which sank within the original depression is the result of spasmodic subterranean withdrawal of molten magma from the three adjacent volcanoes. In geological terms, Atitlán is a "caldron subsistence."

The lava flows blocking the lake were—and still are—permeable along the southern shores. There are many subterranean outlets in the form of seep holes and channels on the lake floor. Water gushes out year round from the narrow canyons on the Pacific side of the volcanoes.

What this all meant was that Lake Atitlán's geology made it a victim. This entire southwestern area is a preferred seismic zone of earth crust, where catastrophic earthquakes can occur any time. After the 1976 quake, these sublacustrine outlets opened further. Fissures formed on the lake bottom, causing more water drainage. Hydrological equilibrium was lost. Atitlán began to lower. There was no way to plug the cracks. Only nature could do that with debris and driftwood from the hills over time. Neither rain nor springs could compensate.

When only one to two feet of water were left in the mouth of the refuge, the pocs *had* to be released. The screening was removed from the iron gate, and the reeds beaten to flush the birds out. No one saw them leave, but no one ever saw them *inside* the sanctuary again. After so much work to catch them, Edgar and I were filled with despair at the irony of having to let them go free. We stood in the visitors center, looking over the empty refuge. I cried. Two years later the refuge was so dry that our guardian, Salvador, and his Indian neighbors planted the bottom with corn and beans. The plants flourished in the rich muck. The lake gives, and the lake takes away. . . .

Edgar was not an expert agronomist for nothing. As he saw the reed beds yellow and die, he conceived a plan. In his usual calm, precise, and well-reasoned manner he said to me one morning, "Anna, if I can grow coffee and avocados, I should be able to grow reeds."

I just stared at him morosely. "What do you mean?"

"Let's go out in the boat and I'll show you."

We got in and headed for a stretch of shore where the vegetation was dying and the water was shallow. Pulling the boat in to shore, he helped me jump out. Then he reached for a shovel, string, and a stone which he'd brought along. "My idea is to dig up these plants where it's dry. Then tie a stone to the root stock, put them in Indian canoes, paddle out to deeper water, and drop them in. The weight of the rock should cause the root part to sink into the soft mud bottom."

As he spoke, Edgar went through the process, using his shovel. It took exactly five minutes to transplant one ten-foot reed plant from the beach to six feet of water.

"That's brilliant!" I exclaimed.

"Well, maybe," Edgar said cautiously. "It remains to be seen if the reeds will take hold and grow."

"It's worth a chance," I said. "What other hope have we got to stop the loss of habitat?"

Therefore, Edgar called the reed cutters of Santiago Atitlán together—the same ones who'd met with us ten years before to pound out the reed law—and asked them to volunteer their time and effort. It wasn't just for the pocs, he said, but for all the wildlife and fish of the lake, and for their own cottage industry as well. Sixty men stood in a semicircle around Edgar, faces impassive. I couldn't figure out what they thought. The Tzutujiles were sharp bargainers and generally wanted to get paid for their labor. How would they take to this notion of reed planting for free?

The sun beat down on their sombreros, some brown, some white, some woven with metallic headbands. Almond-shaped eyes glinted underneath the brims. Their shirts and embroidered purple and white pants made a kaleidoscope of color on the beach. The red sashes wound round their slim waists hung with tasseled ends to their knees. Most of the men were barefoot. Behind them, a battalion of dugout canoes were drawn up on the sand. It was an impressive work force.

When Edgar had finished his explanation, there was a long murmuring among the men. Then the head cutter spoke. "Yes, Don Edgar. It is a good plan. We will work on our free days and do it voluntarily. When shall we start?"

They began that weekend, and I was able to photograph the

MAMA POC

procedure before I left for the States. Two and a quarter years later, they were still planting—Edgar and sixty Tzutujiles. During that time, the lake went down another four feet. More reeds died. More pocs disappeared. But the reed cutters transplanted 75,000 clumps of reeds! Edgar calculated a 75 percent survival rate from his method.

At the time I read his letter telling me this, I was negotiating with *National Geographic* to do a story on the national parks of Central America. At once I realized that I should include Lake Atitlán National Park and highlight Edgar's valiant campaign. So I expanded my outline and itinerary and sent along a selection of photographs.

The assignment was approved. In January 1980, I left for Panama, to work my way north to Guatemala with the contract photographer. By March we had covered ten of the finest parks of the existing thirty-six up and down the isthmus and had only Atitlán and Tikal awaiting us. We saved them for last.

15
Warnings!!!

THE FIRST WEEK AT Atitlán the photographer, Loren McIntyre, took hundreds of pictures of Indians, landscape, and wildlife. Edgar finally received the recognition he so richly deserved when Loren devoted three days to filming him with the Indian volunteer team transplanting reeds. Dressed smartly in khakis and windbreaker, Edgar maneuvered the World Wildlife Fund boat and directed the Tzutujiles where to paddle and drop their reed clumps. He chauffeured us all over the lake, pointed out its most scenic areas, and invited the photographer to stay at his chalet. It was a hectic schedule for Edgar. He had to oversee his farm, pick up his guest in the morning and drop him off at night, buy and deliver food to the chalet at Chuitinamit, ferry me back and forth to my hut, and work with us all day. He seemed nervous. Rather edgy. Not his usual placid self. But I put it down to the workload.

I was so happy to be back at my *ranchito*. Salvador had taken good care of it. The lawn was green, the small forest thriving. He had swept the cement floor, and there was a stack of firewood inside. Where leaks had started in the roof, he had purchased more sheaves of bunch grass and retied the roof tighter. Even the

two drums under my bed were untouched. I opened them to air out my khaki uniforms, sleeping bag, and look over old field gear. The only sign of use was from a wood rat, ensconced in the rafters, who'd nibbled holes in the *petates* on the bed. I wondered if it was a relative of the one who'd taken up residence when Armando and I were so much in love.

The weather was beautiful all week. Loren and I felt sure we'd given Lake Atitlán the best coverage possible. Even though it was only a park on paper, and a park filled with people living in it, its magnificence, its role as home of the pocs, the unique geology, all made Atitlán one of the most interesting places we'd worked in Central America. The night before Loren McIntyre left, we ate in Edgar's chalet and tried to sum up our three and a half months' assignment. Afterward he said to me, "I couldn't have managed without Edgar, you know. But I'm worried about him. He seems so uptight. He sleeps part of the week at his farm, part here, and sometimes in the office at the refuge. Why is he doing that? What's he afraid of? Or is he simply having insomnia over a business problem?"

So I wasn't the only one who'd noticed the change. I resolved to talk with Edgar during the coming two weeks while we made our censuses.

The findings of our work were shattering. The pocs had dropped from 232 in 1975 to 130 or less in 1980. That meant 100 birds had disappeared in five years! Then we found only six and a half miles of shoreline vegetation, as compared to fifteen miles in 1968. This was a decrease of about 60 percent in twelve years! Clearly, the loss of habitat was severely affecting the giant grebes, as well as small fishes, crabs, and other water birds. The loss wasn't just in *length* of reed beds, but in *width*. Knowing that the pocs

---

A volunteer transplanting program was introduced in an effort to save the reed habitat. Edgar Bauer directs from his World Wildlife Fund boat.

preferred very dense, thick, deep beds of vegetation made me
think that the loss of habitat for *them* was greater than 60 percent. Many of the reeds were simply too thin for them to nest in
safely. Those planted by Edgar, were still scraggly. But without
the transplanting, parts of the lake would have no reeds at all.

By far the greatest surprise was to see the number of elegant
weekend homes now standing at Lake Atitlán. Beyond the twelve
shoreline villages, all of which were clustered in their formation, I
counted 308 houses. It was obvious that real estate development
had suddenly mushroomed here. Approximately 15 percent more
building was under construction, some houses very large and elaborate. I checked back to my first count of chalets—28 in 1960.
Then 144 in 1974. This was a 1,100 percent increase in twenty
years!

Edgar and I sat in the boat, drifting under the sun and considering the ramifications of this. We could see that new chalet
owners were ripping out reeds in favor of walls, docks, artificial
sand beaches, and boat houses. There was no law to stop them.

"You can't blame people for wanting to have a vacation
place," Edgar said.

"Of course not," I agreed. "But, Edgar, there don't seem to
be any rules or regulations over what property owners can or cannot do. Simple things like painting their places to harmonize with
the landscape. Complicated things like disposal of sewage. The
kind of pesticides and chemical fertilizers permitted on lawns and
gardens? How can we get them to protect the reed beds and not
yank them out?"

"I don't know," he admitted. "We need a new reed law. As it
is, only the Indian reed cutters are obliged to obey the existing
one."

"Not only that, I'll bet they're finding it harder and harder to
get access to the waterfront. With all these private homes along
the shore, where can they go to wash their bare feet after hoeing

in the fields? Where do they pull up their canoes after fishing? Where can they fill up watering cans?"

"That's true," Edgar said. "Salvador told me recently that the only place between Santiago Atitlán and the grebe refuge where he and his people could have free access to the lake was *at* the refuge."

"You mean every yard of lakeshore has been privately purchased along those three and a half miles?" I gasped.

"Apparently. Land prices have skyrocketed. If you tried to buy your place today, you'd pay thousands, not hundreds, for an acre or two."

There were new houses near my hut, handsomely built of cut rock, with tile roofs. I had counted seven or eight houses around the bay of Xecamuc. When I'd purchased my land a dozen years before, not one building had been in sight.

"Another thing, Anna," Edgar went on, "INDE is planning to run an electric line right by the refuge to service that whole area. The Division of Fauna office asked if we wanted to hook up and have lights at the visitors center."

How swiftly "civilization" was coming to the lake, I thought sadly.

"You can have electricity at your place too, Anna, if you want it."

"No way I'll *ever* use electricity there," I said firmly, "but I think it would be wonderful to have more room. I want to stay longer at the lake each year, Edgar, and do some serious writing."

"Then why don't we go over there now and plan it out?" he said immediately. "I could start the foundation of a little house while you're still here. I've always felt you should have more space, and I'd enjoy building something for you."

Trying to put my worries aside, I agreed. Edgar started the engine and we cruised back to the sanctuary. As we climbed the hill to the hut, I kept looking across the lake toward Panajachel. I wasn't thinking about the changes to the landscape; rather, I was remembering Armando. He had finally faded from my life, yet he was walking around in Panajachel, only nine or ten miles across the water. But he might as well have been on the moon, so different was life in Panajachel. Wistfully I wondered why Armando couldn't have offered to build me a little house? It wouldn't have been such a difficult enterprise. If Armando had done this ten years ago our lives might have been far different.

Edgar and I had just reached my hut when I realized that the worst eyesore on the entire lakeshore could be seen right from my green-shuttered windows: a fourteen-story, three-tower condominium right next to Panajachel. Without vegetative screening or earth-tone colors, it loomed upward stark, white, and bare. How

A three-tower condominium, built on the shores of Lake Atitlán, intrudes on the natural landscape. The project remains unfinished, but one of the towers is used for tourists.

could anyone in their right mind build such an edifice in an earth-quake-prone region, next to a lake like Atitlán, with no thought for the overall visual impact across the lake? Moreover, from this distance the entire town looked bigger and more crowded.

In addition to the old lakeside hotel and the few small pensions, there was now a huge modern hotel with a swimming pool, belonging to a major chain, as well as several new smaller inns back toward town. Tourist shops had multiplied dramatically, as Guatemalan textiles were all the rage.

Perhaps I could position my new chalet so that I couldn't see the blasted condo or hotel. I said as much to Edgar, and we spent the next couple of hours roaming over the land, checking different sites. Finally we chose a spot to the west of the hut, shaded by the avocado tree, with a soothing "no-condo" view of the water.

While we were deciding where the door should be Edgar suddenly changed the subject and said, "Anna, can we walk down by the lake? I want to talk to you."

I sensed he had come to some inner decision and had broken through his deep reserve. "Of course, Edgar," I said, and led the way down to the rocks where Armando and I had skinny-dipped long ago. The sun was slanting down the sky as we settled ourselves on the still warm stones.

Edgar looked out at the lapping waves for several moments without saying anything. I reached over and patted his shoulder.

"Whatever it is, Edgar, you know I'll keep it confidential. Look how long we've known each other, dear friend."

Without looking at me, he picked up a piece of pumice, chucked it in the lake, and then said, "Anna . . . Well, it's like this. I met a girl from California. She is teaching in a small *pueblo*. She really loves Guatemala—she's a lot like you that way. She learned to speak Spanish and lives simply. She has stayed on all this time, so we could be together.

"It wasn't possible to invite her to the farm," he said, "but after I bought the land on Chuitinamit, I could invite her to the chalet. And, recently"—he raised his head and smiled at me for the first time—"we went to California for two weeks.

"It was exciting. We saw a lot. So much wealth and beautiful houses. But I could never live there, Anna. It's too busy, too artificial. I like being a farmer here."

His words reminded me of Armando and the dilemma we had faced.

"Well, couldn't she stay with you at the farm then?" Blinking back sudden tears, I knew the answer before he spoke.

"No. It wouldn't work, I think. The farm is too isolated. Her term is nearly up and she doesn't want to renew another time. She wants a home and a family, but she's used to telephones, electricity, a car, a job. Well, you know, all those American things."

"Yes, I know, Edgar. But if you love each other and can make a strong commitment, it might work."

For a moment there was a glimmer of hope in his eyes, but then he shook his head. "There are other things. I don't know how the farm will do. These are hard times in Guatemala. It might not be safe for her."

"Safe?" I asked. "What do you mean safe?"

"Well, nothing certain really. I just meant, well, financially, and . . . well, who knows. . . ." he finished lamely.

"I don't understand why you're worried about her being safe," I persisted. "Your farm is so far from anything. And you have it fixed up so nicely, Edgar. She'd be comfortable," I predicted. "You could buy her a little car so she could go visiting and run into the city. So far as people are concerned, I've never seen so many American tourists here, and new shops, and buses. Just look at the guest register at the refuge."

I didn't know what else to say. The situation seemed so much like what I had known with Armando. Yet, I would have done anything to spare my friend this kind of heartbreak. Now it was clear, I thought, why Edgar had seemed so keyed up. But before I had a chance to ask him why he moved from place to place at night, he stood up and turned back toward the hut. He offered me a hand and pulled me up. Impulsively, I gave him a hug. "Edgar, believe me, I understand about the differences in lifestyles and places. Maybe if she leaves for a while it will show her how good a life she could have here."

"Maybe . . ." was all he said.

As Edgar climbed the hill ahead of me, there was a dejected slump to his shoulders that I'd never seen before. He had always been so poised and self-confident. With a visible effort, he pulled himself into the present and said, "I'll gather some workmen together and bring them over—perhaps tomorrow. They can clear the area for the chalet and start breaking rocks. I'd like to start now because next week," he said pensively, "I'm taking her to the airport. She's going home for a visit. To decide."

Next morning Edgar was there at 6 A.M. "There's something I want to show you on the lake before the workmen arrive. Come with me, Anna," he said. We sped over the calm surface toward Santiago. Edgar veered off behind the Lions Rocks and steered slowly toward a low island.

"You see that?" he pointed. "That island was an underwater shoal for years. Remember how careful you had to be with a boat and motor in there? Well, since the lake's gone down, the Lions Rocks are sticking way up above the surface and this island has appeared. The government recently leased it for ten years from the Indian who claims it. We want to build a new refuge there."

"What a good idea," I said enthusiastically. "The Ministry of Agriculture is honoring its commitment to our program."

Edgar eased the boat carefully toward a dense stand of cattails surrounding the island. A narrow channel had been cut through to firm ground and there was a little dock. We clambered out and walked inland. In the few years that the soil had been exposed, willows were growing vigorously among the newly emerged, smooth gray rocks. A trail had been cut and leveled, meandering toward the center of the island. There stood a rustic *ranchito*, made entirely from cornstalks and bunch grass. Only the floor was cement and rock.

"This is where we hope to bring visitors," said Edgar. "The Peace Corps is offering to send volunteers to fix it like the old visitors center with a natural history display."

"What happens if the lake comes back up?"

"I doubt it will that fast," said Edgar. "It's taken four years to go down and is still lowering. So even if it reversed next year, it would probably take five years to cover up the island again. By then, the lease would be up. It's all the government could find or afford, given the price of land around here now."

We wandered around and I could see it had possibilities. There was a charm to being on an island, and the cattails acted as a barrier from waves, boat traffic, and the bustle of nearby Santiago. One felt protected here.

"Are there any pocs nesting in the cattails?" I asked.

"Pedro, my assistant, says he's heard them calling nearby, but hasn't seen any chicks. I leave things pretty much in his hands while I do the patrols, poc censuses, and reports."

Backing out from the dock, I asked Edgar if I could borrow the boat to do a little detective work over in Panajachel. I promised to have the boat back at his farm by 5 P.M. That way he'd know I was safe and wouldn't worry.

"Of course," he said, "but you'll be gone all day. Let me go find Pedro and give him some instructions." He headed for the Santiago dock and tied up.

I stayed in the boat while Edgar walked up to Pedro's home. Dozens of women were gathered along the shore, washing their clothes in the shallows with big round balls of brown soap. The smell of it wafted in the air. Rank and antiseptic—it was made of pig's fat and lye. The water where the sudsy clothes had soaked was cloudy yellow. Along the shore, women beat and pounded their materials on the smooth rocks with a rhythmical, wet,

smacking sound. Higher up, wet trousers, *huipiles,* sashes, and
odd scraps of cloth lay festooned on the rocks, drying in the sun. It
made a picturesque scene that tourists never tired of photographing.

Nearby, several small naked boys cavorted in the water, slapping spray at each other and yelling with glee whenever one got

**Further pollution of Lake Atitlán. Most of the local soaps are nonbiodegrada-
ble and contain lye and pig fat.**

hit. They looked like nimble brown monkeys playing on the shore, never going in too deep. Meanwhile, little girls were dutifully following their mothers to market, carrying firewood, bringing water in jugs. They pattered along the dusty streets barefoot, exact replicas of their mothers. Little girls were never seen splashing naked in the lake.

Canoes came and went from the spindly docks of Santiago, bringing fresh vegetables, laying hens, firewood, and corn. Each paddler wore a wide sombrero, and from time to time the stiff straw glinted in the sunlight. How I loved this place, with its bustle and colors and the two majestic volcanoes brooding behind it all. I looked forward to the day when I could spend much of the wintertime in my hut and new chalet.

I saw Edgar coming down the hill with a short, robust young Indian whose eyes seemed mere slits in a moon-shaped face. His hair was jet black and hung straight to his neck.

"This is Pedro," Edgar said. "He's helped me with the reeds."

I shook hands with Pedro and told him how glad I was that he'd been part of the massive transplanting project. He nodded shyly. Then Edgar gave him the keys to the van and told him to be at the refuge in a couple of hours. I was surprised that a country-bred Indian knew how to drive, but Edgar assured me Pedro could also run the boat, repair an engine, and type. "He's a tremendous help, Anna, and speaks fluent Spanish."

"Where did he learn all this?" I asked.

"Partly in a vocational school run by a religious group, and partly just watching me. He's very intelligent."

After dropping Edgar back at the refuge, I crossed the lake alone and tied up to a long dock at Panajachel. Then I walked into town and out the other side toward the condominium towers. Soon the paved street turned to dirt and led through shady old groves of coffee trees. When I reached the condo property, I found it was fenced off with barbed wire strands. Slinging the camera over my chest, I gingerly parted two strands and slipped my leg to the other side. Then I eased between the wires, trying not to snag my shirt. No one was about. That made it easier. Nonchalantly, I strolled up to the towering buildings and looked over the construction. The walls rose sheer above me on all sides. In front, every floor was broken by a balcony. What a million-dollar view, I thought. Until it starts to rock in a quake. Rumor had it that a one-bedroom unit cost about $40,000—a high price for this part of the world. But I wasn't finding what I was looking for. I walked out back, searching for septic tanks, leach fields, trenches—anything that would indicate sewage disposal. I couldn't find any septic system that would accommodate 400 or more units, or around 1,200 people, if you averaged three persons per unit.

I started exploring the area toward the lake. Cement blocks, wires, pipes, plastic tubing lay all over the place, and I picked my way with care. It would not do to get hurt here while I was snooping around. Then I noticed a deep, long culvert that ran directly from the base of the condos to the lake.

Not being an engineer or construction worker, I couldn't be sure what this was for. But at last it dawned on me this *might* be an outfall for sewage and stormwater to go into Atitlán! I followed the culvert down to the lake shore. It got more shallow and ended just a few feet from the water.

This was the exact spot where I'd spent my first weeks watching pocs—that lone pair. I scanned the shoreline for reeds; I saw that there were none. Only a bare beach edged this section. This was also the spot where I'd collected the pair for the Laboratory of Ornithology at Cornell. Now the birds were preserved in formaline inside a deep jar, available only to scientists. The guilt I still felt for shooting them was somewhat lessened now as I realized that their habitat had been obliterated for the benefit of swimmers and sunbathers.

Styrofoam cups and empty outboard motor oil cans lay washed up on the sand, and a tattered sheet of plastic was wrapped around the stilts of a small dock. The freshly exposed lake bottom was raw enough without having these ugly reminders of a throwaway society.

After taking several pictures and resolving to do further research when I got to Guatemala City, I left. I was still stewing with anger over what was being done to this beautiful lake when I saw Edgar later that afternoon. "I'll find out who owns the condo," he promised. "If you can't make contact while you're here, I'll let you know by letter."

"Isn't there some government agency that looks after water pollution in Lake Atitlán?" I stormed.

"I don't think so," was his sad answer.

My last few days I spent quietly at the *ranchito*. Mornings I watched the workmen begin the foundation of the chalet. Afternoons I planted more flowers and trees. It was a peaceful time. My anxiety about Lake Atitlán lessened. We had been successful before in saving the pocs, and perhaps we could be again. The lake couldn't go down forever—all 1,200 feet of it. The combination of Edgar's reed-planting program, the new refuge site, and the natural resilience of plants and animals gave me cause for hope. Perhaps I could also get new grant funds to prepare a natural resource survey and land use plan of the lake. Then I could make specific recommendations about how to control the abuses which always accompany a growth in human population.

For now, though, I woke with the doves at dawn, dipped into the lake, and carried water to the hut. I drank Edgar's excellent coffee with my guava paste and tortillas made by Salvador's wife. I imagined how the volcanoes would look through the tall, slim, south window in my new house. Pictured what furniture I'd place in the fourteen-by-fourteen single room. Decided what color curtains I'd sew for the picture windows overlooking the lake. Dreamed of a fire in the stone hearth, which Edgar insisted on building himself. I was as delighted with my tiny structure as my neighbors were with their million-dollar vacation homes around Xecamuc Bay.

Every day Edgar brought me new plants, and Salvador worked with me to build terraces and rock grottos where bougainvilleas, flame vine, and poinsettias could take root and hold moisture. His corn was growing all around the buildings, and the green shiny leaves made a soothing whisper in the breeze. We heaped rocks into low walls edging my property. Salvador assured me that the lovely night-blooming cereus cactus, or *pitaya,* would soon cover these. "When you come again, Doña Anna," he said, "if it's May or June, you can eat the purple fruits right in front of your chalet."

By the time I had to fly home, the walls were up to three feet. The floor was done and framing for the windows was ready. The new chalet would only be a few feet larger than the old hut and not much bigger than my cabin in the Adirondacks. It would have solid seven-foot-high rock walls. Now the north wind could not whine through the cracks at night and find me. And the windows would be glass; they would open and close. The door would be stout with a lock. I planned to bring a portable typewriter, some books, pots and pans, blankets. They would be safe from wood rats and snoopers. I wouldn't have to store stuff in those old cardboard drums anymore. With luck, perhaps I'd be back within a half a year to live and write in my backcountry haven.

16
A Long Silence

AFTER I LEFT GUATEMALA in March 1980, there was no word from Edgar for several months. U.S. magazines and newspapers began running more and more articles about political unrest in Central America, especially El Salvador and Guatemala. Friends would send me clippings and ask, "Do you think it's safe for you to go back there?"

I wasn't worried about myself, but my concern over Edgar was mounting. Why didn't he write? He'd promised to send me the name of the construction company and owner of the condos.

Meanwhile, I had sent a proposal for "A Land Use and Natural Resources Survey, Lake Atitlán, Guatemala," to World Wildlife Fund/International Union for Conservation of Nature and Natural Resources (IUCN), Smithsonian Institution, and the International Council for Bird Preservation. I had every hope of being funded since all these organizations had given grants in the past. Moving from the ecology and management of a single endangered species* to a land use and planning study of an endangered ecosystem was a natural progression of events.

*The giant pied-billed grebe was now registered in IUCN's *Red Data Book* on a pink sheet, indicating highly endangered and threatened with extinction.

Moreover, the Director of INGUAT (Guatemalan Institute of Tourism) had given his wholehearted approval and offered all possible cooperation in order to achieve the project's objectives.

As hoped, I received approval and a contract for the job.

Tentatively I planned to leave early February 1982.

Then I received a letter that Edgar had written me on the previous October 7th. Part of the letter said: "This region has had problems with guerrillas and the opposing force, the military. I have had to practice all kinds of precautions to protect myself. I keep moving from place to place, changing my sleeping spot from the farm to the chalet and so on, so as not to maintain a regular, fixed schedule. I have heard rumors about kidnappings, robbings, and assaults by the guerrillas, who are apparently hiding up on the volcanoes. They come down to the pueblos to make trouble for the government. All this keeps me uncertain and agitated. The only tranquility I have in my life is to wake up each new day without incident, and give my thanks to God."

He went on to say that the Institute of Forestry (INAFOR) had continued work at the new refuge and it was almost done. My chalet was almost done as well. The floor, fireplace, chimney, walls, windows, and door were all in place. Only the roof was left to finish. Edgar asked me if I wanted bunch grass, or tin, or tile, and quoted costs and drew some designs.

Then he mentioned how bad coffee prices were and how inflation was starting to eat into his earnings.

Last he told me how great he thought my new project would be and how important for the future of the lake and the country. He ended by saying that he offered me his complete help and support and that I shouldn't worry about him.

When I finished reading, I sat quietly for a while. Edgar was telling me not to worry about *him,* when it sounded as though he was running for his life. Sadly I realized there was nothing I could do to help him and that it would be foolhardy to go to Guatemala at this time. That night I wrote a long letter exhorting Edgar to be

careful, offering to send him money, and asking him to stop work
on my chalet. If there was no roof on it, then no one could hide
out in it. Later, I also had to cancel my February departure and
the contract.

Again, there was no news for months. In February I sent a
cable to Edgar, asking for information. Nothing came back.

Late in May I received a letter from Pedro with a clipping
from the newspaper. On May 7, 1982, Edgar had been killed by
unknown assailants on his farm at night. His buildings were
burned down. The World Wildlife Fund boat had disappeared.

Why had Edgar been killed? What had he done to deserve
this? Had he made politically unwise statements? Had a disgrun-
tled worker sided with the guerrillas and targeted him? Or was it I
who had sentenced him to death years before when I suggested he
become a game warden?

There was no way to find out and no one to help me deal with
the grief. Our State Department had issued a traveler's advisory
against unnecessary trips to Guatemala, especially in out-of-the-
way places. I didn't hear from any of my Guatemalan friends for
over a year. The American press continued its dark coverage of
events there. Amnesty International stated that Guatemala had
the worst human rights record in the Americas. The Inter-Ameri-
can Commission on Human Rights, an agency of the Organization of American States, reported that the Army, in 1983, had
"destroyed and sacked entire villages and massacred inhabitants."

Now I knew that Operation Protection Poc, as I'd created it
and run it, was over. No one wanted to be a game warden at Lake
Atitlán now. And the government was fully occupied with guerrillas, not grebes. Edgar was buried near Santiago Atitlán. I could
not attend the funeral, much as I wished to. All I could do was
nominate him to the World Wildlife Fund International's Roll of
Honor. In 1982 his name was joined to others who'd rendered
outstanding service to the cause of conservation. His name ap-

peared with Dr. René Dubos of France, Dr. Barbara Ward (the
Lady Jackson of Lodsworth, U.K.), U Tun Yin of Burma, Saroj
Raj Choudhury of India, and Dr. Mario Dary of Guatemala, all
deceased. The letter announcing this event stated: "His name was
included on the Roll in recognition of his dedication in supporting conservation projects in Guatemala and, in particular, in recognition of his work for the Atitlán grebe."

Editors I'd known for years gave Edgar due respect. News
releases appeared in *International Wildlife* ("Guerillas Kill
Guatemalan Warden"), *Geo* ("Murder of Warden Poses Threat
to Rare Bird"), Smithsonian Institution *News Release* ("Endangered Bird Threatened by Conflict in Guatemala), and *Audubon*
magazine ("New Candidate for Extinction").

The finest words were written by Smithsonian Secretary S.
Dillon Ripley, who warned: "The plight of the flightless grebe is a
tragic reminder to us that the future of many endangered species
is threatened by wars and revolutions taking place around the
world. Biological diversity is essential to the welfare of man and
we can ill afford to permit the grebe and other endangered animals and plants to become extinct."

But in my heart of hearts, all this publicity was comfortless.
Edgar was dead and gone and no words in the world would make
that better. I lit two candles for Edgar in St. Patrick's Cathedral
when I was in New York City. My wish for him, a Catholic, was
that the God he had believed in was being good to him. As I gazed
into the candle flames, I pictured the face of my gentle, helpful,
considerate friend and knew he must be at peace.

On another occasion I took a boat out on Lake George one
late spring evening and floated in the shadow of Black Mountain.
It was very quiet and calm. Few boats broke the reflection of dark
green forest, gray-blue sky, and pearly pink sunset. With a little
imagination, I could pretend I was at Lake Atitlán, in the World
Wildlife Fund boat with Edgar beside me. I floated there for
hours in a kind of trance. I went over the whole tragic scene again

in my mind. Why was Edgar killed? Had he sensed something was coming long before? Was that what he meant when he said it might not be "safe" for his girlfriend to stay with him? What had he feared most when he slept in a different bed each night? Had he suffered? What were his last thoughts when the bullets penetrated his head and body? Finally, it was pitch-black and getting cold. I rose stiffly and started the engine. Facing the stately mountain, I threw a kiss into the night sky. That is how I said my last goodbye to Edgar.

A year after Edgar's death, Pedro wrote me again. He was now the official game warden for Lake Atitlán, and the World Wildlife Fund boat had been found inside a reed bed. It was faded and battered from sun and waves, and the 70 h.p. motor had corroded. Most of the electrical system had undergone electrolysis and no longer worked. Pedro asked if World Wildlife Fund might send him money for new parts, or the parts themselves.

At once I wrote back and told him I'd do my best to help. Fortunately, World Wildlife Fund International agreed to buy $500 worth of parts. Since I had been unable to go to Guatemala to start the land use and natural resources survey, they had money set aside and simply transferred some of it. I went to my local Adirondack boat service and ordered the replacements. A few days later I mailed a bulky package, clearly marked "Donation— Conservation Materials" to Pedro.

Three months later the parts had not arrived. Six months later they had not arrived. Pedro wrote again, begging me to do something. He explained he had checked at Customs and at the city office of INAFOR, but no one had any record of this box arriving. Since all motor parts were in short supply and inflation was mounting daily, he thought perhaps the box had been stolen and the parts sold on the black market.

This time, I used my own funds to purchase an identical set of parts and sent them down by hand with a colleague of mine working for AID. Pedro received them this time, but by then the boat motor was in worse shape. Many more replacements were needed. I could not afford to buy the rest. The government could not afford to buy them either. So the boat, from what I heard, remained on land for another year. One thousand dollars had been wasted. This neglect was to have serious effects on my next trip to Guatemala.

As it was, four years elapsed. I did not return to Lake Atitlán until March 1984.

17

In the Heat of the Day, In the Chill of the Night

EIGHT OF US sat in the leaky rowboat while an old 40 h.p. motor propelled us toward the far western corner of Lake Atitlán. Small waves slapped noisily on the bow, harbingers of a gusty *chocomil*. The sky was a faultless blue and the fierce sun was already burning my nose red. From time to time, the young student running the engine squatted down to bail the boat. I glanced uneasily at the lake. Only three of the seven passengers had life vests. There weren't enough to go around and two had lost all buoyancy.

Our plan on this first day of research was to start near San Pedro de la Laguna and census both pocs and reed beds back toward Panajachel, a distance of perhaps fifteen miles. My job was to advise the two American scientists, three Guatemalan biology students, one Peace Corps volunteer, and one INAFOR official aboard about how I had conducted my research over the past nineteen years. Through this process we would make new censuses and train the local biologists in how to continue work after we three Americans had gone. My two colleagues would also look into captive breeding possibilities.

This trip had begun with a surprise call from the U.S. Fish and Wildlife Service and its coordinator for International Affairs in the Western Hemisphere, Dr. Herb Raffaele. He had received a request from the Guatemalan government asking the United States for help in saving the endangered giant grebes. Apparently, Edgar's very last census (one I'd not seen since all his files were burned at his farm) had showed only *eighty pocs* left in 1982. No one had counted them since. No one was working to conserve both birds and lake. The government, through INAFOR, wanted to become active but had no funds. Moreover, it was a great opportunity for INAFOR, local conservation groups, and the Peace Corps to collaborate.

When Dr. Raffaele asked me to go back to Guatemala, I was hesitant. Fear still held the upperhand. I still had nightmares about Edgar. Guatemala was still in turmoil. Moreover, the logistics worried me. The U.S. Fish and Wildlife Service was paying travel expenses for us three scientists, but the Guatemalan government would provide a vehicle, boat, and gas. From what I remembered, INAFOR's equipment was limited and old. I knew that the World Wildlife Fund boat was *still* out of service. Having had firsthand experience with how lack of funds and poor equipment could hamper fieldwork, I didn't see how eight people could safely and speedily survey Lake Atitlán in one week. All my instincts said, "Don't go." But my loyalty to the project and commitment to conservation said, "Go."

Even as I was thinking back to these original concerns, our outboard motor died. The student pumped the gas bulb and yanked the starting rope several times. Nothing happened. Gingerly, I stepped around occupants to the rear of the boat while Mike and Gary, the two American scientists, crept behind me. The other four, three women and a young man, sat very still. Those in life vests did not know how to swim or could barely stay afloat. I saw fear on their faces. They had read how deep Lake Atitlán is and how violent it can become.

The three of us tinkered with the engine until we got it going again. The student resumed driving toward San Pedro. A glance at my watch showed it was well after 10:00 A.M. At best, we had two hours to work before the *chocomil* began in earnest. At worst, we should be heading back right now, playing it safe.

That morning had not gone well. I'd requested box breakfasts so we could start at 5:30 A.M. to take advantage of the calm period on the lake. Not everyone had awakened on time—understandable after the exasperating drive from Guatemala City yesterday. The eight of us had come in an old van, with a fifty-five-gallon drum of gasoline sloshing in the back and all our luggage on top. During the seventy-five-mile trip we'd had four flat tires. The drive took seven, rather than three, hours, and everyone was exhausted when we reached Panajachel.

But the bigger problem had been gasoline transfer. To get gas from our van into the boat had meant siphoning from the drum into the single boat tank and four smaller containers. These had to be carried from the parking lot around our hotel, down to the beach, and up onto a high dock. The tank and two containers were then handed down into the rowboat. Each time the boat tank ran empty, gas would have to be siphoned in because the small containers had no pouring spout. This morning the transfer had taken an hour.

Then I had refused to start until we checked for life vests, cushions, oars, drinking water, and tools for the motor. I also made sure everyone had binoculars, notebooks, hats, and sunscreen. By the time we got underway, we had lost three hours. By now, I was sure everyone aboard thought I was an old fuss-budget. None of them had ever been to Lake Atitlán before, and this crystal clear, benign morning appeared to hold no perils.

Because of political unrest, I knew that civilians might be stopped at any time. There were military roadblocks on the major

The 1984 census at Lake Atitlán. I'm playing poc calls, while Mike Lubbock, aviculturist, Gary Neuchterlein, ornithologist, and a Guatemalan student scan the shoreline with binoculars.

highways and truckloads of soldiers with machine guns in the countryside. Vehicles could also be stopped by roving bands of rebels in ambushes. I'd asked for special letters from the government—much like the one the Governor had given us years before—to explain our mission and afford us some protection. But these had not yet appeared. I had my own letter from the U.S. Fish and Wildlife Service, but it was in English and perhaps useless. We were safe on the lake, but what if we needed to go ashore?

By now the first reed beds lay just ahead so we slowed up and cut the motor. I took out my trusty old tape recorder. I went through the three-step procedure, playing the gulping cow territorial call and waiting for the standard five minutes. Out of the corner of my eye, I saw Dr. Gary Nuechterlein fidget with impatience, scanning the water surface. Tall, lanky, dark-haired, he is probably one of the world's leading authorities on grebes and recently had worked on a rare and endangered species in Argentina. He hoped someday to see all of the twenty-one species worldwide. The poc would make his day and he could hardly wait.

Mike Lubbock, an expert in captive breeding of waterfowl, was more interested in the reed beds. He hoped to devise a plan for breeding grebes here. This depended, however, on finding a site with plenty of reeds, shallow water, electricity for incubators and lights, and the right kind of security. Just as tall as Gary, Mike had gray-brown hair, brown eyes, and was very quiet. He'd hardly said two words since we set out. I sensed he was eager to use his talents and not chug around in this old rowboat.

Suddenly, a male grebe answered the call. Every pair of binoculars trained on the spot. Cameras clicked. I played the call again and got another response. Our timing was perfect—early March. Even though it had meant a feverish rush to get ready for this unexpected trip, I'd insisted to Herb Raffaele that we *had* to census the pocs now at the height of their courtship period. True to form, the birds were cooperating fully.

Gradually, we worked our way along the lakeshore, stopping to measure reeds. The motor functioned. Everyone was excited. All thoughts of the *chocomil* had vanished. At last, I thought, we were starting to function as a team, in spite of language barriers, age differences, and lack of expertise. I let the students take over and sat back, thinking about the captive breeding aspect.

In conversations with Dr. Raffaele, we had agreed that the best possible place to try raising pocs in captivity was Guatemala. "It would be extremely difficult to get permits here to *import* the birds," he explained to me, "especially since they are rare and endangered. While it's true we have excellent facilities in the States for this work—like Patuxent Wildlife Research Center, Bronx Zoo, National Zoo in Washington, D.C., San Diego Zoo, and others—it might take months, even years to arrange any transfer. And then you don't know if the Guatemalan government would allow it."

"I'm sure that it would be impossible to *export* the pocs from Guatemala," I answered. "The bird has become such a symbol of conservation. The Guatemalans would never let their precious pocs be taken away from their homeland—even to the States.

By good fortune, however, we had an offer from a wealthy Guatemalan bird fancier who wanted to donate his waterfowl ponds and adjacent facilities to raising pocs! The events behind this invitation were bizarre. Despite not going to Guatemala for four years, I'd kept a lively interest in the grebes, publicizing their plight whenever possible and lecturing to conservation groups. Some of my writings appeared in *Natural History* magazine, *Parks* journal, a Reader's Digest book on birds, and even my own book, *Assignment: Wildlife* (1980), now out of print. Some of my talks had been at colleges, before Audubon groups, and at conservation conferences. Early in 1983 I spoke to an endangered species meeting at Sea World in San Diego. There I met Dr. Frank S. Todd, then Curator of Research, who took an immediate interest in the giant grebes. He strongly urged captive breeding in private lands and suggested I contact Roberto Berger in Guatemala, who raised exotic wildlife for his zoological park. Mr. Berger and I exchanged several letters. Then he died. I was distraught for it had seemed this wonderful opportunity to help the grebes was lost.

By some incredible quirk, his son François was on the evening plane to Guatemala in March 1984 with Mike, and Gary, and me. François was every bit as charitable as his father. He offered to fly us immediately to his coastal ranch to check out the zoological park and ponds. "If we leave at daybreak," François said, "we'll be back by 9 A.M. latest. Then you can start your meetings with the government people and organize your trip to the lake."

It was too good a chance to miss, for it would save us a day and a half travel by car later on. We agreed. Next morning, one surprise followed another. Surprise that François was such a good pilot. Excitement when he landed us at Auto Safari Park, Guatemala's one and only popular drive-through zoo. Amazement when we saw giraffes, flamingos, llamas, chimpanzees, and rare ducks all living compatibly and healthily on his huge lowland ranch. The best part was the three fenced and irrigated ponds which had been dug especially for the pocs. They were edged with thick cattails and, most important, young Atitlán reeds!

"Where did those come from?" I asked.

"I sent my workmen to the lake to dig some up and bring them here," replied François pleasantly. "I wanted to see if highland reeds would adapt to our hot, humid coastal climate. I want to honor my father's wishes and prepare things for the pocs, in case you experts decide this is a good place to try captive breeding."

"It looks fine," said Mike cautiously. "But what about food? Are there any fishes in these ponds? The grebes won't eat anything but *live* fishes, aquatic insects and snails, as far as we know."

"The ponds are loaded with small lowland fishes," François said, "but probably not the same species that live at the lake. The stream that runs through here, and helps keep the ponds full and oxygenated, comes from the highlands. It should bring some food organisms with it."

I could see that the water was murky—with visibility less than one or two feet. Not at all like Atitlán's waters. But at least there was no scum or mats of vegetation. Would the birds adapt to it? And the heat? And the new and different diseases and parasites?

"What about predators?" Mike was asking. "Can they get past this fencing?"

"The worst animal is the big lizard that lives on the Pacific coast," said François. "I think the mesh is fine enough and strong enough to keep them out. We see various hawks and falcons around here, but hopefully they wouldn't single out a few pocs on a small pond when they have thousands of ducks in the Safari Park to choose from. Anyway," he added apologetically, "there's no way I can fence over three large ponds to keep them out. It's so open around here that I doubt any wild mammals could sneak up and climb the fence."

"Fish?" I asked. "Any largemouth bass?"

"No. My father just dug these ponds a year ago, and he didn't stock any bass in them."

We were so fascinated with this place and its possibilities that we overstayed our time. François landed us back in the city at 10 A.M., but when we rushed into the hotel lobby to meet our government counterparts, it was 10:30 A.M. They had been waiting since 8:30 A.M.

"Don't worry," I whispered to Gary as we hurried up. "We are all aiming at the same goal—to save the pocs, by any means we can find."

Egos had been bruised, however, particularly after the officials learned where we'd been. I explained about meeting François on the plane and his sudden invitation to review the coastal site. About saving a lot of time with the plane flight. How there'd been no way to call at 5 A.M. to postpone this meeting. Even so, I felt a chilly reception when we walked into the conference room. Several heads of local conservation groups, plus the Peace Corps volunteer, were waiting. We met for two hours, working out a plan for our fieldwork. Then we decided to leave for the lake that afternoon. The atmosphere thawed, yet I noticed that most of the group was still decidedly cool toward me.

It didn't make sense. We had come to help them, at *their* request, to save the rarest bird in Guatemala. I was their key source of information and experience. They had thawed toward Mike and Gary, but I sensed many were still suspicious of me. Why? Time would tell, I thought, yet I felt strangely uncomfortable.

It was only late that same night, after we checked into our Panajachel hotel, that things felt right again. I opened the balcony door of my second-floor room and stepped out into the night air. Below lay Lake Atitlán, shimmering under a pale moon. The smell of clean water, reeds, sand, and pines wafted into my nostrils. I took a deep breath and spread open my arms. The sheer majesty of the volcanoes, starry sky, and glimmering water filled my heart. I was back at my beloved lake—without Armando, without Edgar, almost without pocs—but I could start to heal. I was home again and ready to do battle to save my beloved birds again.

Now that peaceful nighttime feeling was gone. The boat was bobbing and waves were building. I motioned to the biologists to turn off the recorder and start the engine. We had to get out of there fast. The farther we got from shore, the rougher the lake became. Spray soaked us. Two of the women cowered on the rowboat floor, arms around each other, afraid to look out.

"Don't worry," I called reassuringly. "The waves aren't so bad. We'll make it safe and sound." But in my bones I was worried. This boat did not handle at all like my little *Xelaju* or the World Wildlife Fund boat. It wallowed and yawed and refused to mount the waves. More and more water was sloshing in. "Bail hard," I implored Mike and Gary, trying to scoop with my hands. Suddenly the motor died.

Mike, Gary, and I knelt by the engine. We looked it over as best we could, rocking and rolling. Out of gas! We had to try and siphon gas from the small drum into the motor tank in these rough seas. But someone had forgotten to bring the siphon! Warning everyone not to smoke and not to sit in the bilge water, we sloshed gas haphazardly into the tank, spilling half of it into the rowboat. One of the women began to moan from seasickness. When there seemed enough gas to make it to Panajachel, we choked the engine and got it started again. Slowly, painfully, we inched back to town, sun scalding us, water freezing us. Deep down, I was furious. We were breaking every rule in the book for safety, and it was all due to neglect, ineptitude, and poor planning. We'd be lucky to make it through the week alive.

Back at the dock, I urged the Guatemalans to attend to the gas supply then and there and get everything ready for an early departure next day.

"We can't afford to take another chance like this," I said, "and we'll never finish in a week unless we spend more time on the lake." Shamefaced, they agreed.

The next day was almost a repeat of the day before. A late start, trouble with the motor, more sunburn and seasickness, a scary ride home. Our census was way behind schedule. Worse than that, we'd counted less than a dozen birds from San Pedro all the way around to San Lucas—two-thirds of the lake—whereas once I'd known of thirty to forty pocs in that region.

Our third day called for a trip across the main body of the lake to reconnoiter between San Lucas and Santiago Atitlán. It seemed far too hazardous to try with a full boatload, so three people dropped out. Gary took two of the students to make recordings of grebe calls. These would later be turned into sonograms. By analyzing these graphlike reproductions of poc soundwaves, he could tell whether giant grebe vocalizations were identical to common pied-billed grebes or not. It was an important step in deciding whether the two species were truly separate or closely related. Such information could help us with captive breeding efforts.

When we returned from censusing the southern shore of Lake Atitlán, it was three o'clock. The old boat had given us its usual share of problems that day. As I stepped onto the dock, a wave of dizziness washed over me. I walked into the shade of a jacaranda tree in front of the hotel and lay down on the cool grass. My forehead was burning hot. The sun had fried us all, but I was the worst off, coming from an Adirondack winter with my blond hair and pale skin. As I lay there panting and sweating, a sudden decision formed inside. I simply would *not* put up with working like this any longer. Traveling in a dangerous boat with an undependable motor, sitting exposed all day long to the elements, having to translate, teach, and interpret data. There was no fun, no pleasure in our togetherness. Everyone had his or her own agenda. We seemed to be pulling against each other. I still sensed some suspician on the part of the Guatemalans. I felt as though my years of research had become a mockery. Especially mailing the motor parts, which never arrived. Tomorrow I'd rent my *own* boat at my *own* expense, a good engine, a captain, a sun canopy, and start doing things right!

Fighting off another wave of dizziness, I walked to the public docks. There were boats for rent there and I knew the dock master. Before the afternoon was over, I'd contracted for a speedboat with a 100 h.p. Mercury to meet me at 6 A.M. *on the dot.*

That night at our group supper I announced, "Anyone who wants to come with me in a good, safe, fast boat tomorrow and finish the census is welcome. The most important thing we have to do is establish how many pocs are left. We've only counted twenty-five so far. Let's divide up. Those who want to work with Mike on captive breeding—checking aquatic food organisms, reed beds, and any possible limiting factors—can stay here and use the other boat. It'll be safer with fewer people in it."

Gary, one student, and the INAFOR man voted to go with me. Then, the young official told us, with embarrassment, that our gas was used up. He had no funds to buy more. Gary, Mike, and I looked at each other. Gray reached in his pocket and pulled out some money. "Take this, please," he said. "We brought extra funds for any contingency."

I turned away, upset. It wasn't the minor official's fault. But our whole trip could have ended right there and then if the fuel supply had run out.

All night I tossed and turned, feverish and exhausted. At the break of day, I dragged myself from bed and pulled on my field clothes. Maybe things would improve today, I thought. With the fast boat we could finish our census and still have time to stop at the old refuge. I was anxious to measure the drop in lake level against the refuge walls. That was a known place where I had pictures and data on the former water level.

The speedboat came on time and the four of us zipped away across the lake. Since we were planning to wrap up the census in the Bay of Santiago Atitlán, we passed close to Xecamuc Bay. "Let's stop here first. I want to show you all the old refuge," I shouted above the wind.

We tied up to the dock and I carried one oar and a length of rope over to the empty refuge. "Gary, would you hold this rope at the top of the wall, please?" I asked. "Now you take the other end

After the earthquake of 1976, Lake Atitlán dropped abruptly and continually. Here, in 1984, it had gone down sixteen feet. By 1989, it was another three feet lower.

and pull it taut and horizontal with the ground," I said to the student. I gave the INAFOR man the oar and placed him at the end of the rope, holding the oar vertically. I was then able to measure the perpendicular distance, using my eyes as a level and my body as a known length (five foot, four inches). By repeating the process until we came to the water's edge, we came up with sixteen feet. A sixteen-foot drop in eight years!

Shaking our heads, we walked up to the old visitors center and office-dormitory. The rooms were empty, filthy with dust, debris, and dried cornstalks. I was ashamed to show it, remembering how it had looked the day of the inauguration. It appeared the rooms had been used. But who could have stayed there? In front of the complex, I saw a strange mound of sandbags piled at the edge of the terrace.

"Gary, look here. What can this be?" I called. He came running out and stared at the heap. Then we saw another mound on the refuge wall above the water.

"Those are machinegun emplacements," the student muttered. The other two men nodded in agreement.

The INAFOR official shrugged. "Probably the Army or Navy was defending the lake against rebels," he surmised. "Since this is government property, as well as the first 200 meters of land surrounding the lake, they may have made a reciprocal tradeoff from the Ministry of Agriculture to the Ministry of Defense."

Reacting to what my face must have expressed, he said, "Anna, no one cares about wildlife during times of civil unrest. That's why our department has no money for gas, no good boats, no encouragement for our programs. That's why we had to appeal to your country for help with the pocs."

I began looking around for other signs of military occupation. The small stone temple facing Chuitinamit was still intact but someone had whitewashed a large cross upon it. A barbed wire fence separated the visitors center from the land behind. I stared up toward my *ranchito*, hoping to catch a glimpse of it. But the intervening fields had grown up with weeds and scraggly bushes. I didn't feel right taking time to run up there on a personal matter, so I could only hope to squeeze in a visit before leaving Guatemala.

Seeing the temple defaced reminded me of the stone stela Armando and I had brought to the refuge. I hurried down to the terrace, which once stood at water's edge. It was empty. I scanned the cornfields surrounding me. Nothing. How could an eight-hundred-pound stone piece disappear?

Near where the stela had stood I came upon a metal grill lying flush with the stone terrace. Beneath it was a rock-lined, rectangular pit about ten feet deep. Empty. Perplexed, I walked into the cornfields where several Indian men were hoeing their crops.

"*Óla,*" I called. "*Qué tal?*" I waved with a friendly look.

The men stopped working and looked at me. Slowly two of them approached, touching their sombreros politely. I asked them if they knew anything about the stela or the pit. They stared at me and said nothing.

"Don't you remember the poc refuge?" I asked. "It was here before you planted your cornfields. The water covered all this," I indicated with a sweep of my hand. "It came right to the top of the wall. We had our inauguration in June 1968 right there and Father Roberto gave the benediction one foot above the water."

The men maintained a stony silence.

"There was a stela right here—from Chuitinamit. I brought it down to the refuge. I'm Mama Poc."

There was a flash of recognition on one man's face, and he spoke excitedly to the other. Then he came closer and said softly, "They took it away."

"*Who* took it away?"

"I do not know. Just one day some people came and took it away."

"And the pit?" I pressed him. "Who made that?"

"The military—for the prisoners."

"Oh, my God! You mean prisoners were kept down there?"

"Yes."

No matter how much I pressed him, he wouldn't say more. I imagined how it was—people packed in like sardines, unable to lie down, sit down, urinate, defecate.

As I was staring back toward the pit, the other man sidled closer and said, "Father Roberto is no longer here."

"You mean he went back to Oklahoma?" It had probably been the most sensible thing to do, I thought, with this area becoming so volatile.

"No, Doña Anna. He was shot at the altar of his church." At that, I started sobbing. So much love and caring and cooperation had gone into building the refuge. So many people who had helped and donated their services, including the tall, blond Oklahoman. Now this. My hysteria grew. By the time the INAFOR man reached me, I was totally out of control. He took me in his arms. "Anna, it was war. None of it is right, but it was war," was all he said.

We finished the census that day, chastened and subdued. The final results were between fifty and sixty pocs. The reed beds were still about eight and a half miles long but much thinner in width—a 50 percent reduction.

That night, I couldn't eat. I went to bed at dusk and took my temperature: 103° F. I threw up. Memories of sunstroke flooded my mind. It was either that or heat stroke due to those long hours in the uncovered rowboat, or the terrible strain. Sleep brought horrible nightmares of guns and pits and dead pocs. I couldn't go back on the lake again.

At 3 A.M. I rose and stepped out on the balcony. Perhaps the night air would cool my forehead. It was completely quiet. Only a whippoorwill wailed up on the hill. I leaned against the railing and half closed my eyes. Suddenly there was a rustle.

I glanced downward and saw a dark figure slipping through the trees edging the hotel. At once the peril of our position hit me. We were three American scientists and two Guatemalan men (the women had taken inexpensive rooms in town), completely alone in a large tourist hotel. Every room was empty, except ours on the second floor. The hotel was located in a coffee grove inside a canyon apart from Panajachel. Only a rough dirt road connected it to the paved road to Sololá. There was one telephone and one night watchman in the lobby. That was all. We were sitting ducks. A rush of terror flashed through me. Grabbing the railing to keep from swaying, I watched the figure edge around the pool. A flashlight shone briefly on the patio. Then it was dark. The figure came into the hotel alone.

Relief at realizing that this person was the night watchman was just as strong as my fear. I trembled in the night, trying to regain control. When I finally went back in my room, I had the powerful feeling that I must leave Guatemala. Much as I hated to leave the team before finishing our work, my deepest instincts and poor health dictated my decision.

Next morning, I phoned my doctor in Guatemala City and received instructions what to do. Rehydration, rest, an antibiotic. He forbade me to go outdoors. "Please help me," I said. "Book the first flight that you can get to Miami with Pan Am. I'll explain later." Finally, I rang up another friend in the city who regularly came to the lake on weekends. "Can you pick me up at the hotel tomorrow and take me back to the city?" I begged. "It's urgent."

The group had gone off for the day, realizing I was too ill to join them. When they came back that night, I told them I was leaving.

"I feel badly to go, but actually I've shown you everything you need to know about pocs, censusing, and the lake," I said. "From now on Mike and Gary can make plans for captive breeding. Maybe the rest of you can find ways to help the grebes. Hopefully, you'll have time to drive down to the Auto Safari Park and check out the ponds if Atitlán doesn't work out as a safe spot."

Reactions were mixed. Gary and Mike agreed I was right to

go, considering my health, and the fact I couldn't work outside anymore. The Guatemalans were amazed, disappointed, and even sheepish! How strange, I thought, after they had acted cool and suspicious before. Much later, I found out why. The reason was so ridiculous as to be hilarious. Somehow some of them had gotten the crazy notion that I had come to steal pocs. Either to take them back to the States, or to the private Auto Safari Park, where the Guatemalan government would have no control. Somewhere along the line, signals had gotten mixed. Perhaps it was my grebe talk at San Diego; the correspondence with Berger; or our surprise dawn flight to Auto Safari Park. Something had caused the wrong interpretation. When I finally got sick, they realized I really wasn't a poc 'napper.

Three days after my heat stroke, I was on a flight to Miami.

18
Going, Going, Going...

THE TEAM FINISHED OUT their week's assignment, much to my relief, without mishap. After I'd left, they decided on a two-pronged approach to save the pocs. One avenue was an immediate attempt to cross-foster the pocs with commons; the other to find an ornithologist to begin experimental captive breeding.

The first procedure meant letting *common* pied-bills incubate and raise *giant* grebe eggs and chicks. Since the two species were closely related, it was possible that their incubation patterns and needs would be quite similar. The obvious tactic was to find and remove a clutch of poc eggs at Lake Atitlán and slip them under nesting commons. Then, to hope the "adopted parents" did as good a job of rearing the young as their "biological" ones.

The team took two poc eggs from larger-than-normal clutches and transferred them to Laguna del Pino, a small recreational lake with reeds and cattails owned mostly by the government and within an easy bus ride from Guatemala City. It was one of the few places where commons had been found nesting regularly in Guatemala. However, cross-fostering was a chancy job. No one was exactly sure how old the poc eggs were and when they'd pip.

Nor was it known with certainty when the foster parents had begun incubating their own clutch of eggs.

One poc egg hatched. The chick was fed and led out on the water by its adopted parents for a few days. It was an auspicious beginning. Volunteers from local conservation groups and the Peace Corps kept surveillance. Nine days later, the young disappeared. Observations were discontinued. It was thought that largemouth bass had devoured the chick. Or that the disturbances of humans using this lake (motorboats and paddleboats, plus swimmers) were responsible.

When I had first learned of this attempt back home, I was dead-set against it, although the other two scientists approved of the experiment. There was no thorough year-round environmental study of this new lake to refer to. No one knew what food was available, what predators existed, or what other perils lurked there for a young poc. To put chicks on this other lake with largemouth bass present could be dangerous. Also, there was no restricted area, no sanctuary where the birds could be safe from people. Indeed, Laguna del Pino was one of the sites I'd visited twenty years before and crossed off my list of "Possible Places."

The second alternative—captive breeding at François' Auto Safari Park—seemed the wiser and safer solution. As Mike had pointed out before, the park had electricity and buildings where incubators could be operated, and there was a small outdoor water tank in which the chicks could learn to fish before being put in the ponds. The reeds he'd just planted were growing lustily so there'd be plenty of habitat available. Moreover, François' ranch enjoyed complete security. The best part, as I saw it, was François himself. He was committed to saving the giant grebes and was enormously generous.

The only catch seemed to be—who had the "right" to breed and keep pocs? My hunch, gleaned from the behavior of my Guatemalan teammates, was that a "turf battle" between government officialdom and private enterprise was stalling the start of captive breeding at Auto Safari Park.

In 1985, Gary, his wife, Dr. Deborah Buitron, and a graduate student went back to Lake Atitlán and counted fifty-six adult birds. When an endangered population reaches fifty individuals or less, its chances of survival are minimal for many reasons. Wild animals, depending on which species, have psychological as well as physical and ecological needs. If numbers drop too low, a certain breeding stimulus derived from having plenty of other males and females around may be lost. Colonial nesters in particular, like herons, egrets, and ibis, need lots of company to reproduce well.

It may also become difficult to find a mate if distances become great and habitat is fragmented. This is an ongoing problem with jaguars, for example, in Central America, as multinational corporations and local colonists chop down tracts of virgin tropical rain forests for lumber, pasture, and farms. Then, too, a population sometimes loses all of its females *or* all its males.

This occurred with the dusky seaside sparrow in Florida. In the twilight hours of that species' life, only five males remained along the west coast. Some of the species' genetic heritage was maintained, however, by cross-breeding the five males with females of Scott's seaside sparrow (a close relative). The last male bird, "Orange Band," died in captivity of old age in 1987.

Most important, at low population numbers, a species loses its genetic variability. This means it loses its options for survival. Poor qualities, found in recessive genes, may surface or increase. Other useless or debilitating characteristics may appear and further reduce chances for survival. This is one of the concerns with the captive breeding program for the remaining twenty-odd wild California condors. Their gene pool is very small.

My every instinct said that if we were to have success with captive breeding giant grebes and avoid the problems of Laguna del Pino we had to gamble: go in soon, catch three pairs, take them down the coast to Auto Safari Park, and start an intensive program immediately. There wasn't time to mess around.

Finally, at the very end of 1985, an agreement was signed between François and INAFOR, giving him official permission to take pocs or poc eggs to his ranch and try captive breeding there.

But other problems prevailed. Because of an almost total lack of know-how on how to raise young grebes of *any* kind, whatever was tried had to be done on an experimental basis. For example, no one knew the correct temperature at which to incubate poc eggs. No one knew the exact length of incubation. No one knew how often to turn the eggs in the incubator, or at what humidity to keep them. Only a mother poc knew that.

The philosophical question was: Should we take chances with giant grebes when there were so few left? Or should we experiment on common pied-bills? A lot of mistakes could be avoided by trying to raise common chicks first. But then, could we afford to wait the three or four years such studies would take before transferring the new knowledge to pocs? How much time did they have left? My guess was not much.

Then another of those "super flukes" with which the poc project had been blessed over time took place. A young woman, Susan MacVean, was found to conduct the breeding program. She was a candidate for a master's degree in wildlife biology at Colorado State University (my old alma mater for a M.S.) and had written to Herb Raffaele asking for support in her studies of common pied-bills in Colorado. This was not a priority project for the Fish and Wildlife Service, thus funds were not available, but Herb immediately thought of the giants in Guatemala. As it turned out, Susan had lived for years in Guatemala and spoke fluent Spanish. Her parents still worked there, and she was ecstatic about going. Connecting with François, and with assistance from the Service, she set up an incubator and lab at Auto Safari Park near the ponds. The decision was made to stay on the conservative side. Working only with hunches offered by her thesis advisor and plenty of good common sense, Susan obtained a clutch of common eggs from Laguna del Pino and hatched out four eggs. One died upon pipping, but three lived on. Experimenting as she went, Susan raised the chicks single-handed to about four months of age—an amazing piece of research. Then she had to go back to college. The birds were left with a ranch employee who'd become devoted to the project. Over the first year, one common grebe and two females remained.

Susan had come back and raised another small clutch of commons the following year. Her final step and goal, after she completed course work, would be to raise poc eggs. If these chicks made it to adulthood and formed breeding pairs on the ponds, their young would form a reserve population which could eventually be released on any suitable lake, or reintroduced to Lake Atitlán.

Meanwhile, Gary discovered nylon fishnets set close to the reed beds. These seemed to be a major potential cause of poc mortality in the wild. Use of nets was a fairly new phenomenon on Lake Atitlán. Years ago, nylon nets were simply not available in Guatemala, and none of the Indian fishermen could have afforded them anyway. But now nets were cheap and people were eager to catch more fish. They could double their take using nets instead of hooks. I recalled Edgar saying to me in 1980 that he worried that the use of nets might overtax the fishery. It was already at a low from the introduced predatory bass, and there was no protected season during fish spawning. Moreover, there were *no* controls on the numbers of fish which could be taken, what kinds, where and how long nets could be set out, or how often they must be checked.

Deborah Buitron found a dead ruddy duck in one net set right in front of a reed bed. The net showed signs of having been in the water for days. If there were dozens of nets in use by the one hundred fishermen operating in the Bay of Santiago Atitlán, there could conceivably be many pocs drowned each year. I already knew that fishing nets are dangerous to many diving ducks and loons. Indeed, fishermen have recovered drowned birds enmeshed in nets at depths of over one hundred feet. And Gary had found hundreds of drowned western grebes in Manitoba nets, previously.

But how could this be stopped? People were hungry for protein. The Indian population around Atitlán had more than *doubled* during my twenty years. It was expected to *triple*—27,039 in 1950 to 82,000 by 1990—based on a 2.8 percent annual increment. At the same time, the yearly average income had fallen.

No one could stop net fishing unless a presidential decree was issued and wardens were posted to enforce it. Someone had to champion this cause and work out a careful, considerate compromise between fishermen and the resource, just as we'd done years ago with the reeds and reed cutters. But it wouldn't be so easy this time. Pressures on the lake and its natural resources were mounting daily. There was no money available. Pedro, even though he was the official warden for Lake Atitlán National Park, did not yet have the experience, education, or clout to push through a new law.

Looking at these problems from a long-distance perspective, back in the States, I didn't see much hope for the giant grebes.

19

Gone

R. HERB RAFFAELE'S CALL was a bombshell. "We need you to go down to Guatemala again," he said. "Dr. Laurie Hunter, the biologist we're supporting to check into the poc decline, says she's seen grebes fly!"

"Fly?" I gulped. "But they *can't* fly. I proved that aerodynamically years ago."

"*Some* of them are flying," Herb persisted. "What's more, Laurie has found grebes breeding outside the March-to-May reproductive period you described. And she says some birds look a lot like the commons on Laguna del Pino."

"Weird!" was all I could say.

"The numbers are still slipping," Herb said. "Could you possibly go down, Anne, and make a count? Take a look? See what you think?"

I was silent for several seconds. Did I really want to go back? As if guessing my thoughts, Herb said, "The World Wildlife Fund boat is back in business. Extra funds were sent down by World Wildlife Fund USA, to fix it. Pedro is in charge at the lake. You'll find Laurie a very competent ornithologist and she speaks Spanish. There'll be just the three of you."

Convinced, I agreed to go for one week. Once again, my twenty-one-year commitment won out.

Later, as I watched the WWF boat knife through satin-smooth water at dawn toward my hotel balcony—the same room in fact where I'd stayed two years before—I felt good about being back in Guatemala. Pedro was driving, his moon face and black hair recognizable from afar. A young woman in khakis with long brown hair sat in the bow. I had box breakfasts and coffee ready to go. With luck, we could complete the census in three days and have two more days to go to Auto Safari Park. Maybe I'd even have a free day to see my hut and my roofless chalet.

I hurried from the room and down the stairs. Early rising tourists were already on their way into the dining room. I heard smatterings of Italian, German, French, and clipped English; once again hotel rooms were full of Europeans. Few Americans ventured to Guatemala, however, due to bad press. Out on the patio I glanced right and saw the enormous hulk of condominium towering above the trees. It was empty, abandoned, and bankrupt. I wondered what would become of that tremendous eyesore on the landscape.

The boat slowed and settled into the water gracefully. Pedro tied it to a pier and jumped onto the dock. I raced to meet him and gave him a bear hug. Still shy, he barely touched me, but his eyes glowed with pleasure. "Doña Anna," he said, "welcome back."

"Yes, welcome," added the woman who had also jumped out and was extending her hand to me. "I'm Laurie Hunter."

She looked sensible and pleasant. "Hi. I'm glad to meet you, Laurie."

Pedro handed my equipment and the food down into the boat. I stowed it under the rear seats and looked the boat over. It was years since I'd seen it. The blue color of the fiberglass was faded and the seats were cracked and slit. One window was broken. But it was the same boat Edgar and I had purchased together, and it was still running.

We started censusing at once, working east from Panajachel. "Let me know what you think, the very first poc we see," said Laurie. "I'm going nuts trying to figure out what's going on here."

But in the next fifteen miles of shoreline we never saw a bird. Most of the reeds were gone. It was a sobering morning. Finally, that afternoon near a point of rocks at San Lucas, a male swam out of a cattail bed. Large, brownish, slow to dive, he looked every inch a poc.

"It's a giant grebe all right," I announced after a long look with my binoculars. "And he answered the tape recording as well."

"Yes," Laurie said, "but Gary found that commons will respond to taped poc territorial calls, and vice versa. Apparently the sonograms showed they have quite similar calls."

We cruised farther along, taking note of chalets and reeds, as well as searching for grebes. The next bird we found, near the old refuge, seemed very wary. He called and called but would not approach. "I *think* it's a poc," I said, "but he's kind of a funny color."

"I've seen this one fly a short ways," replied Laurie.

The next bird called at a higher pitch than I remembered, and the call was shorter. This wasn't going to be easy, I saw. Could these be common pied-bills which had eased out the giants, or could they have interbred with the pocs to produce a hybrid? "Let's keep going. Make a complete census. Compare notes with what you feel are *not* pocs and what I think *are.*" I said. "But, as long as we're right by the old refuge, I think we should stop and measure the drop in the lake level again."

Using the old-fashioned technique with rope and oar, we found that Atitlán had now suffered an eighteen-foot drop in the ten years since the earthquake!

When we stopped for lunch at Laurie's rented cottage near Santiago Atitlán, we considered all angles of the problem. "The only way we can tell for sure," declared Laurie, "is to trap the birds and measure their bill lengths and weigh them."

"That's true," I agreed. "We know the sizes and weights of the giant specimens I sent to the States in 1965, and we have hundreds of measurements from commons taken all over the States and even in Central America. A bit of statistical analysis would show if these are truly different birds, if they fall into the parameters for pocs or commons."

"As soon as we get our final count," said Laurie, "I think I'll begin trapping."

"That's a tough job," I warned her, "and it could potentially kill birds. How will you do it?"

"Gary suggested I use nest traps."

"Yes, they'll work, but if there are eggs or young you could sacrifice them with all the commotion and by removing their parents. We can't imperil the population like that."

"Have you a better way?" she countered.

I spent an hour showing her the slip knot technique, which had worked when we wanted to catch pocs for the refuge. "This is guaranteed to be successful," I said, "but it's a hell of a lot of work. Remember, Pedro?"

He nodded. He had been young then and just starting to help Edgar, but he was the only person at Atitlán today who carried the knowledge of what Operation Protection Poc had done. That reminded me of something.

"Pedro," I said, "would you be interested in attending a short course on wildlife management and conservation for a month in Mexico City?"

He looked surprised, but nodded yes.

"I've been thinking for some time that it would do you good to learn more about natural resources conservation and to meet other Latins involved in this work. You won't feel so alone then.

I'm ready to sponsor you for the next course coming up, and I'll bet Laurie would, too."

"Of course," she said right away.

"Herb Raffaele told me about one over the phone," I said. "I think it's this summer in June. If we work fast, maybe we could get the paperwork done in time to get you accepted."

"But how would I pay for it?" Pedro asked. "I earn about 120 quetzals a month, and that's not enough for even a plane trip, even one way."

"Of course it isn't," I said, "but you'd get a scholarship from the U.S. Fish and Wildlife Service, which should pay all your costs. And if it doesn't, I'll make up the rest. The Service sends several students each year. You're a 'natural,' Pedro."

"He's a 'natural' all right," agreed Laurie, "but he'll run into problems in the city office. There are new people in power and their priorities are changing. I'm finding less and less cooperation on the poc project. Emphasis is being placed on saving natural areas, not endangered species. If it wasn't for U.S. Fish and Wildlife, I couldn't continue here. They're paying my expenses and a small stipend and bought me a jeep. Look out there."

I could see a smart red and white Toyota four-wheel parked behind the cottage.

"It's cost them over $30,000 to provide a biologist and vehicle to Guatemala. The jeep will stay here when I leave, and one of the conservation groups will use it."

"When do you think you'll go back to the States?" I asked.

"It all depends on the numbers we census and what we find—pocs or not pocs," she answered enigmatically.

At the end of the third day we had counted thirty-two grebes. There were also 401 chalets. The habitat loss remained between 70 and 80 percent. Laurie told me she had also counted thirty-two birds in her earlier census. This meant we had exact proof of the decline. We looked at each other sadly. We were looking at extinction.

"Do your trapping," I advised her. "Let's see what you find. Meanwhile, I'll go down to François' place and check on the new captive breeding program. I'm anxious to see Susan's hatchlings."

Secretly, I was afraid that her victory might be short-lived. The rate at which the pocs were disappearing would make it touch and go whether she would even find any eggs to incubate and raise. And if Laurie's hunch was right—that some of the thirty-two were really commons or hybrids—Susan might never get to finish her thesis.

After visiting the ranch, I went back to Lake Atitlán to spend a day at my land. It had been seven years since I'd laid eyes on my backcountry home. When Pedro and I landed at the old dock, I noted with relief that the sandbags were gone. Taking a firm grip on my nerves, I walked up to the visitors center. It was swept clean but was still completely surrounded with barbed wire fences.

"Land has gotten so valuable around the lake," Pedro explained, "that everything down to the water and behind the old refuge has been purchased. There are something like fifteen chalets around the bay now."

Together we walked down to the terrace. The grill was still there. The pit lay darkly beneath my feet. Tears rolled down my face as I turned to Pedro and said, "Someday someone has to fill that hole up, stone by stone, pebble by pebble."

He nodded impassively, then followed me back up to the *ranchito*. My little forest had grown up fast. Mature pines sighed in the wind and large eucalypti cast their shade. The view toward the lake was more shielded. The whole place felt green, private, and secluded, despite the many chalets. Thank God for Edgar's seedlings, I thought. The hut still stood with its clay pot atop the grass roof, and behind it the four walls of my *ranchito*. The chimney rose forlornly into the sky, no smoke wafting from its opening.

"Where's Salvador?" I asked Pedro. "Why isn't he here?"

"Salvador died three or four years ago," Pedro said.

Surprised and curious, I asked, "Then who's been taking care of my place? It looks pretty tidy around here."

"Salvador's nephew, Alejandro," said Pedro. "I told him you were coming today. He may be bringing his wife to meet you."

Sure enough, a few minutes later a young man, the spitting image of Salvador, threaded his way through my woods, followed by his bashful, buck-toothed wife. She held the hand of a two-year-old boy and was pregnant. Their clothes were in tatters.

I hastened toward this little group and shook hands. "Thank you for coming and thank you for watching over my land. I haven't seen you since you were a small boy coming here to help your uncle. Are you planting corn here, as Salvador did?"

Alejandro pointed down toward the lake, where a cornfield quivered in the breeze. "Good," I said. "You can certainly use the soil and stay in the hut when I'm not here. That was the deal I had with him, in exchange for keeping an eye on the place. Any extra work you do for me, I'll pay you for."

We all went inside the roofless building to see what needed to be done. The floor was smooth and beautifully made with cut volcanic rocks, just as I'd remembered. The walls were over seven feet high, straight and true. On one side an indentation had been made where shelves could be set for kitchenware. In the far corner, Edgar's fireplace and chimney sat cozily. He had rounded the rock face so it gave a pleasing dimension to the room. The hearth was small but well built to draw.

"Look, Doña Anna," Pedro said, pointing above the hearth. There, cemented into a chimney front, was an ancient Mayan stone in the shape of a small, spirited animal.

"How wonderful," I cried. "What is it, Pedro? How did it get here?"

"Don Edgar placed it there himself," he answered. "One of the workmen found it while breaking rocks. It's a little cat—a *gatita*. Edgar asked me to show it to you, in case he wasn't here when you came back to Guatemala. He said it was a present for your house."

My eyes misted over. How like Edgar. Not only did he know how much I valued the Maya culture, but *gatita* was a nickname he'd once used in a joking way. He said I reminded him of a kitten or small cat because of the quick way I walked, talked, jumped, and did everything else. His thousand-year-old memento meant more to me than the whole chalet.

"Pedro," I said. "Can you help me get a roof on this house and a door, windows, and a sleeping loft installed? Would you be willing to oversee this? Of course, I'll give you a commission in addition to paying for the workmen and materials."

"Yes, Doña Anna. I worked with Edgar on his chalet at Chuitinamit and other places. Tell me what you'd like."

Although it had been seven years since I'd seen this place, my imagination had finished it, decorated it, and lived in it many times over. I knew exactly. In just a few minutes, we'd decided on another bunch grass roof with rustic branches for rafters, a loft, shelves, homemade table, desk, and four chairs. While we discussed the job, Alejandro, his wife, and child squatted in a corner, all eyes, watching everything I did.

When Pedro left to get paper and pencil down in the boat, Alejandro and his wife stood up and hesitantly approached me. I sensed they wanted to talk about something. I smiled warmly and said, "What do you think, Alejandro? Will this be a nice *ranchito* when it's done?"

"*Sí,* Doña Anna," he said politely. Then he said, "Doña Anna, before you go, will you look in the hut next door and see what's in the two drums under the bed? Salvador told me to always guard them, but I was afraid to look inside."

"Sure. We can do that right now," I said. But then the young mother reached out and touched my arm. She glanced at Alejandro and mumbled something swiftly in Tzutujil. He nodded and walked away, saying, "My wife wants to ask you something, Doña Anna."

I took her little hand and drew her into a patch of sunlight on the stone floor and sat down. I could see she was scared.

"Tell me now. What's bothering you?" I said.

In a sing-song, stilted Spanish that left me half-wondering what she meant, the young mother told me she had four children. Two of them were in the village with their grandmother. She had a lot of work taking care of them. Corn was expensive. Alejandro did not grow enough here to feed the family. He had no other land. And now another child was coming. "How do I stop having babies?" she asked.

No one had ever asked me for this kind of help before, but obviously she thought an American woman must know these things. I stared at the girl, no more than twenty years old. As best I could, I explained about contraception. First, I described the pill.

"Ah," she said. "But we don't have enough money to buy pills every month."

"Won't the government give them to you?" I asked.

"No," she said sadly. "Here in Guatemala it is not allowed."

Then I explained about an IUD, and suggested she go to a clinic to be fitted.

She rolled her eyes and blushed. "My husband would not permit me," she said. "A Maya woman will not let any man touch her there, even if he is a doctor."

Mentally I checked off options, a diaphragm, sponge, and foams. I mentioned a condom.

Again, she shook her head. "How afford them?"

Now we were down to one choice, given what I knew about birth control, and that was the rhythm method. I explained. I even offered to leave her my little calendar when I left.

"A calendar? What is that?" she asked curiously. "We do not have one of those in my hut. I do not read or write."

"Surely you must have some way of keeping track of the days, fiestas, Christmas and Easter."

"We know. The village elders tell us, the mayor tells us. The sun tells us. The Maya have a different year—only 260 days."

Nothing I could suggest seemed to be a solution. Here I was a Ph.D., a widely traveled woman, and supposedly a wise person from the most technological nation in the world, yet I couldn't even tell a Third World woman how to control her own biological destiny. She looked at me hopefully. All I could do was shake my head. Outside my back window, the line where cornfields met forest had pushed much higher since I had come to the lake. Edgar had asked me once, "Where will people go to plant corn when the line gets to the top?"

The line was getting closer all the time. And there didn't seem to be much I could do—either for the pocs or for the human population. As a conservationist, I felt like a failure.

Pedro was coming back. The young woman stood up and went out to where her husband and child waited. I stood up wearily and met Pedro. "While you're taking the measurements," I said, "I'll go into the hut and check out my drums."

Inside the shadowy room, I reached under the plank bed. Spider webs and dust clung to the cardboard sides of the drums. Alejandro helped me unsnap the lid bands and pry open the tops. There was a soft rustle in the corner. No doubt the wood rat still had his home here. I smiled.

I started pulling out old clothes—khaki shirts and pants, beat-up sombreros, sneakers, a khaki poncho, a khaki ground cloth. I could give these to the family to help out a little. Alejandro stood back in alarm. "Doña Anna, what are those?" he gasped.

"Why they are the field uniforms and rain gear I used to wear with Operation Protection Poc," I said, throwing them into a heap on the floor. I reached in and found the old styrofoam decoys and some fish netting. But Alejandro's face was ashen. "What's the matter?" I asked in alarm.

He did nothing but point at the pile of clothes.

"Pedro," I called. "Can you come here and help us?"

He walked into the hut and stared at the floor. "Where did

those come from?" he asked harshly.

"What's going on?" I cried. "All I did was pull out these faded old uniforms I used to wear back in the 1960s."

"But those are the same colors the guerrillas are using now," muttered Pedro. "We must burn them at once."

"Not again!" I groaned, flashing back to the day twenty years ago when we'd terrorized the Indians of Santa Catarina in our new Operation Protection Poc outfits.

Alejandro was still shaking when Pedro grabbed up the clothes and threw them out the door. *"Leña* (firewood)," he ordered. "Make a fire." Then he turned to me and said grimly, "If any soldiers had come into this hut, opened these drums, and found khaki clothes here, whoever was in the hut would have been suspect and probably shot."

The twist of fate settled on me in all its enormity. I could have sentenced the two guardians to death in complete innocence. Now everything in the drums was tainted. Before it was time to leave, we had burned, chopped, smashed, or buried it all. There was nothing left of Operation Poc except Pedro and the boat, my field notes, and my memories. There was nothing left of my political naiveté either.

Always I'd considered myself nonpolitical; my concern had always been more for the natural world than the sociopolitical arena. But now I saw that ethics and politics are critical to the safekeeping of the environment, as much so as the natural activity of soils and precipitation. The crushing blows of the deaths of Edgar and Father Roberto, the pit, and the drums, finally forced me to become politically aware and shook me out of my ecological preoccupation. While I doubt that I will ever become a political activist, I now realize that a good scientist must recognize social and political issues.

What remained was the bitter recognition that the entire time I'd been working in Guatemala, a relentless covert conflict had been underway between the military and insurgents. Almost a quarter of a century old, this civil war, which I'd been scarcely aware of, had left tens of thousands dead, disappeared, or displaced. Ultimately I was forced to acknowledge it as it touched my work and life. Although conflict had lessened at this time, it still flared up in remote corners of the country and at unexpected times. Peace seemed a long way from returning to Guatemala.

As I got ready to leave for Panajachel, I wondered whether I would have done anything differently in trying to save the giant grebes. I don't think so. So much of it came from the heart, as well as the head. I also wondered if the Maya living here 1,000 years ago had ever had to contend with such human craziness. The only answer was the doves in my avocado tree cooing softly and sadly as I headed back to the States.

20
A New Beginning

LAURIE WROTE ME at my cabin in the Adirondacks that summer with sad news. "I trapped for three months after you left," she said, "and it was *hard*. The nest traps were the best technique, because if I caught one bird, my results were valid for two, that is, the mated pair. The six birds I captured, measured, and weighed were all well within the parameters for commons. That meant twelve of the thirty-two grebes we saw were *not* pocs. Moreover, grebe eggs measured at Lake Atitlán and Laguna del Pino were similar to each other and to eggs of commons in North America."

I stopped reading and stared out my picture window at the somber spruces dripping with rain. It was a fitting day to read what I knew was next.

"In June I finally announced that the giant grebes *as a species* are extinct. The government people didn't like it. They refused to believe it. Especially since the poc was chosen as official mascot, in caricature, for the Central American Olympics in 1986. Dr. Raffaele flew down later and met with key officials of the various conservation groups. He offered to support a *Guatemalan* biologist for the rest of the year to continue the investigation. That way they could see for themselves. The only conditions were that they hire this person permanently afterward and hold a conference on the pocs and their extinction."

I stopped reading and stood up to get firewood. Anything to hold back the sorrow that threatened to wash over me. Twenty birds, even *if* those remaining *were* pocs, would never make it without the most dedicated of efforts and tons of money. From what I knew of the California condor program, an endangered species down to twenty individuals could cost hundreds of thousands of dollars, employ dozens of technicians and scientists, and need the facilities of the most sophisticated zoo or wildlife laboratory. At what point was the effort no longer worthwhile? At what point did other social and ecological needs become more important? What was the cut-off point—economically and emotionally—when humans stopped fighting for an animal's life?

When the fire was going, I sat down to finish reading Laurie's letter. The rest held a bit of good news. "Pedro was sent to a Wildlife Management and Conservation course in Mexico City, as we'd hoped. He was chosen over many senior people on the INAFOR staff. Maybe our letters of recommendation carried some clout."

I lived through a new kind of grieving that summer. At times I contemplated rushing down to Guatemala and seeing if I could find a few more pocs among the twenty still identified. Then I would sit back and realize it would do no good. The infrastructure, money, and support system to save them was unavailable. Really, the only two questions that remained to be answered were: (1) Was the giant grebe really a separate species from the common pied-billed? and (2) Had the poc population been overwhelmed by the more adaptable commons until they were completely replaced, or had they disappeared by hybridizing?

Those were both questions I was unprepared and unqualified to answer. I had assiduously avoided taking any genetics courses at Cornell, thinking they'd never be of value in my work. Now I wished I had. Brand-new techniques exist to unravel the DNA pattern of a species: electrophoresis and mitochondrial DNA analysis, using muscle tissue, blood, or feather follicles of living birds; polymerase chain reaction and sequencing of DNA. But if all the pocs were gone, what material could be used to run a test?

Laurie had collected blood and tissue samples from a few of the "strange" grebes at Lake Atitlán and sent them to a zoologist at the University of Copenhagen, Dr. John Fjeldsa, for analysis, so that he can study the differences in DNA variation. But comparative data is needed from *real* pocs. Possibly the genetic clues are locked inside those four adult specimens at Cornell and Yale. Or in the two young females at the University of Michigan. Unfortunately, the formalin I used in the field to preserve them may have caused chemical changes in the DNA, thus making the test impossible or invalid. If nothing comes of this experiment, I feel that these six specimens are proof that once upon a time flightless giant grebes did live at Lake Atitlán.

That fall of 1986 my sorrow metamorphosed into a desire to make *something* positive come of this loss. A lesson might still be learned from the experience. I got to thinking of all the boxes at my cabin filled with letters, reports, negatives, and sketches of pocs and Operation Poc. Of course, I planned to give them to a museum of science. But wasn't there something else I could do with them? Gradually, the idea of donating an exhibit to Jorge Ibarra's Museum of Natural History developed.

I wrote to Herb Raffaele and asked if the Service would have any interest in funding an educational exhibit for Guatemala. "I think we can use the poc as a biological indicator of what went wrong over time at the lake and what's still going wrong. Not only can I let the people know how their symbol of conservation disappeared, but I can alert them of the dangers to Lake Atitlán."

Herb told me to write up a proposal. It was accepted. U.S. Fish and Wildlife Service, through the International Council for the Preservation of Birds, would fund the preparation of the exhibit, its transportation, and the actual installation at the Museum. But now I needed a *place* to prepare it. My cabin, still with less than 300 square feet of living space and no plumbing or electricity, was hardly the spot.

At the September meeting of the Adirondack Park Agency, a state land use planning agency for which I'd worked as a commissioner several years, I asked our Executive Director if I could possibly work there. I promised to not take space during work hours, to pay any staff I needed, and to trade an ecology lecture a week to the staff for the privilege of using these facilities. Moreover, I'd give full credit to the Agency in the exhibit. Once again, I was lucky.

So it came about that I spent the month of November mounting huge poster prints of my grebes, learning to make captions in English/Spanish on a Leroy lettering set, hanging my poc rug, and designing a habitat set with styrofoam grebes for the centerpiece. Snowy nights saw me working till midnight, my mind and heart 2,000 miles away from the wintry Adirondacks. Finally, it was done. Thirty-six large prints, along with all the rest, were packed in stout wooden crates and shipped to Guatemala.

I went down in March 1987 to retrieve the exhibit from Customs, store it at the Museum, and make preliminary arrangements for the inauguration. Plans were made to hold the opening in November, after the rainy season, but before Christmas. I took a flying trip to Lake Atitlán to measure the lake drop and see my *ranchito with* a roof, windows, and door. The lake had dropped nineteen feet in eleven years! Signs of pollution were growing— along the shores of Santiago Atitlán where women washed, in front of Panajachel where sewer pipes were suspected of entering the lake, on the shores with styrofoam and plastic litter. It was certainly time to save the lake even though we had lost the pocs.

21
Birds of Paradise

FOR A FEW MINUTES, the dark, stuffy lab of the Museum of Natural History became a ludicrous dressing room. The odor of moth balls, formaldehyde, and old feathers was overpowering. Spraying the air and myself liberally with perfume, I slipped on a ruffled skirt, lacy blouse, and high heels. All around the room mounted owls and hawks stared stonily down. From one dim corner, half a deer peered out, waiting for its back half to be stuffed and attached. A spider monkey with no tail hung haphazardly from a branch.

Car lights slanted across the window as vehicles began parking outside. In the intermittent glare, I groped in the gloom to pull free bobby pins and comb out snarls. My nails were filthy. No time to scrub them clean. I heard the faint tinkle of a marimba tuning up downstairs. Dark circles lay under my eyes, the result of ten days' nonstop work setting up the giant grebe exhibit and preparing for this inauguration night. Working mainly by feel, I dabbed on some mascara and stumbled toward the door.

The staccato tapping of stiletto heels sounded hurrying up the stairs. Diana appeared in a stunning red dress and called to me in her lilting Spanish. *"Apurate, Anna* (Hurry up, Anne)!" She

minced toward me with a wide smile and open arms. *"Qué guapa*
(How pretty)." Then the young executive secretary began bab-
bling nervously.

"The guests are streaming in. The waiters are starting to serve
drinks. But they had to put the champagne in a laundry tub full of
ice to chill it for later. I can't find the toilet paper and soap you
bought today for the rest rooms. Oh, and the extension cord to
your projector doesn't work. Anne—*hurry!"*

I caught her hand reassuringly and together we teetered down
the stone stairs in our impossible shoes toward a blaze of lights
and sounds. The rippling cords of "Xelaju" played by the
marimba band and the guests' polite chatter washed over me like
a mighty wave. The inauguration of the Giant Grebe exhibit had
begun!

Beatriz Zuñiga, Director of INGUAT (Guatemalan Institute
of Tourism), was smiling up at me warmly. She was co-hostess for
the inauguration and had made this gala event possible. Together
we had sent out 300 invitations with a handsome woodcut of a
giant grebe, hand-delivered by a special motorcycle team throughout Guatemala City. Her staff had worked with me to set up the
exhibit at the Museum (which had limited funds) and to hire a
catering service and band. The cost of the exhibit itself, which I'd
prepared in the States, was borne by the U.S. Fish and Wildlife
Service, Pan American section of the International Council for
Bird Preservation, and me.

Composing myself, I mixed into the crowd, shaking hands
with elegantly clad millionaires, polo players, photographers, and
Maya Indians in traditional costumes. From time to time I
hugged an old friend or whispered instructions to the Museum
staff. Nibbling at an hors d'oeuvres, I flowed with the press of
people along our exhibit route around a fern-filled patio at the
Museum's center. Its beginning was our masterpiece—a habitat
display of grebes and lake. A striking oil painting of Lake Atitlán
was framed by tall live reeds. We had cut them two days before

and placed them in huge clay pots. In front, on an aquamarine cloth simulating the lake, was a nest of giant grebes woven from reed and cattail fronds. On this, a female styrofoam grebe incubated two plastic eggs while a tiny black and white chick peeked out from her side. A handsome male "floated" on the blue water near her.

Two tape recorders lay beside the birds, inviting guests to play them. Over and over, the taped territorial call of an adult male grebe resounded above the party noise. At this sound, my heart tightened, remembering the sunny days and moonlit nights when I had followed the riveting, mysterious calls, trying to census pocs at the lake.

Around the corner, a row of big color Kodak prints were displayed upon a banner of aquamarine cloth which encircled the patio walls. It was as blue as Lake Atitlán; yet nothing artificial could even begin to duplicate the opalescent, shimmering, transparent blue of that great mile-high lake on a calm morning. The prints along one patio wall showed the natural history of these odd, flightless water birds. The next wall showed how our conservation campaign had been developed to protect the grebes. Between the two sections hung my brilliant red handwoven rug, made by local Indian weavers, featuring the stylized giant grebe. Also, there was a reproduction of that charming primitive painting in oils with the pocs, large as battleships, and a minuscule Indian holding a slingshot.

As I came to the auditorium door, I excused myself from well-wishers and eased inside. The faulty electrical cord snaked across the floor like a sinister orange snake. Without it, I would not be able to present my slide show tonight. An enormous tension filled me as I moved the plug to a new outlet and turned it around. Suddenly, the projector burst into life. Everything else seemed in order, yet worry stayed with me. Would there be enough chairs for all these people? Had I baked a sufficiently large chocolate chip cake—shaped like a giant grebe? Six boxes of cake

For the inauguration of the grebe exhibit in 1987, I made a chocolate chip cake in the shape of a poc.

mix was all I could squeeze into my overloaded suitcases. Plus six cans of chocolate icing. Would the icing hold the huge cake together? More importantly, could I give my forty-five-minute speech in Spanish intelligently and correctly?

I checked the podium and microphone. All okay. The remote control cord was in place and the auditorium wall had been freshly painted for a screen. Three hundred chairs were neatly lined up. The table looked lovely with dozens of glittering plastic champagne glasses, aquamarine plates, matching napkins, and candles. These, too, had been crammed into my bags and brought to Guatemala. A cheerful yellow floral arrangement stood as centerpiece, thanks to Mrs. Ibarra. Still my feeling of unease persisted.

I slid back into the crowd and completed the route around the patio. The last row of photos depicted environmental problems at

Lake Atitlán which affected both grebes and humans. One poster listed the ways in which these threats might be resolved; another, suggestions for the future management of the lake and its watershed.

Finally, in a small alcove filled with flowers, was the last part of the exhibit. I tried not to look that way. At that moment, Diana rushed up and announced that a large contingent of Peace Corps volunteers working in conservation had just arrived. She assured me that there was standing room for fifty more people at the back of the auditorium. She clapped her hands in glee. The inauguration was going to be much bigger and better than we'd planned.

Someone was tugging at my arm. I turned and saw Jorge Ibarra, the director of the Museum, standing behind me, his blue eyes wide, holding a big box. Pencil-slim in his dark suit, he looked the same as the day I'd met him twenty-two years ago. Only his graying temples and slightly stooped shoulders marked the passage of time. "Here," he said breathlessly, "for you." And he thrust the box with a card into my hands.

I tore away the wrappings and saw a gorgeous bouquet of birds of paradise. Who had sent it? Several other arrangements had arrived from friends and were placed near the podium. But this one was special. The gold-embossed card was from the President of the Republic of Guatemala, Venicio Cerezo Arévalo. Low exclamations came from the people around us. A prickle of tears filled my eyes as I accepted this gracious acknowledgment. The thought slid through my mind that the symbolism was perfect, and ironical. Birds of paradise were honoring my beloved giant grebes. Yes, President Cerezo had picked wisely and well.

Now guests were streaming into the hall, chairs filling up fast. I glimpsed the many friends who had helped me over the past two decades. In the front row sat Isabela, who'd loaned the generator for night lighting. François passed and blew me a kiss. Behind him walked a former director of Guatemala's Institute of Forestry (INAFOR). He'd been loyal about supplying our game warden with gas, oil, and a salary (unlike some of his successors). How I wished Armando were there to share in our moment of glory. He'd been invited, as had Doña Rosa, of course, but had neither replied nor arrived. A rush of gratitude for my friends swept over me. Deeply moved, I realized with a sinking heart that I could not speak, could not go on with my performance.

Moving calmly in my direction came Beatriz, statuesque in a draped blue gown. Her glossy black hair capped a classic Guatemalan face with the most dazzling smile I'd ever seen. Firmly she guided me to the dais and pulled out a chair.

"You'll do wonderfully, Anne," she whispered. "They've all come to hear you. And remember, we have to convince them to take the Second Step!" Giving me a comforting embrace, Beatriz sat down next to me.

Four of us now sat before the buzzing audience—Mr. Ibarra, the Vice-Minister of Culture (whose Ministry finances the Museum of Natural History), Beatriz representing Tourism, and myself. The room hushed. Jorge gave the welcome; the Vice-Minister, words of support for conservation of nature. Then, it was my turn. *What* I said and *how* I said it in the next forty-five minutes might determine the fate of Lake Atitlán. It could bring to fruition my years of research as an ecologist here. Linking strongly to my slide show, Beatriz would then make an impassioned plea to save the lake and its watershed from ever increasing degradation. She would plead the case that the natural resource base supports foreign tourism and local people everywhere. Both depend on a healthy environment and a beautiful landscape for survival. Together, we had the chance to make a real difference in this developing nation.

After Beatriz's speech, we planned to introduce the concept of the Second Step, or the saving of Lake Atitlán. We would pass out Certificates of Honor to all those who wished to become Friends of Atitlán. The plan was to capture the cooperation on a *voluntary* basis of people who owned weekend homes and farms at the lake. The Certificates contained Ten Commandments—steps by which the lake could be protected against pollution, eutrophication, and siltation, and its fauna and flora conserved.

After people signed their Certificates, our plan was to toast the Friends with a glass of champagne, a slice of giant grebe cake, and a free T-shirt which said "Save Lake Atitlán." But first, before this glittering finale, I had a graver task to perform.

My slide show was the culmination not just of twenty-two years of research in ornithology and ecology, but also data on the customs and diet of local Maya Indians, the perils of weather and lake, geology and an earthquake, a fluctuating fishery, and social strife. In short, it represented a fascinating web of life where birds, fish, humans, rocks, water, and reeds wove into a troubled tapestry. My story was pure ecology at its most elemental level. It demonstrated how one small water bird could become a biological indicator of impending disaster, and then become a martyr to conservation. And how the decline of one small microcosm could affect the lives of tens of thousands of humans. More than this, my message was that, be it *grebes* or *gorillas*, this pattern of decimation is being repeated around the world, every day, every year, in every country, in every ecosystem.

I stepped to the podium and adjusted the microphone. A deep silence fell over the room. "Why do you think a *gringa* came to Guatemala years ago to study an unknown bird?" I began. "What was her purpose? Was she a crazy birdwatcher? Or was there more to it?"

Then I quoted a sentence from an ecology book which summed up my slide show perfectly.

"Man's morals and politics are ecologically as important as rocks and rainfall in fashioning the environment."

I took up the remote control of the projector. The room went dark. A striking slide of Lake Atitlán hit the white wall. Gathering confidence, I told the audience how I'd first come to Guatemala and what I'd found with my censuses and observations of giant

Beatriz Zuñiga, then director of the Guatemalan Institute of Tourism, gives keynote speech at the poc inauguration.

In my own speech, I declared the giant grebe an extinct species, as Jorge Ibarra, director of the Museum of Natural History, looked on. I think these were the hardest words I ever spoke.
Photo by Gabriela Herrera

grebes. The slides clicked by. My tension mounted. The tough part was coming. What I feared that evening of November 11, 1987, were two things. I was memorializing Edgar Bauer, game warden for the giant grebes, who had been murdered in 1982 after fourteen years of loyal service to our conservation campaign. And that was his photograph and warden's shirt out in the alcove by the exhibit. Moreover, tonight I was formally declaring the giant grebe as a species extinct. These were the hardest words I had ever spoken.

22
Testing, Testing

A SLICE OF OLD MOON setting behind the thatch of my *ranchito* threw fringed shadows on the stone patio. Wrapped in a new red woolen blanket, I stared out at the night. Crickets rasped in the underbrush. Far up on the volcano slope a whippoorwill called relentlessly. The Southern Cross rose slowly, its four stars sliding past the stiff-pointed leaves of the yucca beside my door. From time to time I rose and paced up and down the patio. It was the first time in nine years that I had been able to live in the little building Edgar had designed and built next to my Indian hut. During those grim years, so many things had kept me away—my friend had been murdered, the giant grebe visitors center had been used as a military outpost, refuge waters had dried up, and my pocs had dwindled away. Now finally—March 1989—the country was relatively calm. How long that would last, no one knew, but I had come to stay awhile.

On this first night, however, sleep did not arrive easily. My beloved German shepherds, Condor and Chekika, were back in New York State at a kennel, leaving a big void in my life. My usual support system of mail, an enormous personal library, telephone, close friends, and good neighbors was missing. Soldiers scouted the countryside of Guatemala, carrying Uzis and grenades, presumably watching out for the welfare of tourists and residents. Rebels also still roamed the land but were scattered in small groups away from the population centers.

The official position of the U.S. Embassy was that tourists should avoid the *southern shore* of Lake Atitlán. Government military forces and guerrillas had clashed often in this area, and night or off-road travel was not recommended. Otherwise, the U.S. Travel Advisory claimed that the general security situation in Guatemala had steadily improved since August 1981.

The *un*official consensus was that if local folk said local conditions were untroubled, then one could go there. Nothing I'd heard since arrival in Guatemala indicated danger. So here I was, at my own risk, on my own initiative, at my own expense, in my own house, on the southern shore of the lake. I just prayed no armed men would come stealing through my dark forest during this three-week stay. I planned to make one more thorough census, searching for any remnant giant grebes, measuring reeds and cattails, counting chalets, talking to fishermen, and looking for signs of lake contamination.

A great horned owl hooted nearby in an avocado tree—"Whooooooo-who-who." The solemn sound raised the hairs on my arms. Its mate answered across the bay. A ponderous duet followed. I listened awhile and yawned. It was time to go inside, climb up into the sleeping loft, and try to rest. Pedro would be here with the old World Wildlife Fund boat shortly after dawn. I must be sharp and full of energy to begin our reconnaissance of this huge lake.

I took a few more deep breaths of fragrant tropical air. Back at my cabin, trees would be cracking with cold and barred owls might be serenading each other. Snow would be three feet on the level, with Black Bear Lake cloaked in two feet of ice. I shivered at the thought and stood up. The little old moon had slid down the sky and disappeared behind the clay pot on top of my Indian hut.

The Southern Cross was edging its way up past the roof thatch of the *ranchito* and rested on the shoulder of Volcano Tolimán. I threw the blanket over my shoulder, shut the door, and climbed up a ladder to the loft. Snuggling down among heavy blankets atop a freshly woven *petate*, I fell into an uneasy slumber.

A clear lemon light filtered into the loft about 6 A.M. White-winged doves cooed in the pine trees, and boat-tailed grackles began their imperious trumpeting atop the cypresses bordering my land. The lavender blossoms of my jacarandas were already alive with bees, hummingbirds, and flycatchers. They made a soothing buzz high above the outhouse, where I paid a call before breakfast.

Laying a fire between the three cooking rocks in my small hut, I set a coffee pot to boil and the flat iron drum top to heat. Any moment a local Indian woman would bring me fresh tortillas wrapped in a handwoven textile and I would warm them on the griddle. Smoke filled the small room and I flung open the three green shutters to let in fresh morning air. Just below one window, a tiny mountain wren jumped around on a cactus, burbling his heart out. The melody reminded me of winter wrens arriving in the Adirondacks each spring and warbling their songs. Everything seemed just as it had twenty years ago when I'd lived and worked out of this hut. Only now, in addition to the many weekend homes around the bay, an electric line sliced through a corner of my land. Gone was the glimmering candle glow I'd admired when arriving at Atitlán late in 1964. However, I'd lived comfortably for years in my Adirondack cabin without electricity, and I was not about to buy into that system here in Guatemala. As far as I was concerned, the lines functioned best as swallow perches. At least two dozen birds sat on them twittering and preening in the rosy dawn light.

While waiting for the coffee, I assembled my field gear for the day. Cameras, binoculars, notebook and pens, tape recorder, bathing suit, towel, sunglasses, sunscreen, and a big sombrero. It would feel so good to be back working on the lake. Yet I must be careful of the sun with my winter pallor. I cracked open a hard-boiled egg and ate it along with hot buttered tortillas. This sturdy, simple breakfast would support me till noon.

Sun was pouring through the glass window of the *ranchito* now and highlighting the new white rug I'd purchased. It lay before the fireplace, and its red, blue, and yellow birds made a

My new ranchito, next to my original Indian hut. It was designed and built from volcanic rock by Edgar Bauer, then finished by Pedro.

cheery splash against the stone floor. The rustic wooden dining room table, desk, and chairs looked drab. Tonight I would sew red cotton curtains for the windows and make tablecloths to match. With a pair of candlesticks, red tapers, and flowers in a pot, my new home would look better.

The sound of a boat engine reached my ears and I hurried down to the shore to greet Pedro. He'd hardly changed since our census with Laurie three years ago. I embraced my old friend and handed him my gear. Before jumping into the boat, I said,

"Pedro, first let's measure the lake level while we're near the old refuge. I'm anxious to see if the water's still dropping."

He nodded, reached for the oar and a long line, and led our way to the refuge wall. The measurement was exactly nineteen feet—same as it'd been in November 1987. "Maybe the lake is slowing down a bit," I ventured.

"I think so," Pedro said. "It came up three feet last rainy season, and it hasn't gone down so much this dry time. But there's a new problem I'll tell you about as we go."

Starting at the old refuge mouth, we began cruising easterly, taking plenty of time. I paid special attention to every weekend home we passed, trying to determine if any were discharging sewage by drainpipes into the lake. The only pipes I saw were small diameter water lines leading from the lake up to pumps and thence into the gardens and lawns which surrounded each chalet.

As we cruised along, Pedro kept up a running commentary. "Many people think that with so many new property owners pumping water to irrigate their flower gardens and grass that the lake cannot fill itself up again. A lot of that water leaves as evaporation. What do you think, Doña Anna?"

I thought a while, counting the dozens of chalets we were passing. They all had water pumps and hoses. "It depends partly on how many houses we find, Pedro." I said. "The bigger part of that issue is the water which filters *back* into the lake. It's bound to contain chemical fertilizers and pesticides, which people are routinely using nowadays. Over time, they could affect water quality."

Pedro nodded. "Most property owners and farmers spray pesticides on their crops and flowers at least three times a year and scatter fertilizers twice a year."

We stopped to talk to a few Indian fishermen and learned that basically the fishery had not changed much. Largemouth bass were still around, up to ten pounds in size. Crappies and bluegills were the main food fish, while a few small crabs could still be caught.

I grinned at Pedro ruefully. "Sometimes I think the most useful thing I ever did down here, other than study long-term ecological trends for the lake, was to stock bluegills. With just the handful Armando and I put into the refuge in 1968, we unintentionally are now feeding thousands of Indians."

Pedro and I continued censusing the main body of the lake for four days in this manner. When we had finished that much, we paused for a day so he could give a conservation talk to the sixth-grade children in Santiago Atitlán. His speech was clear and convincing. With only a blackboard and two charts as props, Pedro explained the importance of forests in the watershed and pleaded with the kids to plant new trees. He urged them to use latrines and put their garbage in a dump spot. He explained how soap and chemicals could hurt their drinking water and the fishes they ate. I sat beaming at him and the kids, proud of the way he'd taken hold of Lake Atitlán National Park and its problems since Edgar's death.

After he had finished and we were back in the boat, I asked Pedro why he didn't use the projector and slides that the World Wildlife Fund and Peace Corps volunteers had provided to augment his talk.

"The bulb has burned out and I have no money for a new one. They cost 125 quetzals each down here," he said sheepishly.

I remembered that was a whole month's salary for him just a few years back. "Can't the government send you one?" I asked.

"Apparently not," he answered shortly. "I haven't been sent gas or oil for the boat in several weeks either. You'll have to buy all your own fuel, Anna."

I made a mental note to talk to his chief when I went back to Guatemala City.

Pedro left the World Wildlife Fund boat with me that Friday afternoon because I had an important guest to pick up and bring to my *ranchito* on Saturday morning. Beatriz Zuñiga, my benefactor from INGUAT for the inauguration, was paying a weekend visit. I planned to meet her in Panajachel with the boat. Pedro tied it securely to a chalet dock near the old refuge after asking permission to use it. Just before dusk, I strolled down to double-check the lines. After a calm day, small waves were lapping fitfully against the shore. I glanced up at the volcano tops. Caps of clouds hung over the peaks. I turned and looked across the lake. A line of whitecaps was racing across the purple-blue lake.

Galvanized into action, I raced toward the nearest chalet and burst into the Indian watchman's hut. "Please help me," I shrieked. "There's a sudden *norte* coming and the boat will tear loose and crash!" The Indian, whom I knew as Gaspar, ran outside to look. One glance and he tore off to the next watchman's hut. In the space of five minutes, three men gathered to help me. Together we untied and paddled the boat away from the rocky shore just before the wall of waves hit us. Two minutes later and it would have been swept against the rocks. We struggled for half an hour to bring the boat into a nearby reed bed. Slowly we poled to shore and dragged it by brute strength onto the beach. As an extra precaution, I piled rocks in the bow so the waves could not shift the boat from behind. Exhausted, I returned to my *ranchito* and sank onto the bird rug in front of the fireplace. Atitlán was testing me.

She tested me again next morning as I shoved the boat back into the water and headed into five-foot waves toward Panajachel. If Don Emilio had been alive, he'd have been livid. Whitecaps crashed over the bow, flew above the windshield, and dumped on my head. I didn't dare take my hands off the wheel even to wipe my eyes. Gaspar, who had come along to help, was on his hands and knees bailing furiously. The eight to nine mile trip took one hour and ten minutes. When we arrived at Panajachel, I was trembling from head to foot. Gaspar looked faintly green. Beatriz was standing on the dock, stately even in her blue jeans, Reeboks, and Totonicapan straw hat. The lake was flat calm along the north shore, so she couldn't understand why we and the boat were late and soaked. "Let's go get some hot coffee," I suggested, giving her a big hug. (I wanted to give me and the lake time to calm down.) "Do you swim?" I asked nonchalantly. "It's a little rough on the other side."

By the time I'd relaxed, the lake had indeed calmed and the wind abated. We had an uneventful crossing. I smiled to myself— the lake was playing with me, reminding me of her capricious fury and her lethal power. I was nothing but a little mouse between the paws of a jaguar.

Beatriz came to know this fury that evening, when the north wind rose again and slammed against the *ranchito* walls. It tore underneath the thatch roof to set the candle flames guttering. My guest put on a wool sweater and borrowed my heavy jacket. I stoked the fire and carried two blankets down to the rug. There was no sofa in my *ranchito,* so we snuggled up on the floor to have cocktails. Chattering amiably, we caught up on each other's lives since the inauguration.

Then I turned serious and asked Beatriz what had become of "Friends of Atitlán." "Did anyone take charge and organize the chalet owners to obey the Ten Commandments?" I asked.

"I'm so sorry, Anna," she began, "but no. No one ever called me. As far as I know our campaign died, at least publicly. Maybe some individuals who signed the Certificates still honor and obey them. I'm ashamed to say, I was too busy at INGUAT to devote time to Friends of Atitlán.

I nodded understandingly. How could I fault Beatriz? She'd done so much to make the Giant Grebe Exhibit a success. Lake Atitlán was not her responsibility. With a high-ranking job that took her all over Guatemala, and much of the world, she couldn't take on anything more. What was needed was *one person,* or *one group,* committed to help the lake and be available full time for the next five years.

"What about the photos and text that the Banco Industrial asked you to write? About the conservation problems of the lake?" she asked. "Didn't you tell me a year and a half ago that the bank president wanted to feature "Saving Lake Atitlán" in his 1988 annual report? Did you do it? That might alert a lot of people to the problems."

"It's not printed yet," I replied. "And when it does come out I don't know what sort of distribution the bank normally makes. Perhaps only their clients get copies."

"Yes, but many of their bank customers are chalet owners," Beatriz said, "as well as hotel managers and industrialists. It may help."

The fire flickered and flared as we sat in companionable silence. It turned her smooth skin to warm bronze and danced in her dark eyes. "There's one more shot I can try," I said. "When I finish my census here next week, I'll write up a report. If it's as serious as I think, I'll send it to every private conservation group and government office here, in the States, and in Switzerland. Maybe I can arouse international concern that way. The same way we alerted the conservation community to the hydroelectric project twenty years ago."

"What do you mean 'as serious as you think it is'?"

I murmured, "Beatriz, it's so *silent* out there. How can I describe it to you? There are hardly any aquatic birds, only coots. The habitat is severely depleted. The lake's still down nineteen feet and most of the reed and cattail beds are mere scraggly clumps. If only you could have seen it before. Reed beds thick and green. So many ducks, gallinules, fish, crabs, grebes, and . . . oh, I almost forgot to tell you. I've found one pair of pocs so far in four days of censusing."

Beatriz let out a yelp. "One pair of pocs! Then they're *not* extinct! Anna, that's wonderful!"

I shook my head. "What good is one pair? Do you think a whole species can keep going with just one pair?"

"Well, we could captive-breed. Catch them and put them down at Auto Safari Park. Or make a new refuge here around them. Let's—"

I interrupted her brusquely. "No, my friend. It won't work. The pocs have come to the point of no return. Twenty-four years of work is enough. We don't have the luxury to expend more effort. There's not enough money, or expertise, or facilities here to possibly pull off a successful survival campaign. If we try, it would only sign a death warrant for those birds."

"You're right." she conceded. "There has to be a balance. With so many children orphaned from the earthquake and strife in my country, so many homeless Indians, so many beggars and dump pickers, I feel that humans have to help humans instead of animals when starvation is at hand."

"There's more bad news about the lake, Beatriz," I continued, "but I'd rather wait to tell you when the census is complete and I have all the data analyzed. Now, how about some dinner?"

We spoke little while we ate, deep in our own thoughts. Then I retired to the sleeping loft. Beatriz slept by the fireplace, hoping she'd stay warmer there than in the drafty loft. Next morning, after a tour of the old and new refuges and a stop at the hot springs, I brought her back to Panajachel at noon. We embraced and said goodbye. I promised to call her when I came to Guatemala City with my report. As I put the clutch in reverse and started to back out, my steering wheel gave a funny jerk and started spinning freely. The heavy 70 h.p. motor turned aimlessly from side to side. The steering cable had snapped!

Shouting to Beatriz, I waved her back to the dock, cut the engine, and paddled in. "I can't go back across the lake now. And I don't know how to fix the cable," I cried up at her throwing her a line. "Thank God it happened right here and not in the middle of the lake with a north wind."

Beatriz took charge. "Stay here, Anna," she said. "Watch your boat. It's almost time for the *chocomil* to begin. I'll go find a mechanic. My car's right up near the big hotel. Don't worry. You'll be back at your *ranchito* before dark."

True to her word, two mechanics appeared in ten minutes and

began tracing out the problem. The first breath of south wind wafted by. I knew by experience that within an hour the lake would be heaving under the *chocomil.* It took two hours to fix the boat. By then, I was fending off the craft from the dock with my oar, cursing every wave. Beatriz supervised up on the dock until the men announced it safe for travel. "Are you sure you want to go back alone?" she asked nervously. "It's awfully rough today."

"It is," I agreed, "but there's no way we can leave the boat at the dock, and it's a bitch to pull onto shore. I'd rather take my chances to return now than wait till night. For all we know, the norther may start again. That would be worse."

Extracting a promise that I'd send her a telegram from Santiago Atitlán telling her I was safe, Beatriz waved goodbye. The trip back took an hour and ten minutes, just as it had the day before, only this time I was soused and doused by smaller waves from all directions. Again, I was trembling with fright when I reached the old refuge. My hands, face, and legs were burned crimson. As I tied up the boat in the reeds, I threw a salute toward the lake. "You tried *again*, Atitlán. You don't want me to forget you, lovely lady."

23
The Last Census

NEXT DAY, I ran the boat to Santiago to send Beatriz the telegram. As I waited for the postal clerk, I saw a list of zip codes on the wall. Pixabaj was 07024! It had arrived in the modern world of communication. After sending my message, I strolled to the market to stock up again on avocados, mangos, papayas, carrots, onions, and potatoes. For less than three U.S. dollars I soon had enough food for a week. I decided to find Pedro and plan the rest of the week's censusing. His brother told me he'd gone to the city unexpectedly for a conference at the INA-FOR office. He'd be back and ready to work on Wednesday.

Feeling at loose ends, I suddenly had an urge to go back over to Panajachel. I could check on the small rental car I'd left there, buy some gifts for friends back home, and find green paint for the shutters and door of my Indian hut. They hadn't been cared for since 1969. The lake was flat calm and the sky brilliant blue as I raced across. With luck, I'd be back well before the *chocomil*. This time, I took the boat over to the big docks of the daily mail boats. An old friend operated the line, and he'd helped in the past on stormy days.

"Gregorio," I yelled. "May I tie my boat here for a couple of hours? I just have to run into town."

"Of course, Doña Anna," he called back, coming down to greet me. We stood chatting on the dock while I looped my lines around the posts. Then I noticed a dreadful stench.

"What's that smell, Gregorio?" I asked.

"Why it's the *toma* (drainage ditch) over there." He pointed toward shore. Following his hand, I saw filthy gray water coursing down a ditch directly into the lake.

"That can't be rainwater because it's not raining," I said. "What is it?"

"It's dirty wash water, sewage, and kitchen wastes from the old part of Panajachel," he said. "Maybe even some of the smaller, new hotels."

"My God! You mean they're discharging that right into the lake without treatment?"

"I'm afraid so," Gregorio said. "Usually it only runs at night when no one can see."

"But that's dangerously unhealthy!"

"Let me tell you a story, Anna," he began. "I had two operations in the past few years so I had to stop my daily swim in the lake after the morning mail boats depart. When the doctor said I was healed enough to exercise again, I went down to the beach right there," he indicated the section near the ditch. "After a couple of days, I noticed an awful rash on both my arms. I went back to the doctor and asked him what it was. He said something I'd eaten. But I assured him I eat very simply. Then I mentioned swimming. At once he knew what the trouble was. An infection from the dirty water. He gave me a fungicidal cream and forbade me to swim anymore. Imagine! Right here at my own docks. After so many years of enjoying the lake."

I couldn't believe what I was hearing. "Doesn't anyone try to stop it?"

"No. Not only here, Anna, but at the other end of town. The

waste water and sewage from San Andres Semetebaj up on the hills behind Panajachel have been directed into a small creek and now flow down the slopes and into the River Panajachel."

"But that empties into the lake right beside the public beach!"

Gregorio nodded. "Rumors say even the hospital waste of Sololá runs down here. Lake Atitlán is being used as a giant septic tank."

I resolved to come back with my cameras and document this crime. Maybe I could include photos with my report. But now I had to hurry or the south wind would catch me unawares again.

I started along the beach toward the street where I'd left the rental car, planning to drive down the street with several gift shops. Suddenly I saw a medium-sized brown, skinny dog dragging itself toward the lake. I stopped horrified and watched. Its back legs were twisted sideways, useless, and old blood stained its skinned up paws. The dog moved by digging its front legs into the ground and dragging its rear end along like a sack. Possibly its back was broken and body paralyzed from the center down. Never had I seen such a pitiful sight. The animal reached the water, heaved itself in, and began drinking frantically.

Some Indian boys stood near the beach. I cried to them, "What's wrong with that dog? Has it just been hurt?"

One boy ran up to me and looked at the dog. "I think it was just run over with a car," he said.

"Oh, no," I groaned. "I have to help it. Will you give me a hand? What's your name?"

"Rolando," he said. "Yes, I'll help."

"Quick. We must pick it up carefully in a piece of plastic like you use for a rain tarp. I have a car nearby and we can take it to a veterinary. Is there one in Panajachel now?"

Rolando ran over to a dugout canoe and pulled out a plastic. "I think there's one at the end of town."

I shuddered at the thought of the pain the dog was enduring. Reaching into my *morral,* I pulled out a bottle of aspirins. "Hold

Close-up of a storm sewer at the public beach.

him," I instructed. Together Rolando and I managed to pry the dog's mouth open and force two aspirins inside. Being bitten and getting rabies flashed through my mind. This poor creature had never seen a veterinary's care or gotten vaccinations, that was clear. Then we tried to slide the dog onto the sheet. He thrashed and slithered off.

I was beside myself. Any extra movement might injure the

Ditch carrying raw sewage and domestic wastes beside the major tourist boat dock in Panajachel.

poor animal more. I began crying. Rolando tried again to slide the
dog on the makeshift stretcher. No luck.

Suddenly a burly, older Indian ran up. "What are you doing?"
he asked menancingly. "That's my dog."

Rolando broke out into a torrent of Cakchiquel while I tried
to explain in Spanish. The older Indian just stood there. "Help us.
I want to take him to the doctor in my car," I pleaded.

The other Indians who had been attracted by the commotion
broke into laughter. The dog's owner, too. Only Rolando didn't
laugh. I turned beet red. To hell with them, I thought. They think
I'm a crazy *gringa*. They don't give a damn about this dog.

I turned to Rolando and asked, "What shall we do?"

"If you like, señora, I can cut off its head with a machete," he
said.

The thought nearly made me hysterical. Forcing myself not to
bawl, I said harshly. "No. Ask that man to pick up his dog and
take it to my car. Tell him I'll drive and he can come with us."

The older Indian's eyes widened. Probably he'd never been in
a car before. He reached down, picked up the dog around the
belly, and hurried after me. "Be careful," I screamed at him.
"Don't let its legs swing so much." He paid no attention. When I
opened the car door, he sat down rather pompously on the back
seat with the dog beside him. Rolando got in, too. I drove fast to
the other end of town. After repeated questioning and stopping, I
finally determined that no vet existed in Panajachel.

I screeched to a stop before the post office and went in to ask
advice. The clerk there suggested I try two small medical clinics,
plus a dental clinic. The first two were closed and the surgeons
were away seeing patients in other villages. The dental clinic was
closed for lunch. I stopped the car and rested my head on the
steering wheel. Someone, somewhere, had to treat the poor animal, or put it out of its misery. Meanwhile, the dog lay quietly on
the back seat, only whimpering occasionally, while its owner
looked importantly out the window toward his acquaintances.

Starting the engine again, I drove down a side street, hoping inspiration would strike. The houses here looked familiar. I remembered that a Canadian woman had come to Panajachel to retire about the same time I'd begun work on the pocs. She'd been a nurse and a Quaker. We had become friends, but after I went back to college, we'd gradually lost touch. I wondered if she still lived here. *She* would know what to do.

On impulse, I stopped beside a charming cottage. Signaling to the gardener I asked if Doña Margaret still lived there. He nodded yes and said she was resting. "Please wake her up," I begged. "Tell her it's an old friend and I have an emergency."

A few minutes later, Margaret appeared in a dressing gown. Her hair was silver and her eyes a distant blue. She had aged beautifully. She seemed not at all surprised to see me. Tersely, I outlined the situation. "Do *you* know where a vet works, Margaret, or where I could get medicines to put the dog to sleep?"

"The closest vet is in Quetzaltenango, two hours away or more," she said. "I don't know anyone around here who'd help. You have to drop it, Anne. It's not your problem."

"What do you mean it's not my problem?" I asked in amazement. "Any animal that's hurt is my problem. I can't bear to see their pain, and they can't help themselves."

"It's the karma of each life that decides what happens," she murmured. "You can't change fate."

How could a former nurse and a Quaker be saying this?

Margaret went on. "I've studied the Eastern religions for years now. I've learned to meditate. The longer I live, the surer I am that we must not interfere with karma."

The afternoon was taking on nightmarish tones. My nerves were about shot. I looked quickly around the simple room, hoping this wasn't happening to me. Two huge, sleek Labrador retrievers lay on Margaret's bed, gently snoring. I looked back at my old friend. She was taking a tea pot from a cupboard.

"Will you stay and have tea with me?" she asked dreamily.

"Let the dog go home with its owner. If it lives, it lives. If it dies, it dies."

"No, Margaret," I said stonily. "I won't be staying for tea. Goodbye." But as I shut the door, I couldn't help snapping, "What if it were *your* dogs? Would your karma work then?"

Back in the car, I started the engine and headed blindly down the road. The scarecrow dog panted in the back seat. His owner looked at me questioningly. I stared at him in the rearview mirror and spat out, "She can take her karma and stick it up her ass!" He looked back out the window.

At my wits' end, I turned a corner, then jammed down the brakes. Armando stood in a doorway, chatting briskly with a younger man. I hadn't seen him in twenty years, but I'd recognize him anywhere with those blue eyes and brawny shoulders. Only his shoulders were slumped and his head mostly bald now. Flinging open the door, I jumped to his side and grabbed his hands.

"Armando. It's me. Anita. How are you?"

He looked as if a thunderbolt had hit him, then recovered sufficiently to shake both my hands at once. "When did you come here? Why are you here?" His eyes crinkled as he smiled.

"I'll tell you everything later, Armando," I said. "But right now I need help. If anyone will know what to do, you will. You always did." And I poured out the story of the crippled dog.

Armando stuck his head through the back window, chucked the dog under the chin, and said something to the owner. Then he turned back to me and said, "I'd take it up to the police station and see if one of the men can shoot it with a pistol."

My heart fluttered. It was sound, practical advice, but it hit hard. "Is there no one who could put it to sleep?" I asked.

"You could try old Dr. Gonzalez," he said, "but I doubt he'd deal with a dog."

"Armando, you're wonderful," I cried, sliding back into the car. "I'd forgotten him. Let me try. Can we have dinner together next Sunday before I go back to Guatemala City?"

He nodded yes and squeezed my hand as I threw the car into gear and headed for the doctor's office.

Dr. Gonzalez remembered me and my amoebas. "Doña Anna de los Pocs. Welcome back." Then he kindly offered to put the dog to sleep. He prepared a large injection of sodium pentathol and slipped it into his jacket pocket. "I'll do this for *you,* Anna, but I will see the dog in the *car,*" he informed me in a businesslike way. "It would not do for my patients to see a dog come in here. After all, I treat humans, not animals."

Tears streamed down my face as I followed the doctor out. He opened the door and felt the dog's back hind legs. "I could probably operate and cure your animal, but it would cost lots of money and he'd have to be cared for for several weeks. This man couldn't afford it." Then he told the Indian that he had an injection which would make the dog sleep. He could take it home and let it die in peace.

The Indian shoved himself back on the seat and shook his head. The doctor repeated himself. But the Indian kept shaking his head. "It's against the wishes of God," he announced piously.

I couldn't believe what I had heard. After the frenetic afternoon, I had at last found the solution and now the dog's owner stubbornly refused to help his pet. The doctor tried once more. "Your dog cannot get better. He's in pain. It is better he go to sleep."

"But why?" the Indian suddenly demanded. "He's been like this for two months!"

There was a moment of stunned silence, then everyone began talking simultaneously in Spanish, Cakchiquel, and English. I turned to Rolando. "You told me the dog had just been run over, and there was blood on its paws." He turned to the doctor. "Someone told me the dog had just been run over." The older Indian said, "He was run over two months ago." The doctor said to me, "You told me he was just run over." Bedlam!

Finally, I made profuse apologies to Dr. Gonzalez, paid for a
"house call," and drove back to the beach. Letting the Indian and
dog out, I gave him a parting lecture. "You be sure and give him
plenty of water so he doesn't have to drag himself down to the
lake. He needs more food. You treat him nicely." The Indian
didn't say anything. He hoisted the dog across his back like a
large, brown fanny pack and trudged away. Rolando walked with
me down to my boat, which miraculously was still afloat. I gave
him a tip and thanked him. Then I headed in a daze through the
dusk across the heaving lake.

The string of heavy happenings continued throughout the
week. Pedro and I finished the census. Conditions looked bad
indeed. We had counted *449 chalets*—up 11 percent from the
total two years before of 401. Since my first count of 28 homes in
1960, that meant an increase of 1,600 percent! Land prices ran as
high as $10,000 per acre. Even the old refuge buildings had been
sold for a weekend retreat! Maybe the new owner could deal with
filling up the pit.

Real estate development was bound to escalate further; there
was a new road under construction which would encircle the *entire lake.* Already, piles of dirt and rocks were sliding down the
slopes toward the water. It didn't take much imagination to see
that siltation and water degradation would threaten Atitlán as
soon as the rainy season started. Furthermore, more chalets would
mean less cropland for the local inhabitants.

The reed and cattail beds around the lake were reduced by
half—from 15.4 miles in 1967 to 8.0 miles in 1989. But thick,
wide, good habitat had *decreased by 83 percent!* No wonder it was
silent at Lake Atitlán. There was nowhere for wildlife and fish to
live.

The contamination of water was much worse than in earlier
years, principally in the bays of Santiago Atitlán and San Antonio
Palopo. There, on any given morning, as many as one hundred

women might be washing their clothes at the lake's edge and using the smelly pig fat soap mixed with lye. Moreover, the runoff into the lake from human excrement and urine on the ground in and around these large towns had to be substantial. Few homes had latrines. Those that did sometimes used them as chicken coops or corn sheds rather than as bathrooms. Filamentous green algae, almost psychedelic in color, grew like cotton candy among

Chalets, or weekend houses, have proliferated at Lake Atitlán, from 28 in 1965 to 449 in 1989. As of this writing, there are no local zoning laws or sewage controls, no land use plans, no architectural codes in operation yet.

the aquatic plants. It was a sure sign of pollution and eutrophication. At San Antonio it extended out fifteen yards from shore, but
at Santiago it filled the bay and extended in a mile-long streak
from the docks. The south wind and lake currents pushed the
algae toward the main lake. Another source of contamination
could be coming from the several mail and tourist boats which
now plied the lake. None of them had sealed heads (toilets), so
sewage could be flushed right into the water. Only one or two had
trash pails for litter, and probably they all pumped their oily bilge
water into the lake.

On our last morning in the boat, I counted fifteen pieces of
plastic floating on Lake Atitlán during a half-hour crossing. That
meant one piece every two minutes! I'd never seen anything like
this on the lake's surface. Moreover, beaches everywhere were
becoming littered with empty plastic bags which held soap or soft
drinks, tin cans, glass bottles, plastic containers, empty boxes,
broken baskets, old clothing, and plastic sheeting.

Pedro dropped me back at the *ranchito* and stayed to write up
our report. When he'd finished, I said sadly to him, "Everything's
happening so fast. The entire shoreline is changing. Wherever we
look there are stone walls, boat houses, pumps, gazebos, terraces,
green grass, balconies, exotic trees like date palms, stone steps,
and flower gardens springing up. How I wish there were an Adirondack Park Agency down here to oversee things."

I thought of how it had felt a few days back finding the last
pocs, and how they'd acted. Two pairs—one on one side of the
lake, one on the other. Both wary. Both entranced by the sound of
that taped male territorial call echoing out of the recorder, just as
hundreds of other giant grebes had been mesmerized over the
years.

These males had swum to the edge of the reeds, listened intently, and done their accordion alarm dives. Then they made
several short periscope surveys with only their heads peeking

above the surface, while they skirted our boat cautiously. What fun it had been in those first days at the lake when I was a young scientist describing grebe behavior. I'd taken such pride being the first to name the poc displays.

Reconnaissance complete, each male had returned to its mate sitting silently at the edge of the shoreline vegetation. Each pair gave their pretty hen-flicker duet. Then, with powerful slow dives, each pair of pocs disappeared into its scrap of reeds. Proud, alert, jaunty, doomed.

Turning away from Pedro so he wouldn't see my eyes, I took

Pedro Mendosa Tacaxoy, the present government game warden at Lake Atitlán, during our 1989 census.

the tape recorder, removed its batteries, and slipped out the poc tape. It was of great value to me as a memento, but it served no useful purpose anymore. I wrapped the recorder and my binoculars in a towel and tucked them in my suitcase.

There will be no need ever to run a census again on Lake Atitlán.

Epílogue

I N MARCH 1989 I went to Guatemala City to make one last plea
for protection of the environment. I took along my report
with the ten recommendations that I believe will save Lake
Atitlán.

On the way, passing through Sololá, I saw a family planning
center and went in to speak with the doctor. He told me that
these clinics have sprung up all over Guatemala and are supported
by private donations as well as by United States A.I.D. grants.
Contraception is now accepted in the country, and Indian women
are gradually learning how to limit their families. In fact, several
patients were lined up in the waiting room as I left. It was a far cry
from the day I sat with Alejandro's wife, trying to counsel her
about birth control.

In the city I discovered that President Vinicio Cerezo had
recently signed into being the Comision Nacional del Media Am-
biente, (CONAMA), Guatemala's equivalent of the Environmental Protection Agency. Although the organization is still very
small, young, and underfunded, its Director, Jorge Cabrera
Hidalgo, has already established a national decree on sewage control. He's now working on legislation to stop contamination by

non- biodegradable soaps, such as the pig fat soaps used at Atitlán. Cabrera is also in charge of the Commission for Protected Natural Areas (CONAP) and has identified twenty-six of the most valuable sites in the nation. CONAP is seeking to buy, lease, obtain by easement, or by outright gift, those parcels.

On February 19, 1989, President Cerezo signed a bill creating forty-four nature conservation areas in tropical forests, coastal zones, savannahs, wetlands, lakes, and rivers. Part of this will include thirty-three new national parks. The same day, the President established the Maya Biospheric Reserve (2.5 million acres) in the Petén region. It includes Tikal National Park. The reserve will now be designated an international biosphere reserve as part of the Man and Biosphere (MAB) program of UNESCO in Paris. Because of these two laws, almost 15 percent of the nation will be protected.

It is significant that the National Geographic Society through its editor, Wilbur Garrett, gave President Cerezo an award in 1989 for his attention to the conservation of natural resources and archeological sites and routes. The Society's magazine also printed "La Ruta Maya" in its October 1989 issue and mentioned my research on the grebes and the decline of Lake Atitlán.

I learned there are sixty-four new nongovernmental conservation organizations (NGOs) functioning throughout Mexico and Central America. In Guatemala alone, fourteen NGOs have formed the Conservation Federation of Guatemala. Some have only a dozen members and protect only special birds or orchids. Others number in the hundreds and fight for reforestation or against pesticide poisoning. Some are urban, some rural, some elite, some political. Sometimes they seem to be competing, or without guidance, but they are proof that citizens *are* concerned. If they can organize and harness their energies, they can do far more. At least they are there.

So it is clear that a conservation consciousness has arisen in Guatemala. The very fact that the Banco Industrial chose as its

1988 theme "Let's Save Lake Atitlán" is proof.

The views of different people I spoke with were diverse. There are as many ideas about how to save natural resources as how to save a crippled dog. But the important thing is that most Guatemalans *want* to save living things: whether dogs or pocs or beautiful lakes. The critical need is to organize and encourage individuals toward a common goal.

People from *all* walks of life can be conservationists. Each can help in her or his own way. The well-to-do of Guatemala are surely the environmental hope of the future because they have the resources, education, and power to act.

But everyone can serve conservation by obeying laws, by forming grass-roots operations, and by letting politicians know their views. Look at how the Indians of Lake Atitlán obeyed the reed-cutting law, refraining from ruining the nests of the giant grebe and volunteering to replant reeds.

A *single determined human being* can be a tremendous catalyst and force in fighting for an endangered species or an ecosystem. Dian Fossey proved that with her gorillas; Jane Goodall with her chimps; Eugenie Clark with her sharks; Roger Payne with his whales; George Schaller with his pandas. I was successful, too, with my pocs. For a short span. I did edge them back up to 232 birds and improved their habitat. For a little while. But I could not fight an earthquake, civil war, uncontrolled real estate development, and a human population explosion.

Recently, as I was analyzing the percentages of shoreline on Lake Atitlán for type of land use, I was surprised by these estimated figures. Approximately *10 percent* is taken up by working farms, *10 percent* is rough, uninhabitable terrain, and *10 percent* is accounted for by clustered and crowded Indian villages. Almost 39 percent is now occupied by chalet owners. The remainder is small crop farmlands, pastures, and woodlots. The figure 39 percent is remarkably similar to the estimated 34 percent of arable land controlled by the top 1 percent of landowners in Guatemala.

Therefore, it is the movers and shakers who must take the lead, people like the late Ramiro Castillo, visionary president of Banco Industrial, who wanted to save Lake Atitlán through his bank report. Clearly the affluent must decide whether or not *they* want Lake Atitlán to be a beautiful and environmentally healthy place or a giant septic tank.

Before I left Guatemala, I had dinner with Armando. I was able to tell him that he'd been one of the most important men in my life. That I'd always be grateful for how he had helped me with Operation Protection Poc and with buying my first parcel of backcountry land.

I also visited Edgar's gravesite and said my last goodbye to him. Both these encounters left me with a peaceful sense of closure.

Just before this book went to press, I learned that in September 1989 a Commission for the Conservation of Lake Atitlán and Watershed was established by presidential decree. While I cannot claim any credit for this, I've long promoted the notion that an Adirondack Park Agency-type group be set up to guide land use and control pollution at the lake. I've distributed more than twenty APA master plans and maps to Guatemalan colleagues and high government officials. And I secretly cherish the thought that somewhere along the line a tiny seed was planted, one fragile idea cross-fertilized.

In addition, the European Economic Community has promised $10 million to fund work in agriculture and soils, forestry, sanitation, and access roads and bridges to Indian villages. (The perimeter road around the lake, thank heavens, has been stopped).

Lastly, I learned that young people in Guatemala City are continuing the fledgling "Amigos de Atitlán" group that Beatriz and I initiated during the Giant Grebe Exhibit and Inauguration.

Such welcome news gives hope, a silver lining to the dark and sinister events of the past decade.

Acknowledgments

DURING MY EARLY YEARS in Guatemala, I was deeply indebted to the following persons in the Guatemalan government: Ministers of Agriculture, Lic. C. H. de León and Lic. F. Montenegro Girón; Vice-Ministers of Agriculture, Lic. R. Acinena Salazár and Lic. H. Cavarrus Conde; Directors of the Department of Forestry and Natural Resources, Ing. G. Jiménez, Ing. O. Porres, and Ing. B. Brusti; Director of the National Tourist Commission, Sr. R. Porres; former Head of the Division of Fauna, Sr. M. Saavedra and Assistant, J. Ovalle Arevalo, and former Head Ing. Julio Aparicio, and Assistant, Sr. J. Ovidio. Other government personnel who contributed to the program were the Governors of the Department of Sololá, Colonel A. Muñoz and Colonel J. C. Monterossa; Directors of the National Postal Department, Colonel M. A. Mendosa and Lic. R. Cabrera, and the head of the Philatelic Department, Sr. A. Cuyún. A special acknowledgment must be accorded the late Edgar Bauer, official game warden, for his dedication to our conservation campaign, Operation Protection Poc, and for his loyal friendship.

Throughout my fieldwork, much needed financial aid was generously provided by the International Council for Bird Preservation, Smithsonian Institution, World Wildlife Fund, International and U.S. National Appeals, National Geographic Society, Wildlife Management Institute, and National Wildlife Federation.

Thanks are due to Dr. William Dilger, Laboratory of Ornithology at Cornell, and to Dr. Robert Storer, grebe expert, and Dr. Reeve M. Bailey, Director, Museum of Zoology, University of Michigan, for their review of giant grebe specimens and analysis of wing loading capability. It is also my great pleasure to acknowledge Dr. D. Q. Thompson, chairman of my graduate committee, for his encouragement and enthusiasm.

Later in my research a great many people, both professionals and friends, helped me. I am grateful to David G. Allen, contract photographer to *National Geographic* magazine; Charles Cordier, who advised me about trapping; and to G. Cummings, Refuge Manager, and staff members of the Montezuma National Wildlife Refuge. In 1973–74, Louis A. Krumholz, then Editor of the Wildlife Monograph series, was helpful in assisting me to prepare my doctoral thesis for publication. It appeared as Wildlife Monograph no. 37 in August 1974, entitled "Ecology and Management of the Atitlán Grebe, Lake Atitlán, Guatemala." The cost of publication was defrayed by the U.S. Fish and Wildlife Service and the Rob and Bessie Welder Wildlife Foundation.

Other friends and colleagues who were particularly kind during my early years in Guatemala were Juan Rosales, my patient and willing houseboy; Coronel Antonio Batras, President, Aviateca Airlines; Alfonso de León, head of the La Selta Navigation Line; Father Juan Manuel Amezaga, priest to Panajachel; Don Manuel Maria Herrera, owner of the Palace Hotel; David Vela, owner and editor of the newspaper, *El Imparcial*, and Lucy Whitbeck Sturgil of Guatemala Unlimited Travel.

During the 1980s, a number of scientists, students, and institutions became involved with the survival of the species and contributed to the body of knowledge about grebes. They include Dr.

Frank Todd, former Corporate Curator of Sea World, San Diego; Roberto and Francois Berger, owners of Auto Safari Park, Guatemala; Dr. Herb Raffaele and Larry Mason of the International Affairs office, U.S. Fish and Wildlife Service; Susan MacVean, graduate student, Colorado State University; Frank Zadroga of USAID, Guatemala; Mike Lubbock, aviculturist; Dr. Gary Nuechterlein (who supplied the sonograms) and Dr. Deborah Buitron, ornithologists; Dr. Laurie Hunter, ornithologist; and Lorena Calvo, zoologist and Director of La Aurora Zoological Park in Guatemala.

Thanks are also due to a number of Guatemalan government personnel who aided me in recent years: Guillermo and Martha Pacheco, former Director of INAFOR; Guillermo Zepeda, former head of the Wildlife Division of INAFOR; Juan Carlos Godoy, former Head of CECON; Victor Hugo Garcia, Head of the Peace Corps in Guatemala; Beatriz Zuñiga Seigne, former director of INGUAT; Ramiro Castillo Love, former President, Banco Industrial; Pedro and Benjamin Mendosa Tacaxoy, rangers at Lake Atitlán National Park, under DIGEBOS; and, most of all, Dr. Jorge Ibarra, Director of the Museum of Natural History, and his executive assistants, Diana Madariaga and Luisa de Prado, who facilitated the Giant Grebe Exhibit and Inauguration.

Lastly, thanks are due to the Adirondack Park Agency and its former Executive Director, Thomas Ulasewicz, and staff members for arranging preparation of the Giant Grebe Exhibit at Ray Brook, New York; to the U.S. Embassy in Guatemala for assuring safe transportation of these educational materials; and to my wonderful editor Carol Houck Smith who, with her editorial expertise and instincts, gallantly spearheaded our second book together.

Some people may have been overlooked in this long list, and I apologize for that. To all of these, my deepest gratitude for their attempts to save the pocs and Lake Atitlán.

ABOUT THE AUTHOR

ANNE LABASTILLE *is a wildlife ecologist and consultant with a doctorate from Cornell University. She is a commissioner of the Adirondack Park Agency and an honorary consultant to the World Wildlife Fund. She is also a Fellow of the Explorers Club, from which she received a citation of merit in 1984; and a registered New York State guide. In 1990, she was awarded the Honorary Degree of Doctor of Science from the State University of New York, Plattsburgh.*